HUMAN RIGHTS

A Reference Handbook
Second Edition

Other Titles in ABC-CLIO's
CONTEMPORARY
WORLD ISSUES
Series

Books in the Contemporary World Issues series address vital issues in today's society such as terrorism, sexual harassment, homelessness, AIDS, gambling, animal rights, and air pollution. Written by professional writers, scholars, and nonacademic experts, these books are authoritative, clearly written, up-to-date, and objective. They provide a good starting point for research by high school and college students, scholars, and general readers, as well as by legislators, businesspeople, activists, and others.

Each book, carefully organized and easy to use, contains an overview of the subject; a detailed chronology; biographical sketches; facts and data and/or documents and other primary-source material; a directory of organizations and agencies; annotated lists of print and nonprint resources; a glossary; and an index.

Readers of books in the Contemporary World Issues series will find the information they need in order to better understand the social, political, environmental, and economic issues facing the world today.

H U M A N
RIGHTS

A Reference Handbook
Second Edition

Nina Redman and Lucille Whalen

**CONTEMPORARY
WORLD ISSUES**

ABC-CLIO

Santa Barbara, California
Denver, Colorado
Oxford, England

Library of Congress Cataloging-in-Publication Data

Redman, Nina.
    Human rights : a reference handbook / Nina Redman and
    Lucille Whalen.—2nd ed.
        p. cm.—(Contemporary world issues)
    ISBN 1-57607-041-7 (alk. paper)
    1. Human rights.   2. Human rights—Bibliography.   I. Redman,
Nina.   II. Title.   III. Series.
K3240.4.W46   1998
323—dc21   98-27691
                                                                 CIP

04 03 02 01 00   10 9 8 7 6 5 4 3 2

ABC-CLIO, Inc.
130 Cremona Drive, P.O. Box 1911
Santa Barbara, California 93116–1911

This book is printed on acid-free paper ∞ ·

Manufactured in the United States of America

To the Crane men:
Steve, Max, and Jackson
N.R.

Contents

Preface

Since the first edition of this book was published in 1988, the world has experienced major human rights events. There have been massive killings in Bosnia, Rwanda, and Somalia. But formal apartheid in South Africa has ended and the citizens of the former Soviet Union and Eastern Europe are enjoying the return of the right to self-determination. This book is designed to help in researching events, examining the status of human rights in various countries, and understanding some of the theories scholars have developed about what rights are universal and why rights are often violated.

Human rights encompass many issues, and not everyone agrees about what rights are universal. Perhaps the most agreed-on set of rights is contained in the Universal Declaration of Human Rights, formulated in 1948 and as of 1998 ratified by 122 countries. Since that declaration there have been many more declarations that have expanded rights, including rights for prisoners, rights of the mentally ill and of retarded and disabled persons, and the rights of women and children. Not all governments have ratified each declaration, and certainly ratification of a declaration does not ensure compliance. But these declarations are acknowledgments of the norms of acceptable behavior. Perhaps some of the most controversial rights are the rights of children and the right to development. These rights apply to all and imply responsibility of governments to take care of their citizens by supplying food, clothing, and medical care to all. The children's declaration implies a worldwide commitment to the protection of all the world's children.

In addition to the declarations made by the United Nations, there are regional organizations that seek to protect human rights in different areas of the world: The Organization of American States (OAS) has human rights treaties and declarations that apply to North, Central, and South America. The Organization of African Unity (OAU) established the African Charter on Human and People's Rights. The Council of Europe oversees human rights issues in Europe.

In addition to governmental rights organizations like the United Nations and the Council of Europe, there are thousands of nongovernmental organizations (NGOs) that work for human rights at local, national, and international levels. Some organizations have won the Nobel Peace Prize, including the International Committee to Ban Landmines and Amnesty International. These organizations use a variety of strategies—direct aid to victims, victim advocacy (as in Amnesty International's use of letter writing campaigns to improve the status of prisoners of conscience), government lobbying, careful documentation and publication of human rights abuses (Human Rights Watch is a good example of this), media campaigns to raise awareness, and documentary filmmaking. Many human rights workers have endured threats, imprisonment, torture, and even assassination. Yet exposing and documenting problems sends a message to governments that they are accountable for their actions, and this can result in positive change.

Many questions arise as we work to make our own countries humane places and endeavor to interact with other countries in humane ways. For example, do we purchase goods from countries that operate abusive sweatshops? Do we sell items that can be used for torture to other countries? Do we grant political asylum or citizenship to anyone who asks? How do we balance security issues with human rights? How can we provide humanitarian and other types of aid in ways that encourage human rights?

This book aims to bring together materials that will help the reader explore this complex area. Materials have been chosen without regard to political or other perspective. Since there is a considerable amount of print and nonprint material on human rights, this handbook is necessarily limited in scope. Except for some basic reference tools, most works cover the period 1993–1998. Useful earlier works can be found in the bibliographies listed and in the earlier edition of this book. The focus is on human rights in general; no attempt was made to cover works on specific rights, for example, women's rights, minority rights, or children's rights, except from a general human rights perspective. Works considered to be primarily on civil rights were also excluded, as were technical works on international law.

Since this book is intended for researchers, students, and activists, an important consideration was whether material is likely to be available in academic or public libraries or directly from a publisher or producer. The books and periodicals selected range from the popular to the scholarly, but much information will only be found in journal articles, which can be accessed through indexes or online systems, both of which are listed. Prices for both print and nonprint resources are included when available, but readers should be aware that these are subject to change.

Chapters 2 and 3 contain a chronology and a selection of biographical sketches. The chronology lists some of the key dates and events in the development of human rights in our time. The biographical material is included primarily for students and those who might be unfamiliar with important names in the area of human rights and attempts to provide examples of those who have been active in promoting human rights or have been victims of human rights abuse. People included have appeared in news articles or were suggested by those active in human rights work, although it should be noted that those who do the real work of preserving human rights are most often unknown— peasants in countries where speaking out for labor rights is likely to bring torture or death, doctors and lawyers who jeopardize their careers and sometimes their lives by refusing to cooperate with illegal and inhumane treatment of ordinary citizens, and the men and women representing various religious groups who have spent years of their lives working to maintain basic human rights for the poor and neglected in society. For this reason it is never possible to have an adequate list of those prominent in the field.

Chapter 4 contains copies of the Universal Declaration of Human Rights and some of the other documents important to the study of human rights. As with selection for other chapters, it was difficult to make choices. Since human rights is not an academic field in the same way political science or nuclear physics is, there will always be questions about why some materials are selected and others are not. I have made every effort to ensure the accuracy and completeness of the material and I apologize in advance for any errors or omissions.

Organizations committed to human rights advocacy are listed and described in Chapter 5. They include international, national, and regional groups, most of which have publications available in the United States. Most of the organizations listed have websites that can be very useful for research. Please note that the website information was accurate at the time of publication, but websites change frequently so addresses and content may change.

Chapter 6, on print resources, is arranged with reference tools first, most of which are specific to human rights, followed by monographs and periodicals. Chapter 7 covers videotapes, computer networks, and databases. These nonprint materials can be invaluable for teachers and those who plan programs or small group discussions on human rights. Those listed are meant to be samples of the types of material available. Little is found on human rights in general; most audiovisual materials focus on one or another right or, more frequently, on the deprivation of specific rights. Included is a list of producers and distributors that should facilitate locating material of this type. Databases and the internet can be very valuable research tools.

I am extremely grateful to the libraries at the University of Southern California (and to Phelix Hanible for arranging borrowing privileges) and the University of California at Los Angeles and to the International Monitor Institute for graciously allowing me to view their extensive videotape archive. I thank the many people who so patiently answered my questions on the telephone and sent helpful material, my colleagues at the Glendale College Library, and our director, Jan Naumer, for her encouragement. Lucille Whalen, the author of the first edition, has been a tremendous support and inspiration. Thank you, Lucille. And most of all, thanks to my husband and children, Steve, Max, and Jackson Crane, for their kind patience and support during this project.

Nina Redman
Manhattan Beach, California

Introduction

1

Most people consider "human rights" to be a good idea. But what exactly are human rights and how are they enforced? Human rights is an abstract concept that means different things to different people. The year 1998 marks the fiftieth anniversary of the creation of the Universal Declaration of Human Rights, the most basic and comprehensive international human rights instrument. Yet in these fifty years human rights atrocities have continued to occur—one only has to pick up a newspaper to find many examples. This chapter will provide a basic definition of human rights, introduce the Universal Declaration of Human Rights, provide historical background, present information on international law as it applies to human rights, describe major governmental and nongovernmental bodies that work to improve human rights, and discuss some current human rights issues.

Human Rights: A Definition

Human rights are laws, customs, and practices that have evolved over time to protect people, minority groups, and races from oppressive rulers and governments (Humana

1

1992, 4). Further, human rights are held to exist even when they are not recognized or implemented in the customs or legal systems of particular countries (Nickel 1987, 3).

Human rights derive from two sources. Certain rights are considered inalienable and inherent to humanity. These moral rights are the implicit rights to which each human being is entitled. Other rights—legal rights—are established by local, national, and international law. Legal rights are based on the consent of the governed. The goal of human rights, both moral and legal, is to ensure the dignity of every human being.

Historical Foundation of Human Rights

Human rights derive from three main interrelated sources: religion, philosophy, and law. These rights are often classified into three generations of rights. The first generation, civil and political rights, requires governments to make and enforce laws. Second generation rights, or economic rights, imply that people have rights to certain basic necessities, such as food, shelter, and medical care. Governments must take an active role to ensure the economic well-being of their citizens. Third generation rights, the rights to development, peace, disaster relief assistance, and a good environment, require governments to cooperate with each other. Each of the three major foundations of human rights—religious, philosophical, and legal—contains elements of at least the first two generations of rights.

Religious Foundations of Human Rights

The world's major religions all have a humanist perspective that supports human rights. Many writers credit the development of monotheism, the belief in only one god, with being the step that created the moral force to respect the rights of others. The idea that one god created all the people on the earth made all peoples worthy of dignity and respect. Polytheistic religions, by contrast, had one set of rules that applied to the treatment of their own peoples and another set of rules for the treatment of other peoples (Swidler 1990, 14). The covenant people (Hebrews in the Old Testament, Christians in the New Testament, and Muslims in the Koran) are chosen not to enjoy special privileges, but to serve the people of all nations (Ishay 1997, xv). In addition to this altruistic underlying philosophy in the biblical tradition, the ten commandments represent a code of morality and mutual respect that strongly influenced the Western world.

The prohibition against killing implied a right to one's life, and the prohibition against stealing implied a right to one's property. These rights are civil and political rights, first generation rights, but there are other places in the Bible and the Koran that extend these rights to economic and social rights, so-called second generation rights. The Koran expresses deep sympathy for the downtrodden, oppressed, or weak classes, including women, slaves, orphans, the poor, infirm, and minorities (Wronka 1992, 40). Leviticus 19:18 states, "Thou shall love thy neighbor as thyself." Proverbs 25:21 reads, "If your enemy be hungry, give him food to eat, if he be thirsty, give him drink." These instructions are further echoed in the teachings of Christ.

Buddhism, similarly, contains many humanistic and moral codes. Although Buddhists do not study one particular book as Christians study the Bible, there are certain moral codes that are shared by all Buddhists. Buddhists must abstain from killing, stealing, lying, ingesting intoxicants, and partaking in harmful sex. The goal of Buddhism is to achieve six perfections: generosity, morality, patience, vigor, concentration, and wisdom (Ishay 1997, xv). Since Buddhists are working toward a selfless attitude, an appreciation of human rights is a natural consequence.

Philosophical Development of Human Rights

The secular philosophers were also beginning to recognize the idea of human rights, starting with the Greek philosophers Plato (427–348 B.C.) and Aristotle (384–322 B.C.). Plato was one of the earliest writers to advocate a universal standard of ethical conduct. To Plato, this meant dealing with foreigners in the same way one dealt with one's compatriots. It also implied conducting wars in a civilized fashion—no ravaging lands or burning houses. *The Republic* (c. 400 B.C.) proposed the idea of universal truths that all must recognize. People were to work for the common good (Ishay 1997, xvi).

Aristotle wrote in *Politics* that justice, virtue, and rights change in accordance with different kinds of constitutions and circumstances. He concluded that mixed constitutions and a strong middle class are likely to be fairer and more stable. He also believed that states and laws should encourage leisure, peace, and the common good.

The Roman statesman Cicero (106–43 B.C.) laid out the foundations of natural law and human rights in his work *The Laws* (52 B.C.). Cicero believed that there should be universal human rights laws that would transcend customary and civil laws. In Cicero's view, a person should be a citizen of the whole universe as if it were a single city (Ishay 1997, xvii). Interestingly, Sophocles (495–406 B.C.) was one of the first to promote the idea of freedom of expression against the state: a character in *Antigone* stands up for his beliefs against the government (Wronka 1992, 43). St. Thomas Aquinas (c. 1225–1274) advanced human rights further when he took the position that the individual alone has ultimate value (Wronka 1992, 48). Dignity and the power of man are expressed in natural law.

During the Enlightenment, several philosophers refined and extended the theoretical basis for human rights. Thomas Hobbes (1588–1679) defined the state as an entity designed to protect individuals and defend their natural rights to life and security. Jean-Jacques Rousseau (1712–1778) and John Locke (1632–1704) argued that the role of the state is to secure the individual's right to property, political representation, and equality before the law.

Hugo Grotius, a Dutch jurist (1583–1645), set out conditions for just and unjust wars in *On Laws and Peace* (1625). He began by distinguishing between national and international laws. Grotius was the first to conceive of international laws that could offer greater protection to the citizens of the world. Although Grotius conceived of these laws as advisory in nature, he believed that they could set forth standards of permissible actions. A nation could therefore compare its actions to standards to determine whether its actions were just (Ishay 1997, xx).

Legal and Political Foundations of Human Rights

The English Magna Charta (1215) was created in response to the heavy taxation burden created by the third Crusade and the ransom of Richard I, captured by the holy emperor Henry VI. The English barons protested the heavy taxes and were unwilling to let King John rule again without some concessions to their rights. They drafted the Magna Charta as a power-sharing document. The overarching theme of the Magna Charta was protection against arbitrary acts by the king. Land and property could no longer be seized, judges had to know and respect laws, taxes could not be imposed without common council, there could be no imprisonment without a trial, and merchants were granted the right to travel freely within England and outside. The Magna Charta also introduced the concept of jury trial in clause 39, which protects against arbitrary arrest and imprisonment: "No freeman shall be seized or imprisoned, or dispossessed, or outlawed, or in anyway destroyed excepting in the legal judgment of his peers, or by the laws of the land" (Wronka 1992, 53). Although the Magna Charta was only enacted as a political tool, it became working law in England. Over time its tenets were incorporated into common law (Davidson 1993, 12).

In 1679 Habeas Corpus was enacted. A writ of Habeas Corpus, which means literally "you are to bring the body," entitled prisoners to a justification of their imprisonment. Therefore, no one could be imprisoned without just cause. This is often referred to as due process of law.

In 1787, the drafters of the U.S. Constitution looked to the ideas of Locke and Rousseau to create the Bill of Rights, the most extensive set of rights granted to individuals at the time. Perhaps because it was so forward looking and because it is taken so seriously in the United States, most U.S. citizens believe the Bill of Rights offers sufficient protection of human rights.

The French Declaration of the Rights of Man and Citizen (1789) specified rights that were fundamental to individuals and were therefore universally applicable (Ishay 1997, xxiii).

Development of International Human Rights

International human rights evolved from several sources, including three organizations that worked for the protection of human rights. In 1863 the Red Cross was founded, later sponsoring two international conventions to protect victims of wars and to proscribe treatment of prisoners of war. The International Labour Organization was created by the Treaty of Versailles in 1919 to develop conventions and standards related to labor issues. It is now part of the United Nations and has sponsored over 150 conventions since its founding on such subjects as conditions of work, remuneration, child and forced labor, provision of holidays, social security, discrimination, and trade union rights. The League of Nations, established after World War I, had no specific human rights charter, but the covenant committed members to work toward establishing humane working conditions, prohibited trafficking in women and children, worked to prevent and control disease, and worked for the just treatment of native and colonial peoples (Davidson 1993, 9).

Momentum for the creation of the United Nations and for strong human rights protections ironically came from the Nazi atrocities. Although the pogroms against the Jews in Imperial Russia and the Turkish massacre of the Armenians had shocked world public opinion at the time, the Nazi Holocaust forced the international community to recognize outside responsibility for what happens within other countries' borders (Haas 1994, 2–3). In January 1942, the Allied Powers claimed that complete victory over their enemies was essential to defend life, liberty, independence, and religious freedom, and to preserve human rights and justice in their own as well as in other lands. This corresponded to Franklin Roosevelt's four freedoms articulated in January 26, 1941, in his speech to Congress: freedom of speech and expression, freedom of religion, freedom from want, and freedom from fear (Wronka 1992, 85).

After World War II ended in 1945, the United Nations was established. The new organization acted quickly to formulate a bill of rights. On December 10, 1948, the Universal Declaration of Human Rights was adopted.

The United Nations and Human Rights

The United Nations is made up of six principal organs and many subsidiary organs and agencies. The General Assembly is structured to give each nation one vote. It is an important forum for nations to be heard. The General Assembly has no powers to compel member states to act—the effectiveness of the debates and resolutions is entirely dependent on the willingness of the members, especially the major powers, to comply.

The Security Council is composed of five permanent members, the United States, Great Britain, France, China, and Russia. There are also ten rotating members elected by the General Assembly that serve two-year terms. The rotating members are chosen to reflect a balance among the major geographic regions not already represented. Usually three African, two Asian, three European, and two Latin American countries are chosen. The Security Council's mission is to maintain international peace and security by resolving disputes by peaceful means. The council is empowered to impose binding economic and military sanctions to back international decisions. The structure of the council is such that substantive decisions require a yes or abstention from the permanent members of the council. In practice, the permanent members have veto power.

Agencies of the United Nations involved in human rights include the High Commissioner for Refugees, which sets standards and works to provide humanitarian aid for refugees; the United Nations Children's Emergency Fund (UNICEF), which works to improve the well-being of children worldwide; the International Labour Organisation; the World Health Organization; and the United Nations Commission on Human Rights (CHR).

The CHR has been empowered to make thorough studies of situations that reveal a "consistent pattern of violations of human rights." Rules prohibit the commission from disclosing research on particular countries until the commission is ready to make public its findings. Unfortunately, this tends to delay action until human rights violations are well under way. Confidentiality also deprives the United Nations of one of its most powerful tools: adverse publicity. The CHR has undertaken thematic investigations—for example, forced disappearances, summary executions, and torture studies—that do not require the same level of confidentiality. The CHR drafted the Universal Declaration of Human Rights, the two covenants that when agreed upon will make the Universal Declaration enforceable, and also a large number of standard-setting declarations and conventions regarding human rights.

In addition to the United Nations, there are three regional systems that work to enforce human rights. These agencies are the Organization of American States (OAS), the European Convention on Human Rights, and the African Charter on Human and People's Rights. The OAS and the European Convention have active courts that can be petitioned when human rights are violated. The African Charter is primarily investigative at this writing. As yet there is no similar body in Asia.

The United States and Human Rights

The U.S. government, along with many other governments, has as a policy the promotion of rights in the conduct of its world affairs. Within the Department of State, the Bureau of Democracy, Human Rights, and Labor monitors human rights around the world and issues an annual report to Congress. Human rights are only one of the factors, and not always the dominant one, that go into creating and implementing foreign policy. However, human rights are used as a bargaining chip, and the United States has been able to improve human rights in various countries through negotiation. For example, in the late 1990s the U.S. government was able to get China to release several dissidents and agree to sign the Universal Declaration of Human Rights.

Nongovernmental Organizations

In addition to the official bodies described above, there are numerous nongovernmental organizations (NGOs) that work to protect human rights. The largest and probably the most famous of these organizations is Amnesty International. Amnesty International started in London in 1961 after a lawyer, Peter Benenson, read about a group of students in Portugal who had been jailed after making a toast to freedom in a restaurant. Benenson launched a one year "Appeal for Amnesty" in the *London Observer* asking others to write letters to governments requesting them to release "prisoners of conscience." (Amnesty International defines prisoners of conscience as those prisoners jailed for their political or religious beliefs or gender, racial, or ethnic origin who have neither committed nor advocated violence.) One year was not long enough to release all the prisoners, so the organization became permanent.

Amnesty International has chapters all over the world. Each chapter works to free specific prisoners of conscience by conducting letter-writing campaigns to the governments holding the prisoners. Each letter is written in a respectful tone. The Amnesty organization researches each case extensively to ensure that each prisoner is a legitimate prisoner of conscience and has not committed any violent or criminal acts. The letter-writing campaigns are often successful because it is more difficult to incarcerate someone without just cause when others around the world are watching.

Amnesty also works to prevent and reduce torture around the world. The organization carefully documents cases and publishes reports. In this effort it campaigns for humane treatment for all prisoners, not just prisoners of conscience. Amnesty International strongly opposes the death penalty.

Human Rights Watch (HRW) is another major human rights organization. HRW was founded as Helsinki Watch in 1975 to monitor compliance with the Helsinki Accords. HRW works primarily as a monitoring and lobbying organization. Its coverage of the world is fairly comprehensive, investigating all kinds of human rights violations, including summary executions and torture, restrictions of freedom of expression and association, prison conditions, religious persecution, women's issues, the environment, and war-related issues. Although HRW started out lobbying the U.S. government, its influence has expanded to the United Nations, the European Union, the World Bank, and the Japanese government. The primary lobbying tool is the painstakingly documented reports that the organization produces (see Chapter 6 for examples). HRW sends fact-finding teams all over the world to investigate human rights abuses. These teams interview witnesses, victims, government officials, labor leaders, journalists, lawyers, relief groups, and doctors to get firsthand information. Human Rights Watch also works extensively with other human rights organizations in other countries and often collaborates on reports.

Because HRW documentation is so reliable, the organization has been able to use the reports to effect change all over the world. HRW is organized around both regions and issues. It has five regional monitoring divisions: Africa, Americas, Asia, Helsinki, and the Middle East. Projects and initiatives include arms, children's rights, women's rights, academic freedom, corporate accountability for human rights, drugs and human rights, freedom of expression, and prison conditions. Human Rights Watch was one of the original six organizations that formed the International Committee to Ban Landmines.

International Law and Human Rights

Perhaps the most basic concept in international law is the idea that nations have sovereignty over themselves. Thus individual states have a total right to conduct their internal and external affairs in whatever way they choose. A related concept is nonintervention: no state or states have the right to intervene in the internal or external affairs of any other state. Sometimes states agree to reduce their individual sovereignty to accomplish certain aims. Numerous treaties have been signed to facilitate trade, to protect the environment, to make it possible to extradite criminals, and to protect human rights.

When a state makes a treaty, it is bound by the provisions of that treaty unless it decides to breach the treaty, in which case the treaty is generally canceled. A distinguishing feature of human rights treaties is that they are not canceled when a breach occurs. This provision was created because there would be no protective character to human rights treaties if a single human rights violation nullified the agreement. States may also denounce human rights treaties by following certain procedures spelled out in the treaty, but states are still held responsible for any violations committed before the denouncement.

In addition to denouncing a treaty, a state may sign a treaty subject to particular reservations. It is then not bound to the treaty provisions that relate to these reservations. Some treaties also contain conditions in which the state is not obligated to honor treaty provisions. This is called derogation. Rights to freedom of association might be derogated in a time of war, for example. Certain rights may never be derogated, including the right to freedom from torture.

Although treaties cover most human rights protections, there are some crimes against humanity that are considered too heinous to ever be tolerated. These crimes include genocide, apartheid, and summary executions. Therefore these crimes are considered to have universal jurisdiction. Besides sanctioning governments, individuals committing these crimes are also subject to universal jurisdiction. This is a legacy of the Nuremberg Tribunal. Nazis were held responsible for their acts even when they were following orders. Following orders may not be used as a defense in these crimes.

International Criminal Court

In July 1998, the United Nations convened a diplomatic conference to establish a permanent International Criminal Court (ICC) to prosecute human rights abuses including genocide, crimes against humanity, and serious war crimes. Until that time, there was only the International Court of Justice in the Hague. This court (often called the World Court) addresses disputes between states. Special tribunals had to be set up to prosecute individuals perpetrating genocide and other crimes, for example, the tribunals to try Yugoslavian and Rwandan war criminals.

The tribunal system has suffered organizational problems—lack of funds, failure to arrest and extradite the vast majority of those indicted by the tribunal, shortages of qualified personnel, limited training, weak investigative procedures, and lengthy lead time needed to set up a tribunal. It is hoped that a permanent court will solve many of these problems (Carter 1998, 165).

Although 120 nations signed the treaty approving the creation of the court, 60 countries will have to ratify the treaty before it will take effect. The United States did not sign the treaty in part because of fears that the treaty could expose U.S. military personnel to politically motivated charges. Another provision to which the United States objected is the way investigations leading to prosecution are initiated. Signatory nations, the U.N. Security Council, and the prosecutor may all bring matters before the court subject to the approval of a pretrial panel of judges. The U.S. government fears this will undermine the strength of the U.N. Security Council. It is not clear at this writing whether the United States will actively lobby other nations against ratifying the treaty.

Universal Declaration of Human Rights

Although the Universal Declaration of Human Rights is not legally binding, it has over the years been transformed into a potent legal instrument. Its precise legal status is still subject to debate (Davidson 1993, 13). The declaration protects five categories of rights: civil, political, economic, social, and cultural. The most developed rights in the Universal Declaration are civil rights. These rights center around two concepts, the right to equality and the right to life, liberty, and security of person.

Civil Rights

- Discrimination: Three of the articles, 1, 2, and 7, deal with equality and nondiscrimination. The articles state that people are born free and equal in dignity and rights, are equal before the law, and are entitled to equal protection against discrimination. Article 2 explicitly defines categories of discrimination—for example, racial, sexual, religious—and Article 7 also provides for protection against incitement to discrimination. Discrimination has been and continues to be one of the most difficult impediments to human rights.
- Life, liberty, and security of person: These articles are meant to remove arbitrary government interference and to protect the rights of those in custody.
- Slavery: One article abolishes slavery. Slavery has been particularly difficult to completely eradicate because some slavery takes the form of enforced labor contracts or indentured servitude. A recent case in the United States involved Thai garment workers used as sweatshop labor

and confined in an apartment building in a suburb of Los Angeles. Some countries have used debt bondage in agricultural settings with stiff penalties when workers revolt (Levin 1981, 49).

- Cruel, inhuman, and degrading treatment: Article 5 states that no one shall be subjected to cruel, inhuman, or degrading treatment or punishment. Torture continues to occur in many parts of the world. A survey by the Human Rights Watch Prisons Project found that substandard prison conditions exist in most parts of the world (Human Rights Watch/Prison Project 1993, 3). The death penalty is also considered as cruel and unusual treatment, particularly when it is applied unevenly as in the high execution rates of minorities and poor people in the United States.
- Legal recognition: An interesting feature of Article 6, which states that "everyone has a right to recognition everywhere as a person before the law," is that noncitizens should be able to make contracts and start proceedings that ensure their legal rights. Currently, refugees who enter the United States without proper papers can be detained and have few legal rights.
- Enforcement of constitutional rights: If a fundamental constitutional right is violated, the Universal Declaration gives individuals the right to go before a national court to correct the situation. This does not imply that rights from the Universal Declaration are enforceable, just that rights that are stated in a country's own constitution should be enforceable.
- Arbitrary arrest, detention, exile, and fair trials: Further provisions protect citizens from arbitrary arrest, detention, exile, and provide the right to a fair trial, including the presumption of innocence, right to a public trial, and freedom from retroactive justice. Article 12 seeks to protect people from arbitrary interference with privacy, family, home, or correspondence and to protect people from slander. This article covers modern electronic devices such as wiretapping, since telephone conversations and electronic mail are forms of correspondence (Levin 1981, 60).
- Movement between and within countries: Article 13 affirms the right to move within and between countries. There are many legitimate exceptions to this right—in times of natural disaster or epidemics, civil or international wars. Similarly, people facing trial may not be permitted to

leave a state or country. Freedom of movement is often denied within countries because of work-related needs. These may be legitimate or may be a mask for discrimination. In Kuwait, the Bedoons, who are not recognized as citizens, are confined to certain areas (Human Rights Watch/Middle East 1995, 5).

- Asylum: All are granted the right to seek asylum in other countries unless they are being prosecuted for nonpolitical crimes. Provisions in the declaration stop short of granting the right to *gain* asylum because countries were unwilling to open their borders to potentially large numbers of people (Levin 1981, 62).
- Nationality: A nationality is granted in Article 15. Nationality provides people with an identity. This identity is related to geographic location and the implicit entitlement to the protection of the laws in operation within the jurisdiction of the state. The state is also responsible for the treatment of its nationals by other states (Levin 1981, 64). The Bedoons, who compose one third of Kuwait's native population, were "denationalized" in 1985. As illegal citizens they live in apartheid conditions (Human Rights Watch/Middle East 1995, 2).
- Marriage: Other civil rights include the right to marry and found a family and to mutual spousal consent.
- Property rights: Property rights include the right to own property and the protection from being arbitrarily deprived of one's property.
- Religion: The declaration also makes freedom of religion and freedom to change religions fundamental rights. Sometimes states have limited religious rights thinking that religion leads to subversion or as another means of control. In China citizens must register their religion, and if they participate in religious ceremonies, it must occur only in a proscribed way (Human Rights Watch/Asia 1997, 3).

Political Rights

- Opinion and expression: Some rights are both civil and political, such as freedom of opinion and expression as defined in Article 19. This right includes the right to seek, receive, and impart information and ideas through any media and regardless of frontiers. This article speaks directly to freedom of the press, but it also looks at persecution of writers and journalists, banning of books, state ownership of the media, and censorship.

- Association: The article describing freedom of association also includes the freedom not to belong to an association. Freedom of association is often abridged in repressive governments.
- Participatory government: Article 21 affirms the right to participatory government. This is expressed through the right to periodic and genuine elections, equal access to public service, and direct involvement in government or election of representatives. Foreign domination or support of tyrannical governments is an abridgement of this article since it helps to remove governments from accountability to their citizens.

Economic, Social, and Cultural Rights

The next group of rights—economic, social, and cultural rights— sometimes referred to as second generation rights, requires positive action on the part of states to implement. Nickel identifies three beliefs that support government responsibility for second generation rights. The first belief is that poverty, exploitation, and discrimination are threats to human welfare and dignity as serious and deliberate as violations of political rights. The second is that misery and inequality are not inevitable but come from social, political, and economic conditions that can be subjected to moral or political control. The wealthy economies of Europe, North America, Japan, Australia, and North America and the accompanying welfare rights are cited as examples supporting this belief. The third belief is that government power is often used to create and maintain economic institutions that favor certain groups. Therefore political, economic, and social systems cannot truly be separated (Nickel 1987, 8–9).

- Social security: The economic rights set forth in the Universal Declaration include the right to social security. The article is phrased in such a way as to mean a more complete guarantee of these rights in richer countries than poorer countries.
- Work: Article 23 concerns the right to work. It incorporates free choice in employment, equal pay for equal work, sufficient pay to ensure dignity, and freedom to join trade unions. As a further work-related protection, the Universal

Declaration calls for the right to rest and leisure, including reasonable working hours and periodic paid holidays. An adequate standard of living, including food, clothing, housing, medical care, and social services and unemployment security, is also considered to be an important economic right in the declaration.

- Education: Article 26 grants the right to a free education, at least through elementary school. Parents should be able to choose the kind of education they want for their children and human rights education should be included in all curriculums.

- Culture and copyright: Cultural rights include the right to freely participate in the cultural life of the community, to enjoy the arts, and to share in scientific advancement. Interestingly, this right also incorporates copyright, because it states that everyone has the right to the protection of their interests resulting from scientific, literary, or artistic production.

- Social and international order: The last major right in the Universal Declaration is a third generation right: "Everyone is entitled to a social and international order in which the rights and freedoms set forth in this declaration can be fully realized." These are third generation rights because they require not only active change by individual governments but international cooperation to fulfill. The idea behind these rights is to enhance the legal and economic situation so that the right to development is guaranteed, as are disaster relief, peace, and a healthy environment (Davidson 1993, 6).

As it now stands, the declaration is the ideal for human rights, but only some parts of it are enforced. They are enforced through two covenants that apply to nations that agree to be bound by them.

Current Human Rights Issues

Land Mines

Land mines kill or maim over 26,000 people annually. Ninety percent of the casualties are civilians going about normal activities—gathering water, working in fields, and traveling on rural roads.

Experts estimate that there are more than 100 million land mines planted in 70 countries (Marshall 1998, A-1, A-16).

Land mines were originally developed as countermeasures against tanks. The tank mines were large and easy to detect, so antipersonnel mines were developed to protect the antitank mines. Indiscriminate use of antipersonnel mines began with U.S. use in Indochina during the 1960s and early 1970s, especially during attacks against Laos. The Soviets scattered "butterfly mines" over suspected guerrilla strongholds in Afghanistan after the 1970 intervention. These mines look a bit like toys and many children died after playing with them. Armies like to use land mines because they are simple to use, low-tech, and cheap; mines can cost as little as $3 (International Committee of the Red Cross 1994, 3–35).

Unfortunately, maps of mine fields are seldom made and detection and demining are extremely dangerous and expensive. In Poland, where 15 million land mines were cleared after World War II, 4,000 mine-related deaths and 9,000 mine-related injuries have occurred in the period from the end of World War II to the mid-1970s from uncleared mines. Newer mines are often equipped with antihandling and antidetection devices that make deactivation even more dangerous. Mercury tilt switches can make mines detonate as soon as they are moved, and mines fitted with microprocessors detect movement and detonate. Metal detectors are often used in mine clearance, but not all mines use metal. Some have cardboard or plastic housings. Specially trained dogs can sniff out the explosives used and then the mine can be destroyed. It costs as much as $1,000 to remove each mine and many mine clearing workers have been killed (International Committee of the Red Cross 1994).

Many mines are concentrated in Central America, Africa, the former Yugoslavia, Iran and Iraq in the Middle East, and Southeast Asia. Most of those affected live in rural areas without the medical infrastructure to handle the types of injuries sustained from land-mine explosions. There are two main types of land-mine injuries—direct blast injuries and injuries caused by dirt, clothing, metal, and plastic that get driven into tissue and bone. These deep tissue and bone injuries often result in severe secondary infections. Many victims need to have limbs amputated. There is often not enough money for prosthetics or trained personnel to perform rehabilitation or physical therapy.

Besides the direct impacts of injuries, there are often severe economic effects because land mines limit access to otherwise productive land. It is estimated that one million acres of farm-land along the Mozambican/Zambian border have been ren-dered useless by the Rhodesian crisis, which ended in 1979. In Somalia where it is estimated that hundreds of thousands of mines are planted or scattered, nomadic herdsmen are unable to use their traditional grazing lands. Humanitarian efforts in heavily mined areas are often curtailed because of the danger.

The United Nations has worked hard to get a universal ban on land mines. The United States declared a moratorium on the sale of land mines in 1992. The most effective effort, however, has come from nongovernmental organizations that banded together to form the International Campaign to Ban Landmines. This unique effort started with six organizations and eventually in-cluded over 1,000 NGOs from all over the world. The campaign lobbied governments to sign a treaty banning landmines. For their efforts, the International Campaign to Ban Landmines and its director, Jody Williams, were awarded the Nobel Peace Prize in 1997. More importantly, in December 1997, 122 nations signed a global treaty banning land mines (Marshall 1998, A-1). The United States has not yet signed and is seeking to have exception clauses for mines used in the North Korea/South Korea border and for "smart mines" that self-destruct in time.

Global Refugee Crisis

During the 1980s, there were eight million refugees worldwide. By the 1990s there were 15 million. Most of the refugees today are women and children—many of whom are fleeing from conflict zones where rape and sexual abuse have been used as a tool of war by soldiers. In many instances the United Nations or other countries have set up camps to house the refugees fleeing across national borders. In some cases, life in the camps has not been much better. Hundreds of Somali women were raped in these camps between April 1992 and November 1993. Most were raped by bandits, but some were raped by Kenyan soldiers and police (Barber 1997, 8–10).

Besides the threat of rape, often these camps become bases for opposition guerrilla fighters. The aid that flows from other governments and international humanitarian organizations is sometimes skimmed by militants based in the camps. During the 1978–1991 conflict in Cambodia, the United States and other na-tions funded refugee camps in Thailand that were bases for three Cambodian guerrilla forces fighting the Vietnamese-backed government. One of these was the Khmer Rouge. More than 50,000 Vietnamese solders died in combat or from malaria during the more than 12 years of fighting.

In Rwanda in 1994, 1.5 million Rwandan and 300,000 Burundian refugees who were mostly Hutus fled to Zaire and Tanzania. The refugee camps in Zaire were controlled by Hutu militiamen and former Rwandan army troops who launched attacks across the border against Rwanda's new Tutsi-dominated government. When Tutsis from Zaire smashed the camps in November 1996, more than 500,000 declined to follow the militias deeper into Zaire. They walked home to Rwanda, telling reporters that they had been held hostage for two years. Although this may have been an exaggeration, there is evidence that guerrillas used physical and psychological coercion to keep them in the camps. This included withholding the news that the Rwandan government promised a safe return and spreading propaganda that the Tutsis would slaughter them if they went back.

Bob Devecci, head of the International Rescue Committee, which supplied some of the sanitation and water services at the biggest camp in Zaire, said, "The way the camp was organized, it was militiamen who determined food distribution, access to hospitals. [Militia] police ran the camps. The refugees were more like hostages than refugees getting direct aid." Unfortunately, streams of refugee aid often have the effect of prolonging conflicts and civilian suffering. Many refugee analysts believe that aid has been used as a substitute for political initiatives that would resolve root causes of emergency migrations including war, ethnic conflict, famine, economic imbalance, and environmental damage (Barber 1997, 8–12).

Another dimension of the refugee crisis is the growing difficulty for individuals to emigrate to other countries. Many countries in the West, including the United States, have tightened their immigration laws, severely limiting the numbers of refugees and asylum seekers that are allowed to settle permanently. Anthony Richmond writes that this is a form of global apartheid. However, it is unrealistic to think that the United States and the rest of the West could absorb all the current refugees and those that come after them and provide social services for them. In addition to the question of whether people can emigrate is the treatment of people when they arrive from other countries. Many refugees are detained while awaiting processing of their cases. Since they are not U.S. citizens, they are not legally entitled to due process and other protections set out for citizens.

Some detainees linger in jails (called detention facilities) for more than a year waiting to have their cases heard.

In Britain, refugee organizations estimate that less than one third of asylum seekers whose applications are denied leave or are deported. Experts estimate that around 50,000 people are living in Britain without civil status and with no social or political rights ("Britain's Asylum Shambles: Those Fleeing Persecution Deserve Better Treatment" 1998, 20). This vulnerable group also exists in the United States, where illegal immigrants are extremely vulnerable to exploitation.

In 1945 the U.N. Charter laid out principles of refugee humanitarian aid. In 1951 the Office of the High Commissioner for Refugees was established. One of the principal tenets of U.N. policy is that countries should avoid forcibly returning individuals to countries where their lives or freedom are threatened. This is termed *refoulement*. Although countries have tried to avoid *refoulement*, there are many instances in which it occurs. In the European Union, asylum seekers are often returned to "safe third countries" if they have arrived in Europe stopping in another country first. Many potential U.S. asylum seekers have been returned under the same policy. There are often no safeguards that the "safe third country" will not return them to their original country of origin. In Europe half of all asylum claims were granted in 1984, but by 1998 less than one in ten was granted ("Britain's Asylum Shambles: Those Fleeing Persecution Deserve Better Treatment" 1998, 20). This leaves many refugees with no choice but to go home where they fear persecution. Creative ways to help refugees need to be found that do not prolong conflicts and that improve the odds of bettering their lives.

Labor Issues and Human Rights

Labor is an area that generates many human rights concerns. One of the most difficult problems is slavery, either outright or through debt bondage. Child labor and sweatshops are other areas that have resisted solutions. Debt bondage is the most common form of slavery today. Estimates are that there are millions of slaves, most of whom are women and children. The cycle starts when a worker agrees to sell his labor (or his child's labor) for a lump sum. This could be to cover a major medical expense. Low wages, high interest rates, and cheating by the bondholder make the debt almost impossible to repay. Bonded debt can be passed from one generation to the next and people can be sold to other landlords. If a man escapes, his family can be held until he returns. Bonded peasants can be sold into marriage.

It is estimated that half a million South Asian children are bonded to carpet weaving looms. In Nepal and Pakistan, bonded workers do farm labor. They also supply the brick kilns and mines of South Asia and work in remote areas of Brazil and Peru. In India and Thailand, the threat of AIDS has led to the entrapment of more and more women and children into sexual slavery. Brothel customers are anxious for young girls from the country, thinking that they will be less likely to carry the HIV virus. Some are kidnapped, a few decide to become prostitutes voluntarily, but most are lured under false pretenses. Nepali girls average 13 years of age when they are trafficked to India. In the Sudan, women and children are kidnapped and sold into slavery. The men are killed or left behind to raise ransom. Girls become concubines, children tend animals, and women become servants. Although there are numerous conventions against slavery in place, some governments have done little to stop it. Thailand, India, Myanmar, Pakistan, and Nepal all have laws against slavery, kidnapping, and child prostitution, but enforcement is minimal. In Brazil, the government has spoken out strongly against forced labor but the Amazon region is vast and few policemen and labor inspectors have been assigned to enforce existing laws and policies ("Flourishing Business of Slavery" 1996, 43–45).

Short of slavery, there are many other labor conditions that compromise human rights. One of the most difficult to address is child labor. The International Labor Organization (a U.N. agency) estimates that 200 million children under the age of 14 are engaged in work that is dangerous to their health, morals, or development. A 1994 U.S. Department of Labor study reported that millions of children are involved in producing goods that are imported from Asia, Latin America, and Africa. In India, about 55 million children are at work—many in bondage or in endangering situations of sickness and illiteracy. There is lax enforcement of applicable laws (Harvey 1995, 362–366).

One of the most difficult aspects of child labor laws is that in many situations the family is dependent on the income from the child's labor and cannot survive without it. In many countries children go to work early, either working in the fields or in the home, and childhood is seen as a period for learning employable skills. When labor laws are imposed from the outside, as in the U.S. Harkin bill, they can have the effect of creating even more poverty and misery in the group that they were attempting to protect.

This kind of catch-22 can be seen in many factories around the world. In Haiti, the legal minimum wage is 30 cents per hour. This is not even sufficient to cover the cost of food for one family. Workers live in small shacks, children do not have milk to drink, and there is no money for medicine. Yet the factory workers, although exploited, are desperate to keep their jobs (National Labor Committee 1996). In the past, higher minimum wages have meant that jobs have moved to countries with cheaper labor rates. Medea Benjamin, codirector of Global Exchange, a San Francisco–based human rights group that has investigated sweatshops in the United States and abroad, criticized a 1997 agreement to end sweatshops as inadequate to prevent worker abuse. Global exchange has focused on improving corporate accountability as a method of improving worker rights (Benjamin 1997).

Global Poverty

In 1966 the poorest 20 percent of the world's peoples earned 2.3 percent of the world's income. Thirty years later, this group earned 1.4 percent while the world's richest 20 percent had increased their share of income from 70 percent to 85 percent of the total. Disparity in levels of income are perhaps even more extreme if one considers the increasing participation in the marketplace. In the 1960s there were many fewer participants in the marketplace. A self-sufficient farmer who lived near the forest and bartered did not use much money at all. With increases in population and destruction of forests to make way for development, people have increasingly moved to urban areas to find work.

One factor exacerbating poverty levels is the high level of debt in the Third World. The debt level of the Third World is now over two trillion dollars. Much of the debt was incurred for large infrastructure projects that did not always improve quality of life. Some of the debt was incurred to support oppressive regimes and some was skimmed by these regimes and placed in foreign bank accounts. At various points, many developing countries were unable to keep up with their loan payments. Some debt was forgiven and some was restructured in exchange for the country's agreeing to implement structural adjustment policies designed to make their economies healthier and better able to repay the debts. One of these adjustments is diverting government spending from social services to loan repayment. Other structural adjustment policies imposed by the World Bank and the International Monetary Fund have had the effect of squelching small farmers and independent businesses.

The adjustment policies put in place so that governments could pay off their debts require governments to increase exports and open their own economies to outside businesses. As a consequence, local producers of commodities that are not competitive against global producers are forced out of business. Farmlands are often converted from supplying local needs to growing crops for export and often with large foreign investment. Economies that were once functional have been transformed by debt into poverty creating environments. Unemployment in developing countries has increased dramatically.

Two of the effects of this grinding poverty are increased malnutrition and poorer health care. In some countries, medicines are no longer subsidized and poor families must make difficult choices in their already stretched budgets. Most of the more than one billion people who live in poverty in the developing world receive no effective biomedical care at all. Polio vaccines are unknown to many people, measles and malaria kill millions each year, childbirth involves mortal risk, and tuberculosis is as lethal as AIDS (Farmer 1995, 14).

Even with access to medical care, the poor are much more likely to die from treatable diseases. Even though tuberculosis is curable 95 percent of the time, the poor are often unable to implement the cure. They may not take the full regimen of drugs because they cannot get to their appointments or they might not be able to eat well or sleep in an uncrowded place. Even though the disease is curable, the underlying poverty prevents the cure from working.

Various governmental and nongovernmental agencies have developed health and welfare programs. The Carter Center has worked on many health issues—ameliorating the guinea worm and river blindness and helping to increase the world immunization rate from 20 percent to 80 percent (Carter Center Website 1998). Oxfam has many poverty reduction programs. Countries contribute resources to social development in developing countries from a high of .9 percent of GNP in the Nordic countries to a low of .15 percent in the United States (Benetar 1998, 296). UNICEF sponsors programs to improve the health, education, and well-being of children. There are some signs that these programs help.

The U.N. Development Program has a Human Development Index that tracks human welfare measures, including income, education, and various factors affecting life expectancy. Overall quality of life rose 44 percent in the period from 1980 to 1995 by these measures. This great gain is largely due to 15 countries, mostly Asian, that have greatly improved the standard of living for their people. Incomes have often doubled, people eat better, the water is cleaner, life expectancy is greater, and there are more jobs, better education, and lower infant mortality. Even in Africa there has been a 21 percent quality of life improvement since 1980 ("A Global Poverty Trap?" 1996, 34).

There are many that believe a new world economic order is necessary to eliminate or at least reduce the extreme poverty in the world. Regardless of human rights issues, it is in the best long-term political and security interests of the developed countries to have a developing world that is economically secure. The misery of poverty can often lead to political instability, a greater refugee population, and increasing disease.

Racism and Ethnic Cleansing

Racism exists in almost every country in the world. It can take the form of hate groups in the United States, discrimination in housing and employment in Great Britain, social and ethnic exclusion in France, xenophobic skinheads and neo-Nazis in Germany, and outright genocide in Bosnia and Rwanda. Often the source is poor people who feel that another ethnic or racial group is taking their jobs. However, there is also a great deal of prejudice and discrimination by people who have attained a certain level of success and income and who want to protect this by building social and racial barriers to keep others out (Wieviorka 1996, 10–14). When racism becomes extreme, it can take the form of ethnic cleansing. Andrew Bell-Fialkoff defines population cleansing as the planned, deliberate removal from a certain territory of an undesirable population distinguished by one or more characteristics such as ethnicity, religion, race, class, or sexual preference. These characteristics must serve as the basis for removal for it to be termed *ethnic cleansing* (Bell-Fialkoff 1996, 3). Cleansing can range from pressuring people to emigrate to genocide. Deportation and resettlement are intermediate steps. Often racial pressures increase when a government is destabilizing. Looking to blame some other force, a government losing popularity will often incite racism and intolerance that can often lead to ethnic violence (Human Rights Watch 1995, 10).

Certain organizations are working to discourage racism and violence. The Southern Poverty Law Center in Montgomery,

Alabama, maintains a Klanwatch program that keeps tabs on the Ku Klux Klan and other hate groups in the United States, including those established on the internet. They have also developed videos and teaching materials that they distribute at low cost in their Teaching Tolerance program. The Simon Wiesenthal Center disseminates information about hate groups and operates the Museum of Tolerance in Los Angeles, which seeks to promote intercultural understanding and information about the Nazi genocide. The U.N. Subcommittee on Prevention of Discrimination and Protection of Minorities investigates racial issues and uses advocacy and promotion of human rights to help counter racism.

Prisons and Torture

In the United States, the prison population grew to 1,000,000 in 1995 from 400,000 in 1984. There are now 5,000,000 men in the justice system either imprisoned, on parole, on probation, or awaiting trial. Alabama has brought back the chain gang (Boulard 1995, 24–26) and prison conditions worldwide do not meet minimum standards. Besides not adhering to minimum standards of custodial care, many countries around the world engage in torture. Perhaps the biggest challenge to improving prison conditions is the attitude that prisoners deserve what they get and that prison should be a place where offenders are thoroughly punished for their crimes.

The U.N. Standard Minimum Rules for the Treatment of Prisoners is the most widely known and accepted document that regulates prison conditions. Although these standards are known to prison administrators all over the world, they are seldom fully enforced. Human Rights Watch examined prison conditions using the minimum standards for their 1993 *Human Rights Watch Global Report on Prisons*. They found that the great majority of the millions of persons who are imprisoned worldwide are confined in filth and corruption without adequate food, medical care, with little or nothing to do, and in constant threat of violence either from other inmates or from their guards (Human Rights Watch Prison Project 1993).

In addition to overall low quality of care, there are many conditions that represent more extreme cruel and unusual punishment. Human Rights Watch has documented excessive use of solitary confinement and overemphasis on rules in Japan, often fatal assaults on inmates by guards in South Africa, and sexual abuse of women prisoners in the United States. Children are often abused and shackled in U.S. detention facilities, and super maximum security prisons are sprouting up all over the country. The super maximum security prison in Marion, Indiana, has small, windowless cells where prisoners spend an average of 23 hours a day. Prisoners face extreme social isolation, enforced idleness, and extraordinarily limited recreational and educational opportunities. Some of the prisoners have preexisting psychiatric illnesses (Human Rights Watch Website 1998).

Torture has been documented in many countries around the world. Some countries favor methods that leave little evidence of torture, while others care less about whether the procedure leaves marks. Darius Rejali investigated torture in Iran, noting that torture in Iran has changed in the last 100 years from being an open ritual performed in the streets to being conducted in secret where the torturer works to break the prisoner's soul (Rejali 1994). Torture is often part of a larger plan of terror designed to keep people oppressed. Often it is used in conjunction with disappearances to ensure compliance. Generally torturers view their victims as less than human. When people are dehumanized, it becomes easier to maltreat them. A study of torturers found that torturers felt they were serving their countries by performing torture (Crelinsten and Schmid 1995).

The U.N. Human Rights Commission investigates human rights abuses, including torture. Several human rights organizations also work to pressure governments to make changes. Amnesty International is perhaps the most outspoken against cruel punishments, prison conditions, and torture. An organization in Minnesota, the Center for Victims of Torture, works to help victims recover from their physical and emotional wounds.

The Environment and Human Rights

Environmental destruction poses a grave threat to human rights. Oftentimes destruction of forests, pollution of streams, and other environmental degradation threaten the ability of people who use traditional methods of hunting, fishing, and farming to get food and drink clean water. One person in five in the world does not have access to clean water (Johnston 1997, 5). Additionally, the way that many countries have gone about developing natural resources has involved persecution of peoples protesting environmental destruction.

In Nigeria in 1996, nine environmental activists, including one Nobel Peace Prize nominee, were executed after protesting against Shell Oil Company's environmental destruction (Hammer 1996, 58–69). In Irian Jaya, Indonesia, the U.S. corporation Freeport-McMoRan has been mining copper and gold since 1973. This is the largest gold mine in the world, with an estimated value of $50 billion. Unfortunately, this mine has pitted the interests of the indigenous peoples against those of the Indonesian government. The government has stationed troops at the mine to protect it, and in 1995 the military killed at least 16 people and tortured others near the mine. The mine has created enormous environmental destruction; it is estimated that 3.2 billion tons of mostly acid-producing mine tailings will be dumped in the local river over the course of the project (Bryce 1996, 66–70). Drinking water has become contaminated as a result.

In October 1995, the FSB (the successor organization to the KGB) entered offices in Murmansk and St. Petersburg of the Ballona Institute, a joint nonprofit research agency of the Norwegians and Russians. The institute was investigating industrial pollution and radioactive waste in northeastern Russia. The FSB entered Ballona offices and seized records, computers, floppy disks, and video cameras and then entered scientists' homes and detained several people for questioning. Ironically, all of the information that the agency gathered was public information (Johnston 1997, 322).

On a positive front, the crisis at the Ballona Institute prompted a flurry of e-mail describing the incident, and a formal protest was lodged within two days by the prime minister of Norway. Countries around the world are becoming more concerned about the environment and about overexploitation of resources. The U.N. Human Rights Commission has drafted a declaration on human rights and the environment. This declaration states that human rights, an ecologically sound environment, sustainable development, and peace are interdependent and indivisible. It further asserts that all people have a right to a secure, healthy, and ecologically sound environment. Other provisions cover healthy food and water and safe and healthy work environments. Many NGOs work hard on environmental issues, including the Natural Resources Defense Council, Greenpeace, and the Nature Conservancy.

Conclusion

There are many challenges to improving human rights. Perhaps the best hope lies in working to end global poverty by making income distribution throughout the world more equitable. Global minimum wage laws that offer workers wages that would at least cover basic expenses could go far toward alleviating poverty. A stronger, more independent United Nations would almost certainly be more effective at improving human rights. Currently, the United Nations is an excellent forum for raising international concerns, but the veto power of the Security Council makes it difficult to go forward with enforcement of human rights in many cases. An example of this is the situation in Turkey, where the Turkish government is involved in a long-standing conflict with the Kurds. There have certainly been human rights atrocities on both sides, but the United States continues to supply arms to Turkey, which in turn uses these weapons against the Kurds. The United States has military bases in Turkey and wants to defend its security interest in the Middle East (Human Rights Watch Arms Project 1995).

Were a resolution to come before the United Nations to investigate and potentially take some action against Turkey, the United States, although favoring human rights in principle, would veto any action in the Security Council because it goes against its security interests. Similarly, the only way the United Nations gets peacekeeping forces is through resolutions and agreements. No country really wants to get involved in settling disputes, especially when there could be casualties. There have been situations, particularly in Bosnia, where insufficient peacekeeping forces made preventing violence impossible.

If the United Nations were to become more independent, with an independent, permanent peacekeeping force, and if the veto power of the Security Council members were to be severely reduced, the United Nations would be better able to mitigate and help solve human rights abuses.

Some writers have proposed creating a very small tax on international currency transactions. This would raise enough money to support a permanent peacekeeping force and pay for the International Criminal Court and increased poverty reduction programs.

In 1998 the Universal Declaration of Human Rights celebrated its 98th anniversary. In the time since its inception there have been many human rights violations, but there has also been an increased awareness of human rights. The declaration has raised the international standard of behavior. Perhaps in another 50 years we can look forward to a world with improved health, prosperity and peace, and, consequently, the observance of human rights.

References

Barber, Ben. 1997. "Feeding Refugees or War? The Dilemma of Humanitarian Aid." *Foreign Affairs* 76, no. 4 (July/August): 8–15.

Bell-Fialkoff, Andrew. 1996. *Ethnic Cleansing.* New York: St. Martin's Press.

Benatar, Solomon. 1998. "Global Disparities in Health and Human Rights: A Critical Commentary." *American Journal of Public Health* (February): 295–303.

Benjamin, Medea. 1997. "No Sweat for Companies to Agree." *Los Angeles Times,* April 17 Metro section, p. 1.

Boulard, Garry. 1995. "What's Tough Enough." *State Legislatures* (December): 24–28.

"Britain's Asylum Shambles: Those Fleeing Persecution Deserve Better Treatment." 1998. *Economist* (February 14): 20.

Bryce, Robert. 1996. "Spinning Gold." *Mother Jones* (September/October): 66–70.

Carter, Jimmy. 1998. "A Permanent International Criminal Court Should Be Created." In Mary Williams, ed., *Human Rights: Opposing Viewpoints.* San Diego: Greenhaven Press.

Carter Center Website. 1998. www.emory.edu/CARTER_CENTER.

Crelinsten, Ronald, and Alex Schmid, eds. 1995. *Politics of Pain: Torturers and Their Masters.* Boulder, CO: Westview Press.

Davidson, Scott. 1993. *Human Rights.* Philadelphia: Open University Press.

Farmer, Paul. 1995. "Medicine and Social Justice." *America* (July 15): 13–18.

"Flourishing Business of Slavery." 1996. *Economist* (September 21): 43–45.

"Global Poverty Trap? A." 1996. *Economist* (July 20): 34.

Haas, Michael. 1994. *Improving Human Rights.* Westport, CT: Greenwood Press.

Hammer, Joshua. 1996. "Nigeria Crude: A Hanged Man and an Oil-Fouled Landscape." *Harper's Magazine* (June): 58–69.

Harvey, Pharis. 1995. "Where Children Work: Child Servitude in the Global Economy." *Christian Century* (April 5): 362–366.

Humana, Charles. 1992. *World Human Rights Guide,* 3d ed. New York: Oxford University Press.

Human Rights Watch. 1995. *Slaughter among Neighbors.* New York: Human Rights Watch.

Human Rights Watch Arms Project. 1995. *Turkey: Weapons Transfers and Violations of the Laws of War in Turkey.*

Human Rights Watch Prison Project. 1993. *Human Rights Watch Global Report on Prisons.* New York: Human Rights Watch.

Human Rights Watch Website. 1998. www.hrw.org.

Human Rights Watch/Asia. 1997. *China: State Control of Religion.* New York: Human Rights Watch.

Human Rights Watch/Middle East. 1995. *Bedoons of Kuwait: Citizens without Citizenship.* New York: Human Rights Watch.

International Committee of the Red Cross. 1994. *Landmines: Time for Action.* Geneva, Switzerland: ICRC Publications.

Ishay, Micheline, ed. 1997. *The Human Rights Reader: Major Political Writings, Essays, and Speeches from the Bible to the Present.* New York: Routledge.

Johnston, Barbara Rose. 1997. *Life and Death Matters: Human Rights and the Environment at the End of the Millenium.* Walnut Creek, CA: Alta Mira Press.

Levin, Leah. 1981. *Human Rights: Questions and Answers.* Paris: UNESCO.

Marshall, Tyler. 1998. "Nobel Prize Sets Off Land Mine." *Los Angeles Times,* February 6, A-1, A16–A17.

National Labor Committee. 1996. *Mickey Mouse Goes to Haiti.* Videotape. Available from National Labor Committee, 275 Seventh Avenue, New York, NY 10001.

Nickel, James. 1987. *Making Sense of Human Rights.* Berkeley: University of California Press.

Rejali, Darius. 1994. *Torture and Modernity: Self, Society, and the State in Modern Iran.* Boulder, CO: Westview Press.

Richmond, Anthony. 1994. *Global Apartheid: Refugees, Racism, and the New World Order.* New York: Oxford University Press.

Swidler, Leonard. 1990. "Human Rights: A Historical Overview." In Hans Kung and Jurgen Moltmann, eds., *The Ethics of World Religions and Human Rights.* London: SCM Press.

Wieviorka, Michel. 1996. "The Seeds of Hate." *UNESCO Courier* (March): 10–14.

Wronka, Joseph. 1992. *Human Rights and Social Policy in the 21st Century: A History of the Idea of Human Rights and Comparison of the U.N. Declaration of Human Rights with United States Federal and State Constitutions.* Lanham, MD: University Press of America.

Chronology 2

The idea of fundamental rights and freedoms has existed since at least Old Testament times. The Magna Charta, the English Bill of Rights, the Declaration of Independence, the French Declaration of the Rights of Man and Citizen, and the League of Nations Covenant all express the idea of inalienable, universal rights. It was not until the 1940s, however—particularly at the time of the founding of the United Nations—that the modern concept of human rights came into existence. The idea of international law protecting the rights of individuals and not only states was a new one, brought about by the horrors of World War II. Thus the highlights in the development of human rights for the most part have been the various declarations and covenants to which nations of the world subscribe. It should be pointed out that the declarations and resolutions are generally statements on which nations agree, but they do not have the force of law, while covenants, conventions, and treaties, used somewhat interchangeably, become international law when ratified by a specific number of nations. The following is a chronology of the major human rights documents and events.

1941 President Franklin Roosevelt's State of the Union message includes one of the first references to the "Four Freedoms"—freedom of speech, freedom of religion, freedom from want, and freedom from fear—freedoms that, he states, should prevail everywhere in the world.

1944 Declaration of Philadelphia. Two famous passages are incorporated into the constitution of the International Labour Organisation (ILO), a specialized agency of the United Nations: "All human beings, irrespective of race, creed, or sex, have the right to pursue both their material well-being and their spiritual development in conditions of freedom and dignity, of economic security, and equal opportunity"; and "Freedom of expression and association are essential to sustained progress."

1945 Preamble to the U.N. Charter. Includes the phrase "to reaffirm faith in fundamental human rights, in the dignity and worth of the human person, in the equal rights of men and women, and of nations large and small"— one of the first times human rights are mentioned in an international treaty.

1946 The U.N. General Assembly approves and ratifies the Nuremberg Principles, which establish the right and authority of nations to punish violations of human rights and specify that soldiers may not be acquitted on the grounds of following orders of superiors when they violate the rules of war.

1948 The U.N. General Assembly adopts the Universal Declaration of Human Rights, which prescribes that all human beings are entitled to all human rights and fundamental freedoms set forth in the declaration. This is the most fundamental of all U.N. instruments; most subsequent human rights statements are based on its tenets.

Convention on the Prevention and Punishment of the Crime of Genocide. Recognizes genocide as a crime under international law and states that those accused of it, in wartime or peace, can be tried by the country where the crime was committed or by such international tribunals as have jurisdiction.

1949   American Declaration of the Rights and Duties of Man, based on the Universal Declaration of Human Rights, brought into existence by the Organization of American States (OAS) in Bogotá and adopted for Latin America.

Council of Europe established. Its statutes include the statement, "Every member of the Council of Europe must accept the principles of the rule of law and of the enjoyment by all persons within its jurisdiction of human rights and fundamental freedoms." It also proposes the establishment of an internal organization to ensure the collective guarantee of human rights.

The Geneva Conventions. The four conventions represent a significant attempt to protect war victims. They expressly prohibit violence to life and person, in particular, torture, mutilation, or cruel treatment, the taking of hostages, or any degrading treatment. The conventions also oblige each party to search for those who have committed these abuses.

International Labour Organisation (ILO) adopts the Right to Organise and Collective Bargaining Convention, prescribing for workers adequate protection against antiunion discrimination in respect of their employment.

1950   Convention for the Suppression of the Traffic in Persons and of the Exploitation or the Prostitution of Others. The convention parties agree to punish any person who, to gratify another, procures, entices, or leads away, for the purpose of prostitution, another person, even with that person's consent, or exploits the prostitution of another person, even with the person's consent.

1951   Convention Relating to the Status of Refugees. Parties agree to give refugees "national treatment"—that is, treatment at least as favorable as that accorded their own nationals with regard to such rights as freedom of religion, access to courts, elementary education, and public relief. (Convention covers only persons who become refugees as a result of events occurring before January 1, 1951.)

1952   Convention on the International Right of Correction. Provides that when a signatory state finds a news report filed between countries or disseminated abroad capable of damaging its foreign relations or national prestige, that state may submit its version of the facts to any other states where the report became publicized, and that these other states are obliged to release such a communiqué to news media within their territories.

1953   European Convention for the Protection of Human Rights and Fundamental Freedoms. Requires contracting states to make their laws conform to the provisions of the convention and creates the European Court of Human Rights.

1955   Standard Minimum Rules for the Treatment of Prisoners. These seek to set standards for acceptable treatment of prisoners and management of penal institutions.

1956   Supplementary Convention on the Abolition of Slavery, the Slave Trade, and Institutions and Practices Similar to Slavery. Requires parties to expedite, through legislative and other measures, the complete abolition of such practices as debt bondage, serfdom, and the use of a woman, without the right to refuse, as an object of barter in marriage.

1957   Convention on the Nationality of Married Women. Contracting states agree that neither celebration nor dissolution of marriage between a national and an alien can automatically affect the nationality of the wife.

Convention concerning the Abolition of Forced Labour (ILO). Members agree not to use any form of forced or compulsory labor as a means of political coercion or education or as punishment for holding political views ideologically opposed to the established system.

1958   Discrimination (Employment and Occupation) Convention (ILO). Each ratifying member agrees to declare and pursue a national policy promoting equal opportunity and treatment in employment and occupation, with a view to eliminating any discrimination in respect thereof.

1959   The Organization of American States (OAS) creates the Inter-American Commission on Human Rights to promote respect for human rights. The commission asserts its authority to study the human rights situations of member states.

Declaration of the Rights of the Child. Maintains that children shall enjoy special protection and be given opportunities and facilities, by law and other means, to enable them to develop physically, mentally, morally, spiritually, and socially in a healthy and normal manner in conditions of freedom and dignity.

1960   Convention against Discrimination in Education (UNESCO). Parties agree to ensure, by legislation where necessary, that there is no discrimination in the admission of pupils to educational institutions; to make primary education free and compulsory; to make secondary education generally available and accessible to all, and higher education equally accessible to all on the basis of individual capacity; and to make certain the factors relating to the quality of education provided are equivalent in all public education.

1961   Convention on the Reduction of Statelessness. Specifies grounds on which a state may not deprive a person of nationality; these include racial, ethnic, religious, or political reasons.

1962   Convention on Consent to Marriage, Minimum Age for Marriage, and Registration of Marriages. States must take legislative action to specify a minimum age for marriage and to provide for the registration of marriages by an appropriate official. Marriages may not be legally entered into without the full and free consent of both parties.

1963   Declaration on the Elimination of All Forms of Racial Discrimination. Discrimination against human beings on the grounds of race, color, or ethnic origin is an offense to humanity and shall be condemned as a denial of the principles of the Charter of the United Nations, as a violation of the fundamental freedoms proclaimed in

1963   the Universal Declaration of Human Rights, and as an
cont.   obstacle to friendly and peaceful relations among na-
        tions. Special measures shall be taken in appropriate cir-
        cumstances to secure adequate protection of individuals
        belonging to certain racial groups, but these measures
        may not include the maintenance of unequal or separate
        rights for different racial groups.

1964   Employment Policy Convention (ILO). Parties to the
        convention must declare and pursue, as a major goal, an
        active policy designed to promote full, productive, and
        freely chosen employment.

        Civil Rights Act of 1964. Signed by President Lyndon B.
        Johnson, the act is a landmark in the development of full
        human rights for all citizens in the United States.

1965   International Convention on the Elimination of All
        Forms of Racial Discrimination. The convention con-
        demns racial discrimination and undertakes to pursue
        by all appropriate means and without delay a policy of
        eliminating racial discrimination in all its forms, to pro-
        mote understanding among the races, and to discourage
        anything that tends to strengthen racial division.

1966   International Covenant on Economic, Social, and Cul-
        tural Rights. States recognize rights to which all people
        are entitled, including the right to work, to just and fa-
        vorable conditions of work, to social security, to an ade-
        quate standard of living, to the highest attainable
        standard of physical and mental health, to education, to
        take part in cultural life, and to enjoy the benefits of sci-
        entific progress.

        International Covenant on Civil and Political Rights. Es-
        tablishes a legal obligation on states to protect the civil
        and political rights of every individual without discrim-
        ination as to race, sex, language, or religion. It ensures
        the right to life, liberty, security, individual privacy, and
        protection from torture and other cruel, inhuman, or de-
        grading treatment. The covenant also guarantees a fair
        trial and protection against arbitrary arrest or detention
        and grants freedom of thought, conscience, and religion,

freedom of opinion and expression, and freedom of association.

Optional Protocol to the International Covenant on Civil and Political Rights. A state party to the International Covenant that becomes a party to the Optional Protocol recognizes the competence of the Human Rights Committee to receive and consider communications from individuals subject to its jurisdiction who claim to be victims of violation by the state party of any of the rights set forth in the covenant.

1967   Declaration on the Elimination of Discrimination against Women. All appropriate measures shall be taken to abolish existing laws, customs, regulations, and practices that discriminate against women and to establish adequate legal protection for equal rights of men and women.

Declaration on Territorial Asylum. Asylum granted by a state to persons seeking asylum from political persecution shall be respected by all other states. No such person shall be subjected to such measures as rejection at the border, expulsion, or compulsory return to any state where he or she may be subjected to persecution except for overriding reasons of national security or to safeguard the population.

Convention on the Non-Applicability of Statutory Limitations to War Crimes and Crimes against Humanity. The convention states principles regarding international cooperation in the detention, arrest, extradition, and punishment of war crimes and crimes against humanity; for example, there is no statutory limitation on certain crimes such as genocide, eviction by armed attack, or inhuman acts resulting from the policy of apartheid.

1969   The American Convention on Human Rights. Signed in San José, Costa Rica, but not brought into force until 1978, this is one of the most ambitious and far-reaching documents on human rights issued by any international body. Among other features, it bans the death penalty and authorizes compensation for victims of human rights abuses in certain cases.

1969
cont.
The ILO receives the Nobel Peace Prize for its work on behalf of human rights. The ILO was the first international governmental agency, under the League of Nations, to define and vindicate human rights. It has sought tirelessly to improve the conditions of working men and women around the world.

1971
Declaration of the Rights of Mentally Retarded Persons. The mentally retarded person has, to the maximum degree of feasibility, the same rights as other human beings, including the right to proper medical care, to education and training, to economic security, and to a decent standard of living.

Workers' Representatives Convention (ILO). Workers' representatives shall enjoy effective protection against any act prejudicial to them, including dismissal, based on their participation in union activities, insofar as they act in conformity with existing laws or other jointly agreed-upon arrangements.

1973
International Convention on the Suppression and Punishment of the Crime of Apartheid. Inhuman acts resulting from the policies and practices of apartheid and similar policies of racial segregation and discrimination are crimes that violate the principles of international law and constitute a serious threat to international peace and security.

1974
Universal Declaration on the Eradication of Hunger and Malnutrition (World Health Conference). All men, women, and children have the inalienable right to be free from hunger and malnutrition in order to develop fully and maintain their physical and mental faculties. The eradication of hunger is a common objective of all countries, especially of those in a position to help in its eradication.

Declaration on the Protection of Women and Children in Emergency and Armed Conflict. All states involved in armed conflict or in military operations either in a foreign country or in territories still under colonial domination must make special efforts to spare women and children from the ravages of war.

1975   The Helsinki Agreement or the Final Act of the Confer-
        ence on Security and Co-operation in Europe. Signed
        in Helsinki by 33 nations and the 2 superpowers—the
        United States and the Soviet Union—the Helsinki Ac-
        cords, as they came to be called, pledged respect for
        human rights and fundamental freedoms, including
        the freedom of thought, conscience, religion or belief,
        for all people without distinctions as to race, sex, lan-
        guage, or religion. The signatories agreed to promote
        universal and effective respect for human rights,
        jointly and separately, including cooperation with the
        United Nations.

        Declaration on the Use of Scientific and Technological
        Progress in the Interest of Peace and for the Benefit of
        Mankind. States that the results of scientific and techno-
        logical developments are to be used in the interests of
        strengthening international peace and security and for
        the economic and social development of peoples in ac-
        cordance with the Charter of the United Nations.

        Declaration on the Rights of Disabled Persons. States
        shall protect disabled persons against all exploitation,
        all regulations, and all treatment of a discriminatory,
        abusive, or degrading nature.

        Declaration on the Protection of All Persons from Being
        Subjected to Torture and Other Cruel, Inhuman, or De-
        grading Treatment or Punishment. No state may permit
        or tolerate torture or other cruel, inhuman, or degrading
        treatment or punishment. Exceptional circumstances
        such as a state of war, internal political instability, or
        other public emergency may not be used as a justifica-
        tion for such treatment.

        International Women's Year and the First World Confer-
        ence for the Decade for Women in Mexico City. Marks
        the beginning of the most profound consideration of
        women's rights on a worldwide basis that has ever
        taken place.

1977   The Carter administration emphasizes human rights. In
        his inaugural address, Jimmy Carter makes it clear that

1977
cont.

human rights will be an important factor in U.S. foreign policy. In a speech to the United Nations two months later, he states that he will recommend the ratification of the major human rights treaties. Although he keeps his promise, the human rights treaties are not ratified by the United States. He does, however, create the Bureau of Human Rights and Humanitarian Affairs and appoints Patricia Derian to head the bureau.

1978

Declaration on Race and Racial Prejudice (UNESCO). All individuals and groups have the right to be different, but this right and the diversity in lifestyles may not, in any circumstances, be used as a pretext for racial prejudice and may not either in law or in fact justify discriminatory practices.

Declaration on Fundamental Principles concerning the Contribution of the Mass Media to Strengthening Peace and International Understanding, to the Promotion of Human Rights, and to Countering Racism, Apartheid, and Incitement to War (UNESCO). Journalists must have access to public information for reporting so that individuals may have a diversity of sources from which to check the accuracy of facts and appraise events objectively.

1979

Code of Conduct for Law Enforcement Officials. In the performance of their duties, law enforcement officials shall respect and protect human dignity and maintain and uphold the human rights of all persons. They may use force only when strictly necessary and to the extent required for the performance of their duty. They may never inflict, instigate, or tolerate any act of torture, or other cruel, inhuman, or degrading treatment, nor invoke superior orders or exceptional circumstances as a justification for such treatment.

Convention on the Elimination of All Forms of Discrimination against Women. Parties shall take all appropriate measures, including legislation, to ensure the full development and advancement of women, for the purpose of guaranteeing them the exercise of human rights on a basis of equality with men.

1980   Second World Conference for the Decade for Women. Conference held in Copenhagen to assess the progress made in implementing the 1975 Mexico City conference's plan of action and to adopt guidelines for international, regional, and national efforts to assist women in attaining equality in all spheres of life as part of a plan of action for the second half of the decade.

1981   UNESCO meeting in Freetown, Sierra Leone. A meeting of experts to analyze the forms of individual and collective action by which human rights violations can be combated.

        African Charter on Human and People's Rights. At a meeting of the Organization of African Unity (OAU), the leaders of 51 member states adopt the African Charter on Human and People's Rights. The charter reiterates the basic principles of human rights and stresses decolonization and the elimination of apartheid as top priorities. It seeks to preserve the traditional African social concept that the individual is not considered independent from society but is subordinate to the group.

        Declaration on the Elimination of All Forms of Intolerance and of Discrimination Based on Religion or Belief. All persons shall have the right to have a religion or belief of their choice, and shall have the freedom, either individually or in community with others and in public or private, to manifest their religion or belief in worship, observance, practice, and teaching.

        The Universal Islamic Declaration of Human Rights. Many of the provisions of this declaration are similar to those in other major human rights instruments; the declaration contains references to the right to life, to freedom under the law, to equality before the law, to fair trial, and to freedom from torture. Its basis is religious rather than regional and draws justification from reference to the Koran and the *sunna*.

1982   Principles of Medical Ethics. Health personnel, particularly physicians, charged with the medical care of prisoners and detainees, have a duty to provide for them the

1982 cont.	same standard and quality of physical and mental health care afforded others. It is a gross violation of medical ethics to engage actively or passively in acts that constitute participation in or complicity with torture or other cruel, inhuman, or degrading treatment or punishment.
1984	Convention against Torture and Other Cruel, Inhuman, or Degrading Treatment or Punishment. Defines torture as any act by which severe physical or mental pain or suffering is intentionally inflicted by, at the instigation of, or with the acquiescence of someone acting in an official capacity, whether to obtain information or confession; to punish, intimidate, or coerce; or for reasons based on discrimination. The convention states that parties must prevent torture in their jurisdictions and ensure that it is legally punishable.
1985	Third World Conference for the Decade for Women. Held in Nairobi in July 1985 to assess the progress achieved and obstacles encountered during the past decade and to formulate strategies for the advancement of women to implement through the year 2000 and beyond. International peace and security will be advanced by the elimination of inequality between men and women and the integration of women into the development process.
1986	United Nations Declaration on the Right to Development. Declares individuals to be the center of all economic activity. Therefore development efforts must improve the well-being of the entire population, not just increase economic indicators.
1988	Almost 40 years after the United Nations approves the Genocide Convention, President Reagan signs legislation enabling the United States to become the 98th nation to ratify the agreement. The legislation amends the Criminal Code of the United States to make genocide a federal offense.
1989	Convention on the Rights of the Child. Declares the responsibility of all nations to provide adequate nutrition,

education, and health care for the world's children. Other provisions govern child labor, juvenile justice, and child participation in warfare.

1990   The General Assembly of the United Nations adopts the International Convention on the Protection of the Rights of All Migrant Workers and Members of Their Families. The convention provides for the establishment of a committee to oversee protection of migrant worker rights.

1992   The General Assembly of the United Nations adopts the Declaration on the Rights of Persons Belonging to National, Ethnic, Religious, and Linguistic Minorities. The declaration calls on states to protect the existence and the national, ethnic, cultural, religious, or linguistic identities of minorities living in their territories.

1993   Declaration on Violence against Women. Calls on governments to exercise diligence to prevent, investigate, and punish acts of violence against women. World Conference on Human Rights in December 1993 declares that the human rights of women and girl children are an inalienable, integral, and indivisible part of universal human rights.

The U.N. Security Council officially names Srebrenica the world's first U.N.-protected civilian safe area. Unfortunately, the United Nations does not send sufficient troops to the area and over 7,000 Muslims are slain.

The United Nations responds to human rights violations throughout the world by adopting the Vienna Declaration and Programme of Action at the U.N. World Conference on Human Rights, which reaffirms its commitment to previously recognized human rights, with special recognition of the right to development and to economic, social, and cultural rights. It also calls for an end to discrimination, violence, and poverty.

1994   The United Nations drafts the Declaration on Human Rights and the Environment. This document focuses on the right to benefit from nature, to consume safe and healthy food, and the right to a healthy environment.

| 1994 cont. | The United Nations proclaims the decade 1995–2005 the Decade for Human Rights Education. The purpose of this proclamation is to broaden awareness of human rights and make human rights education a part of the curriculum. |

The U.N. Security Council adopts a resolution re-emphasizing that "ethnic cleansing" constitutes a clear violation of international law. This echoes a 1992 Security Council resolution condemning "ethnic cleansing" in Bosnia and Herzegovina.

The U.N. Security Council establishes an International Tribunal for Rwanda. Eight hundred thousand people are killed in Rwanda in one of the worst genocides since the Nazi Holocaust.

1995   Fourth U.N. World Conference on Women. Held in Beijing in September 1995, the conference focuses on the economic empowerment of women and addresses continuing inequalities in the areas of health care, education, and political participation. The conference has spurred legislative efforts worldwide to enhance the rights and role of women.

South Africa establishes the Truth and Reconciliation Commission to investigate human rights abuses that took place under the apartheid government. Archbishop Desmond Tutu is appointed head of the commission by President Nelson Mandela.

1997   An international treaty is negotiated among 89 countries in Oslo, Norway, to ban antipersonnel land mines. The world has more than 100 million unexploded land mines, which kill or cripple 26,000 annually.

Biographical Sketches 3

It is impossible to even begin to select all of the individuals who have made significant contributions in the field of human rights—many of those who are doing the most to advance human rights are ordinary citizens who do so with considerable risk to themselves and their families. They are most often unknown, as are many in the United States who quietly and conscientiously work for the relief of prisoners of conscience or work to change repressive laws. Nevertheless, there are individuals, known nationally and internationally, who have made important contributions to human rights and who serve as role models for others. The following are biographical sketches of a few of these persons.

Jimmy Carter

Jimmy Carter, the 39th president of the United States, from 1977 to 1981, will be remembered as making human rights an integral part of his administration's foreign policy. The facts of Carter's life are well known—he was a Baptist fundamentalist, a peanut farmer, and a one-term governor of Georgia before becoming president. Born in Plains, Georgia, on October 1, 1924, he grew up in Georgia and attended Georgia Tech

45

and the U.S. Naval Academy, from which he graduated in 1946. He spent some time on battleships and in the submarine service before being accepted into the nuclear submarine program.

When his father died in 1953, Carter returned to take over the family business in Plains and became active in church and community affairs. It was during this time that he began his human rights advocacy. At one time, having refused to join the local White Citizen's Council, he found his businesses were boycotted. On another occasion he and his family were the only ones in his church to vote against a resolution refusing blacks and civil rights "agitators" the right to worship in the church.

During his political career Carter served as a senator and later as governor of Georgia, which gave him the opportunity to open up government positions for women and blacks and set in motion several humanitarian programs. During his primary campaign for the presidency, Carter focused on human rights in many of his foreign policy statements and made them an issue in the debates during the general election campaign. This was one of the factors that stirred enthusiasm for his campaign among young people, church-affiliated groups, broad-based citizen groups, and even some labor groups.

It was not surprising that Carter, on taking the oath of office, pledged: "Because we are free, we can never be indifferent to the facts of freedom elsewhere. Our moral sense dictates a clear-cut preference for those societies that share with us an abiding respect for individual human rights." Nor was it surprising that one of the first steps taken by the new administration was the appointment of Patricia Derian, a long-time civil rights activist from the South, as head of the newly established Bureau of Human Rights and Humanitarian Affairs. As a result of this human rights policy, the United States opposed many loans to foreign countries on human rights grounds, arms transfer proposals to a dozen countries were altered, and diplomatic dialogue on human rights occurred at many levels. Some of the other stands Carter took on human and civil rights issues were supporting the Equal Rights Amendment and universal voter registration, granting pardons to Vietnam War draft resisters, and ending a practice of denying visitors' visas to foreign Communists wishing to visit the United States. These and other factors were the reasons the International League for Human Rights in its report cited President Carter's policies as being responsible for significant improvement in human rights around the world.

Since leaving the Oval Office, Carter has continued to work

for peace and human rights. The Carter Center at Emory University and the adjoining Carter Library in Atlanta are action-oriented institutions with programs on regional issues, health scourges, agricultural innovation, conflict resolution, and human rights. As a private citizen, Carter has made significant contributions toward peace in Haiti, Nicaragua, Bosnia, and Korea. At home in the United States, Carter is very active in Habitat for Humanity and organizes a multihome building project in a different part of the country each year.

Vaclav Havel

Born in Prague on October 5, 1936, Vaclav Havel, now president of the Czech Republic, is a Czech playwright who has used his dramatic skills to further the cause of human rights. When the Communist government nationalized industry in Czechoslovakia in 1948, Havel's parents were forced to give up their property and business and take low-paying jobs. This turn of events also denied easy access to an education for their son, but he managed by working days and continuing his schooling nights to receive his education at a technical college and then the Prague Academy of the Arts. After doing his compulsory military service in the late 1950s, Havel worked as a stagehand, electrician, secretary, and manuscript reader before becoming a playwright in the early 1960s. In his many plays, he frequently tries to show the dehumanizing effects of mechanization on society and the individual spirit.

When the Soviet Union and other Warsaw Pact armies invaded Czechoslovakia in 1968, Havel addressed groups of Czech artists and writers from an underground radio station, urging them to unite in the cause of human rights. He was able to convince a small group to commit themselves to use whatever means they could to protest repression by the government. Havel's plays and writings were subsequently banned and he was twice imprisoned for his human rights advocacy. In 1977 Havel signed Charter 77, a document protesting the failure of the Czechoslovakian Socialist Republic to abide by the Helsinki Covenant on Civil and Political Rights, which it had signed. The government's response was to arrest large numbers of those who had signed the document, among them Havel, who had been one of the three elected spokesmen for the protest. He was jailed for four months and later brought to trial for sending copies of his banned writings out of the country for publication. Although given a suspended sentence, he later founded a movement known as the Committee for the Defense of the Unjustly Persecuted and along with six others was sentenced to four and one-half years at hard labor.

Havel was known principally for his plays before he became president in 1989. *The Memorandum,* a full-length play satirizing official gibberish, and three one-act plays about conformists trying to rationalize their collusion with a corrupt system—*Interview, A Private View,* and *Protest*—are generally thought to be his best. Havel has had a profound influence on human rights, particularly on the rights of artists and intellectuals to criticize the government and their works.

In his presidency he has continued to work for human rights. During the conflict in Bosnia, Havel worked to bring peace to the region. In his own country, he has worked to improve the rights of the Gypsies. There have been over 1,200 attacks on Gypsies in the Czech Republic in the 1990s. Havel has used his position as president to implement plans to improve the social and economic situation of this group.

Bernard Kouchner

Bernard Kouchner was born in 1939 in Avignon, France, grew up in a suburb of Paris, and became an activist as a teenager demonstrating support for Algerian independence and the demands of striking workers. He earned his medical degree in 1964, but demonstrated his interest in world affairs by writing articles and pamphlets on political topics. He traveled to Cuba to meet Argentine guerrilla leader Ernesto (Che) Guevara and interviewed Fidel Castro for *Clarte,* a magazine for young Communists.

Kouchner volunteered to help the Red Cross in Biafra in 1968 where a bloody civil war had claimed many lives. There he became sensitized to human rights abuses. He was frustrated that the Red Cross policy of neutrality prevented the Red Cross from taking a stand against human rights abuses. He helped found Medicins sans Frontieres (MSF, or Doctors without Borders) in 1971 to help heal the wounded and to speak out against human rights abuses. MSF has sent medical teams to Nicaragua after an earthquake had left 6,000 dead and many more injured and homeless, to Lebanon where many were wounded from civil war, and to Vietnam and Turkey, for example. MSF has grown into the world's largest medical relief organization, with over 2,000 doctors of 45 nationalities active in over 60 countries.

After a falling out with some of the leadership of MSF, Kouchner founded Medicins du Monde (MDM, or Doctors of the World). MDM organized relief efforts in the 1980s to Afghanistan, Armenia, Ethiopia, Brazil, Chile, Columbia, Guatemala, El Salvador, Mexico, Poland, Burma, and Mozambique. Although Kouchner is no longer formally associated with MSF or MDM, he has continued his activism. Kouchner held humanitarian posts in the French government from 1988 to 1993. From these posts, he has become active in the United Nations.

In 1988 the United Nations adopted his proposal that set forth guidelines for providing humanitarian assistance to victims of natural disasters and other emergency situations. In 1990, the General Assembly of the United Nations passed a resolution requiring "access corridors" along which humanitarian relief organizations could travel to provide assistance to the needy. Because of these resolutions, Kouchner was able to push through the passage of Security Council Resolution 688 requiring Iraq to permit relief organizations and nations access to Kurdistan to bring supplies in 1991. In 1997 Kouchner left France to run a hospital in the Southern Sudan.

Graça Machel

Born in 1945, Graça Machel grew up in a poor mud and grass hut in Mozambique. It was her father's dying wish that she go to both primary and secondary school. Her brothers and sisters honored this wish, making Graça Machel one of the few children in Mozambique to receive formal education. She won a scholarship to college in Lisbon, where she began her activism in the movement that led to Mozambique's independence from Portugal. In the new government, she was the minister of education. During her tenure, the number of children enrolled in school doubled before civil war destroyed much of the country's infrastructure.

Her husband, Mozambique president Somora Machel, was killed in a plane crash in 1986 under mysterious circumstances. She withdrew from public life for five years until she decided to transform her grief into helping others. She sought to help the children of Mozambique both by directing agencies and projects and by creating international awareness of their plight. She heads the National Organization of Children of Mozambique, which tries to find homes for children orphaned during the war, and heads the Community Development Foundation, which funds development projects designed and carried out by members of poor communities.

Because of her knowledge and experience of wars' effects on women and children, she has become an internationally recognized expert. She was chair of the United Nations Study of the Effects of Armed Conflict on Children. At Graça Machel's recommendation, UNICEF has pushed to set a worldwide minimum age of 18 for military recruitment and made banning antipersonnel land mines a priority.

Rigoberta Menchú

Rigoberta Menchú, born in Guatemala in 1959 into the Quiche, one of 22 groups of Mayans in Guatemala, experienced with her family extreme discrimination and ill treatment from the landowning classes. During the harvest season, Menchú and her family worked 14-hour days on the coffee and cotton plantations for subsistence wages. Two of Menchú's brothers died on the plantations—one from inhaling pesticides and one from malnutrition. Her family was not allowed to bury the child who succumbed to malnutrition and was evicted without being paid for 15 days' work. Life in the city was not much better. Menchú worked in Guatemala City for a short time as a maid. There she endured backbreaking work and slept on a mat next to the family dog.

Her father, Vincente Menchú, was imprisoned for organizing resistance to the landowners who were hiring soldiers to take the Mayans' land by destroying homes, raping women, and killing the family dogs. Menchú and her father came to believe that land reform was the only hope for the indigenous peoples of Guatemala. Vincente Menchú helped found the Committee of Peasant Unity to better the status of the Mayans.

Menchú learned Spanish so that she could exercise her legal rights. She learned three other Mayan dialects so that she could communicate with other tribal groups that suffered similar oppression. Because of the family's efforts to improve the rights of Mayans, Menchú's mother, father, and brother were tortured and killed in separate incidents during 1979 and 1980. Menchú began to organize labor unions and organized several large strikes. In 1981 she became wanted by the police for her alleged subversive activities. It became too dangerous for her to stay in Guatemala, and she fled to Mexico, where she continued to work for human rights for the indigenous peoples of Guatemala.

She wrote her autobiography, *I, Rigoberta Menchú*, while in

Mexico. In 1992 she won the Nobel Peace Prize. Menchú's award was not without controversy. The Guatemalan government had labeled Menchú a communist, and there were many, including American conservatives, who were upset at the choice. With the $1.2 million prize, Menchú set up a foundation in memory of her father. The Vincente Menchú Foundation works for human rights and education of indigenous peoples in Guatemala and the Americas. Menchú's accomplishments have extended beyond Guatemala's borders; she has helped to heighten awareness of the rights of indigenous peoples worldwide.

Partly due to her efforts, a peace accord was signed between the guerrilla groups and the Guatemalan government in December 1996. In the 35 years that the civil war lasted, over 100,000 Guatemalans were killed and at least 40,000 were "disappeared" and are presumed dead, 440 villages were burned to the ground, 100,000 people were wounded, and 200,000 fled to other countries. Menchú now travels safely to her homeland.

Juan E. Mendez

Juan Mendez, a lawyer and educator, was born and raised in Argentina and received his education from Stella Maris Catholic University and the Provincial University in Mar del Plata and later from the American University in Washington, D.C. He was in private law practice in Argentina from 1970 to 1975 and was acting dean of the School of Economics at Provincial University for the year 1973.

Under Argentina's state of siege, Mendez became a political prisoner without charges for 18 months. Adopted as a "prisoner of conscience" by Amnesty International in 1976, he was exiled in 1977. He became director of Centro Christo Rey, a Catholic Center for Hispanics in Aurora, Illinois, and then accepted a position with the Alien Rights Law Project under the sponsorship of the Lawyers' Committee for Civil Rights under Law in Washington, D.C. In 1982 Mendez became director of the Washington, D.C., office of Americas Watch (now Human Rights Watch/Americas), a position that allowed him to participate in many of the Americas Watch investigations of human rights violations, particularly in Latin American countries. He has been responsible for several of the excellent Americas Watch reports and other publications on human rights in Latin American countries.

On a monitoring mission during the 1980s, Mendez was ordered to leave Ayacucho in Peru because he was told he did not have permission from the politico-military command there to carry out such work. Since he had already received approval from the prime minister, the foreign minister, and others, he strongly protested this expulsion. It was of particular concern because during his brief stay there before the incident he had received eyewitness testimony about the military abduction of two men who had themselves witnessed a massacre of peasants that had occurred earlier in the year. In a letter to Peruvian president Garcia Perez, Mendez strongly protested this and other restrictions on the ability of Americas Watch to investigate allegations of human rights abuses.

Mendez left Human Rights Watch in the 1990s to become the executive director of the Inter-American Institute for Human Rights based in Costa Rica. The institute has implemented several education programs to make people aware of their rights to humane treatment. They have been commended by the Organization of American States for their work. Mendez's activities on behalf of human rights, though less known than those of others, are nonetheless powerful.

Adolfo Pérez Esquivel

Adolfo Pérez Esquivel, born in Argentina in 1931, worked for human rights at a time when violence and terror were rampant in his country and rapidly spreading to other countries. After graduation from the National School of Fine Arts in Buenos Aires in 1956, he married and pursued a career as a sculptor and professor of fine arts. Although successful—much of his sculpture is in the permanent collections of various museums in Argentina— he gave up this career in 1974 to devote himself to coordinating various nonviolent peace and justice groups into an organization called Servicio Paz y Justicia (Service for Peace and Justice) and founding its journal, *Paz y Justicia.* Although Pérez Esquivel is a devout Roman Catholic, the organization he founded was ecumenical and not under the auspices of the Roman Catholic hierarchy, which was reluctant to become involved in the political turmoil that was responsible for such grave human rights abuses. As secretary-general of the group, he waged an international campaign to persuade the United Nations to establish a Human Rights Commission that could help bring an end to the flagrant violations of human rights not only in his country but in many others as well. He also championed the cause of the 6,000 *desaparecidos*—those who simply disappeared from their homes or off the streets of Argentine cities during the dictatorial military rule. His speaking out for such causes brought about his arrest without any legal charge and 14 months of imprisonment and torture. Even though he experienced this brutal treatment and worked to prevent it, he pointed out that peasants denied food and land also suffered grave human rights abuses. Under his leadership, Servicio Paz y Justicia sought to break the cycle of poverty that caused this type of abuse by championing the rights of workers.

In his travels throughout Latin America, he strongly supported other groups dedicated to the advancement of peace and human rights. For his efforts in this work, Pérez Esquivel received the Nobel Peace Prize in 1981. In awarding the prize to a relatively unknown human rights advocate, the committee noted that his message was important and valid for the whole of Latin America.

Pérez Esquivel is now president of the Honorary Council of Paz y Justicia, a member of the Permanent People's Tribunal, and president of the International League for the Rights and Liberation of Peoples based in Milan. Using his status as a Nobel Peace Prize winner, this champion of human rights has lent his name to peace and human rights efforts all over the globe from appealing to the United Nations in behalf of the people of Sri Lanka to working to ban nuclear testing.

Ginetta Sagan

One of the stories recounted often in Amnesty International literature is that of a young woman who was in a dark prison cell when a guard threw in a round loaf of bread, which she broke in two. Inside she found a matchbox that had in it a slip of paper with the word *Coraggio!* (courage) on it. Knowing that someone knew and cared, she nurtured the hope that was to sustain her through several more weeks of imprisonment and torture.

The woman in the story was Ginetta Sagan, a small 19-year-old, who had acted as a messenger for the Italian underground during World War II. When she was caught by the police, she was subjected to torture—rape, electric shocks, burnings, and near drownings—and to the terrible realization that she was alone and no one knew she was there. Some time after the matchbox incident, when she was hardly conscious after a severe beating, she heard her captors talking about the imminent end of the war and the necessity of eliminating all witnesses. Before this could happen, however, two German officers informed the Italians that she was to be taken for further questioning—actually Germans in the underground who drove her to safety.

Topolina, as she was then called, spent most of the next two years in the hospital trying to recover from the physical and psychological effects of imprisonment and torture. She did recover and resolved to help others who were held prisoner for their beliefs. To this end she has worked for many years in Amnesty International U.S.A., both on the board and as an active member, and has been one of those responsible for its tremendous growth. Sagan continues her work for human rights in countries all over the world—wherever people are imprisoned for their beliefs.

She received both the Presidential Medal of Freedom and the Grand Ufficiale de la Republica, Italy's highest award, in 1996. Amnesty International started the Ginetta Sagan Fund in recognition of Sagan's efforts. The fund will offer recognition and assistance to women doing effective work to protect the dignity, liberty, and lives of women and children in regions of crisis. At this writing, Sagan is ill with cancer.

Andrei Sakharov

Born in Moscow in 1921, Andrei Sakharov received his bachelor of arts degree from Moscow State University in 1942 and then joined the P. N. Lebedev Physics Institute in Moscow, where he worked with Igor Tamm, who later received the Nobel Prize for Physics. Under Tamm's direction, he obtained his doctorate in physical and mathematical sciences in 1947. From then until 1956 he worked in nuclear physics as a member of a team of scientists engaged in the development of nuclear arms.

Sakharov became increasingly uneasy about the "moral problem inherent in this work" and tried unsuccessfully to bring about open discussion of these problems. In 1968 he expressed his views in an essay titled "Progress, Peaceful Coexistence, and Intellectual Freedom," which, written from a global perspective, was an appeal to responsible citizens worldwide. Following the publication of the essay, Sakharov was dismissed from his position at the institute and began to have problems with the authorities. In 1970 he formed the Committee for Human Rights with friends and fellow scientists who dedicated themselves to changing the repressive measures so often taken by his government. For his work on peace and human rights issues he was awarded the Nobel Peace Prize in 1975. He took the opportunity of his Nobel lecture, which was read by his wife, Yelena Bonner, to speak about the repression in the Soviet Union and plead for the restoration of human rights. In 1980 he was sent into internal exile in Gorky, where he remained until 1986, when Soviet leader Mikhail Gorbachev freed him and allowed him to return to Moscow. Sakharov died December 14, 1989. He is remembered as an important leader in human rights.

Anatoly Shcharansky

A founding member of the Moscow Helsinki Watch, a group devoted to monitoring Soviet human rights violations, Anatoly Shcharansky was outspoken in his criticism of his country's repressive policies on Jewish emigration and other human rights violations. Born in Donetsk, a Ukrainian coal mining town, on January 20, 1948, Shcharansky attended school there until leaving in 1966 to enroll in a special mathematics school in Moscow. He later graduated from the Moscow Physical-Technical Institute as a specialist in cybernetics and found a position as a computer specialist with the Moscow Research Institute for Oil and Gas.

Although he had a promising career, he applied for an exit visa to Israel but was refused on the grounds that his work was classified. Knowing that this was not true—the institute was considered an "open" institution, not one involving secret work—he began to protest the government's treatment and joined the dissident movement. With his fiancée he applied again later while imprisoned for his activities; she was granted an exit visit but he was not, though they married before she left for Israel, thinking it would be only a matter of time before he would be granted permission to emigrate.

When this permission was not forthcoming, Shcharansky became more active in the dissident movement and with a small group founded the Moscow Helsinki Watch to monitor Soviet compliance with the human rights provisions of the Helsinki Accords. He subsequently lost his job, was subjected to constant threats and surveillance, and was accused of being a spy for the CIA. Arrested in March 1977 for "treasonable espionage," he was tried, found guilty, and sentenced to three years in prison to be followed by ten years in a labor camp.

Shcharansky served nine years of his thirteen-year term, suffering from long periods of isolation, hunger, and cold. His open defiance of Soviet regulations lasted until the day he left the Soviet Union as part of an exchange of prisoners. His release was due in part to the constant support given by his wife, his family, and friends. In May 1986 he came to the United States to thank the many who had supported him through his long imprisonment. He also urged the United States not only to continue "quiet diplomacy" but to put public pressure on the Soviet Union to release the thousands of Jews awaiting exit visas.

Aung San Suu Kyi

Born June 19, 1945, in Rangoon (now Myanmar), capital of Burma, Aung San Suu Kyi is the daughter of Aung San, a Burmese general who is largely credited with creating the strong nationalist movement that helped the Burmese people liberate themselves from the British and Japanese in 1948. Aung San was assassinated in 1947 when Aung San Suu Kyi was not yet two years old. She continued to live in Burma until 1960 when her mother was appointed the Burmese ambassador to India.

While in India, Aung San Suu Kyi became familiar with the teachings of Mohandas Gandhi. At St. Hughes College, Oxford University, she read politics, philosophy, and economics because she felt those subjects would be of most benefit to her country. She received her bachelor of arts degree in 1967. Aung San Suu Kyi married, had two sons, and pursued her academic interests in England, Japan, and India until 1988 when she returned to Rangoon to care for her dying mother.

Things had changed dramatically in the time she had been away from Burma. In 1962 a military coup was staged and a junta took over the government. She arrived home in 1988 at a time of great civil unrest. Aung San Suu Kyi had spent much of her time abroad researching the work of her father, and she was particularly distressed to see the condition of the Burmese people. Events culminated for her during a public demonstration where as many as 3,000 people were killed by government forces who shot indiscriminately into the protesting crowds. She decided that the time had come to take an active role in shaping Burmese politics. Her first major public appearance took place on August 26, 1988, before 500,000 people at Shwedagon Pagoda, Burma's most sacred shrine. Aung San Suu Kyi introduced the idea of basic human rights as a political objective for the people of Burma. Although she envisioned a democratic country that included a strong military, the Burmese government introduced tighter controls to discourage her and others from speaking out.

Aung San Suu Kyi helped found the National League for Democracy in September 1988. She continued to hold rallies despite laws banning political gatherings. All through her campaign for government reform, she stressed nonviolence. In perhaps her bravest act, on April 5, 1989, she was nearly gunned down by six soldiers that had been ordered to kill her. She remained calm and asked her supporters to move aside. She then walked directly toward the soldiers. At the last moment a higher-ranking officer countermanded the order to shoot.

In June of 1989 the junta gave the army the right to shoot political protesters without trial. This sparked Aung San Suu Kyi to remark that the government was showing its "true fascist colors." On July 20, 1989, she was placed under house arrest and at times was not permitted to see her husband and two sons. She was not permitted to leave her house until July of 1995. She and her supporters still encounter tremendous harassment from the Burmese government; advisors have been beaten with sticks and chains upon leaving her house, her phone is tapped, and her house has been barricaded. She encouraged the U.S. government to implement sanctions against Burma in an effort to end the government's repressive policies. Aung San Suu Kyi was awarded the Nobel Peace Prize in 1991.

Jacobo Timerman

Jacobo Timerman was born in the Ukraine in 1923 but moved with his family to Argentina when he was five and spent most of his life there. He very early became interested in human rights issues and spent time reading socially committed writers. As a young man he was briefly arrested while attending a film sponsored by an alleged Communist group, the Argentine League for Human Rights. He became a member of the Youth League for Freedom, which supported the side of the Allies in World War II—the government of Argentina supported the Germans. In another instance, he was briefly detained for leading an attack on the headquarters of a Nazi newspaper.

Although for a time he attended an engineering school, Timerman eventually became a journalist and also became involved at various times in radio, television, and publishing. Success in these media led to his founding his own newspaper, *La Opinión*, in 1971. Because the paper was outspoken on various issues, Timerman became a target of harassment by the government at a time when it was moving toward corruption, violence, and gross human rights violations. He was eventually imprisoned and tortured, though no charges were ever filed. Because he was well known, his case received a great deal of attention, and many human rights groups pleaded for his release. Timerman credits his release—at least partially—to the human rights policies of the United States during the Carter administration; under Carter, the United States withheld aid to Argentina because of that country's abuses.

Timerman's story is told in his book *Prisoner without a Name, Cell without a Number.* After his release from prison, Timerman lived for a time in Israel and the United States, but he eventually returned to Argentina and returned to the newspaper business. He, along with hundreds of others, gave testimony during the trials of the members of the military juntas responsible for so many disappearances and deaths during what has come to be called Argentina's "dirty wars"; but little has been done to punish most of those responsible for the gross human rights violations of the period. After his newspaper folded, he moved to Uruguay and became a founding member of the Asociación para la Defensa del Periodismo Independiente, an organization dedicated to freedom of the press. On March 22, 1996, Argentinian president Carlos Menem tried to reopen slander charges against Timerman. Timerman was not extradited to Argentina, and in April 1997 the charges were dropped.

Archbishop Desmond Tutu

There has been no more forceful spokesperson against South Africa's system of apartheid than the Anglican archbishop Desmond Mpilo Tutu. Born on October 7, 1931, in Klerksdorp, Witwatersrand, Transvaal, South Africa, Tutu attended Bantu Normal College, from which he earned a teacher's diploma in 1953, and the University of South Africa, receiving his bachelor of arts degree the following year. After teaching for four years, he entered St. Peter's Theological College in Johannesburg, earning a Licentiate in Theology in 1960. After being ordained to the priesthood in 1961 and gaining some experience as a curate, he received further degrees in theology and began a career in theological education that led eventually to his being appointed bishop of Lesotho, bishop of Johannesburg, and finally archbishop.

Although Archbishop Tutu had been keenly aware of the injustices brought about by apartheid since he was a child, it was not until he was appointed the first black to direct the South African Council of Churches that he became a leader in denouncing the government's proapartheid policies. He spoke out on every possible occasion about the deprivation of human rights that existed because of government policy. In 1984 when he received the Nobel Peace Prize for his heroic and fearless efforts, he used the occasion to describe the plight of black people in South Africa and did so with great eloquence. He was quick to point out, however, that in reality South Africa is a microcosm of the world and that injustice exists in many other countries. As on many occasions since then, he pleaded with the international community, and particularly the United States, to exert pressure on the South African government to end what had become a brutal system depriving thousands of their basic human rights.

Since the end of apartheid, Tutu has played a major role in helping South Africa recover from the wounds inflicted by apartheid. In 1995 Nelson Mandela appointed Tutu head of the Truth and Reconciliation Commission, which seeks to document the crimes committed during apartheid while granting the perpetrators amnesty. Tutu believes that if the crimes and human rights violations that took place under apartheid are acknowledged, the victims will be able to forgive the perpetrators.

Elie Wiesel

Elie Wiesel, born in a small town in Romania in 1928, is well known for his indefatigable zeal in ensuring that the world remembers the horrors of the Holocaust. He is said to be the first to use that term in reference to the killing of some six million Jews by Nazi Germany. The only son of a shopkeeper, Wiesel was brought up with his three sisters in a deeply religious family. In spite of rumors of Nazi atrocities, the family was shocked when they, with the 15,000 other Jews in the town, were deported to the Auschwitz concentration camp in Poland. His mother and youngest sister died in the gas chambers there; he and his father were later transferred to the Buchenwald camp, from which he was liberated. His father died in Buchenwald from starvation and dysentery.

Wiesel ended up in Paris, where he studied at the Sorbonne and eventually became a writer and journalist, a career that took him to many parts of the world. He did not write about his experiences in the camps until ten years later when he published *La Nuit*, in French. It was later translated into English as *Night* but was published in the United States only after many rejections from publishers. This memoir was to be the first of many writings—novels, plays, stories, and essays—designed to raise the awareness of readers to the events of the Holocaust. After recuperating from an accident in New York, Wiesel joined the staff of a Yiddish-language newspaper there and became a U.S. citizen in 1963.

Though Wiesel's works generally focus on Jewish themes, he has at the same time shown deep concern for any violations of human rights wherever they occur. Over the years he has spoken out for the rights of black people in South Africa, of the Miskito Indians of Nicaragua, of the boat people of Indochina, of Argentine political prisoners, and of Soviet Jews. He traveled to many of these countries to show his solidarity with oppressed peoples. For his writings and his ceaseless commitment to freedom and justice, he was awarded the Nobel Peace Prize in 1986, the most prestigious of the many awards he has received through the years. Since winning the prize he has continued to work for peace. He has met with leaders in Bosnia and organized the Tomorrow's Leaders youth conference in Venice, where in 1995 he brought together 30 adolescents from battlefields around the world—Bosnia, several African countries, Northern Ireland, the Middle East, and some of the more violent neighborhoods of American cities—to talk about their lives and make friends.

Simon Wiesenthal

Simon Wiesenthal, a prolific writer and documentor of the atrocities of the Holocaust, was born in 1908 in an Austro-Hungarian town, now part of the Ukraine. He received a degree in architectural engineering from the Technical University of Prague in 1932 and did further studies at the University of Lemberg. He was a practicing architect in Lemberg from 1939 until he was arrested in 1941. Although he escaped execution by the Nazis through the help of a former employee, he and his wife were assigned to a forced labor camp. She was later helped to escape by the underground, but Wiesenthal had to endure life in a series of concentration camps, finally being liberated by the Americans from the camp at Mauthausen.

For a time he was employed by the U.S. War Crimes Commission to help prepare evidence of Nazi atrocities, but when the position ended, he and some other volunteers established the Jewish Historical Documentation Center in Linz, Austria, to continue the work of gathering and preparing evidence against Nazi war criminals. Thus began a life's work of bringing to justice those responsible for the crimes of the Holocaust. Through his efforts and that of the many volunteers who assist him, Wiesenthal has been responsible for finding and bringing to court almost 1,000 war criminals, including Adolf Eichmann.

In addition to his work of gathering evidence that will stand up in a court of law, Wiesenthal has written many books and articles. Among his best known are *I Hunted Eichmann* (1961), *The Murderers among Us* (1967), *The Sunflower* (1969), *Sails of Hope* (1973), *The Case of Krystyna Jaworska* (1975), and *Max and Helen* (1982). The long list of his honorary degrees and various awards from all over the world attests to the esteem in which Wiesenthal is held. His unflagging efforts to make the world aware of the most massive violation of human rights in modern times seem particularly important today, when there is evidence of a resurgence of Nazi terror.

Jody Williams

Jody Williams was born October 9, 1950, grew up in Brattleboro, Vermont, and while a student at the University of Vermont took part in protests against the Vietnam War. After earning a master's degree in Spanish, she visited Mexico, where she was stunned by the contrasts of extreme wealth and poverty.

In 1981 she was working as a temporary employee in Washington, D.C., when a leaflet sparked her interest in Central America. She joined an organization that was working to build public awareness of U.S. policy there. She then earned a degree at Johns Hopkins School of Advanced International Studies. After graduation she took a paid position with the Nicaragua-Honduras Education Project. This in turn led her to the Los Angeles–based charity, Medical Aid for El Salvador. Its mission was to help war victims during that country's 12-year civil war that ended in 1992. Williams's position was to raise funds and deliver prosthetics for thousands of children who had lost limbs due to land mines. Her experiences affected her profoundly and she decided to concentrate her efforts on trying to ban land mines.

In 1991, Williams was approached by the head of the Vietnam Veterans of America Foundation, Robert Muller, to help form the International Campaign to Ban Landmines (ICBL). Its strategy was to leverage their resources by involving humanitarian and nongovernmental organizations from all over the world. Williams traveled extensively and contacted via e-mail over 700 humanitarian and nongovernmental organizations in over 40 countries to create support for a ban on land mines. In 1995, the

International Committee of the Red Cross, at ICBL's behest, took its first activist stance, running advertisements calling for a ban on land mines. In 1997, 89 nations convened in Oslo, Norway, to negotiate a treaty banning land mines. In December 1997, 121 nations signed the treaty.

Jody Williams and the International Campaign to Ban Landmines were jointly awarded the Nobel Peace Prize in 1997.

Selected Human Rights Documents

4

As part of its Blue Book Series, in 1995 the United Nations published *The United Nations and Human Rights, 1945–1995.* This work contains an excellent summary of U.N. activity on human rights and the most crucial U.N. documents in the human rights field. For a more comprehensive treatment without the historical background, consult the United Nations' *Human Rights: A Compilation of International Instruments, Parts I and II.* Human rights covers many different groups and issues and it is impossible to include all documents the reader might need. However, the documents selected here are intended to cover the issues of particular interest to the American public.

No selection would be adequate without the Universal Declaration of Human Rights and its covenants, known collectively as the International Bill of Human Rights, since these form the basis for all the other instruments. They are, therefore, included first, followed by the Convention on the Elimination of All Forms of Discrimination Against Women and the International Convention on the Elimination of All Forms of Racial Discrimination, for somewhat the same reason. One might argue that misogyny and racial discrimination are the basis for many of the world's problems, and

63

though the United States has made great strides in these areas, sexual and racial discrimination persist in various forms.

The instruments relating to prisoners seem appropriate to include—U.S. prisons are filling up faster than they can be built. The resulting overcrowded and sometimes inhumane penal conditions have in a few instances prompted the courts to order prisons to reduce their populations or be shut down. The Optional Protocol aimed at eliminating the death penalty is included as world pressure is starting to mount against the United States on this issue.

The Convention on Freedom of Association seems relevant in view of recent attempts by the government to find a balance between maintaining civil rights and preventing violent events, like the Oklahoma City bombing, by groups known to oppose government policy.

The final instruments relate to the care a society and the world is obliged to give those who frequently are unable to defend their rights—children, the mentally retarded, and the disabled. The Convention on the Rights of the Child is included because it seeks to expand children's rights, an area of current interest in the United States. The Declaration on the Right to Development is included because it is an area of interest within the field of human rights, as development projects change to become more aware of the likely outcomes for all population groups.

Universal Declaration of Human Rights

G.A. res. 217A (III), U.N. Doc A/810 at 71 (1948).

PREAMBLE

Whereas recognition of the inherent dignity and of the equal and inalienable rights of all members of the human family is the foundation of freedom, justice and peace in the world,

Whereas disregard and contempt for human rights have resulted in barbarous acts which have outraged the conscience of mankind, and the advent of a world in which human beings shall enjoy freedom of speech and belief and freedom from fear and want has been proclaimed as the highest aspiration of the common people,

Whereas it is essential, if man is not to be compelled to have recourse, as a last resort, to rebellion against tyranny and oppression, that human rights should be protected by the rule of law,

Whereas it is essential to promote the development of friendly relations between nations,

Whereas the peoples of the United Nations have in the Charter reaffirmed their faith in fundamental human rights, in the dignity and worth of the human person and in the equal rights of men and women and have determined to promote social progress and better standards of life in larger freedom,

Whereas Member States have pledged themselves to achieve, in cooperation with the United Nations, the promotion of universal respect for and observance of human rights and fundamental freedoms,

Whereas a common understanding of these rights and freedoms is of the greatest importance for the full realization of this pledge,

Now, therefore,

The General Assembly,

Proclaims this Universal Declaration of Human Rights as a common standard of achievement for all peoples and all nations, to the end that every individual and every organ of society, keeping this Declaration constantly in mind, shall strive by teaching and education to promote respect for these rights and freedoms and by progressive measures, national and international, to secure their universal and effective recognition and observance, both among the peoples of Member States themselves and among the peoples of territories under their jurisdiction.

Article 1

All human beings are born free and equal in dignity and rights. They are endowed with reason and conscience and should act towards one another in a spirit of brotherhood.

Article 2

Everyone is entitled to all the rights and freedoms set forth in this Declaration, without distinction of any kind, such as race, colour, sex, language, religion, political or other opinion, national or social origin, property, birth or other status.

Furthermore, no distinction shall be made on the basis of the political, jurisdictional or international status of the country or territory to which a person belongs, whether it be independent, trust, non-self-governing or under any other limitation of sovereignty.

Article 3

Everyone has the right to life, liberty and security of person.

Article 4

No one shall be held in slavery or servitude; slavery and the slave trade shall be prohibited in all their forms.

Article 5

No one shall be subjected to torture or to cruel, inhuman or degrading treatment or punishment.

Article 6

Everyone has the right to recognition everywhere as a person before the law.

Article 7

All are equal before the law and are entitled without any discrimination to equal protection of the law. All are entitled to equal protection against any discrimination in violation of this Declaration and against any incitement to such discrimination.

Article 8

Everyone has the right to an effective remedy by the competent national tribunals for acts violating the fundamental rights granted him by the constitution or by law.

Article 9

No one shall be subjected to arbitrary arrest, detention or exile.

Article 10

Everyone is entitled in full equality to a fair and public hearing by an independent and impartial tribunal, in the determination of his rights and obligations and of any criminal charge against him.

Article 11

1. Everyone charged with a penal offence has the right to be presumed innocent until proved guilty according to law in a

public trial at which he has had all the guarantees necessary for his defence.

2. No one shall be held guilty of any penal offence on account of any act or omission which did not constitute a penal offence, under national or international law, at the time when it was committed. Nor shall a heavier penalty be imposed than the one that was applicable at the time the penal offence was committed.

Article 12

No one shall be subjected to arbitrary interference with his privacy, family, home or correspondence, nor to attacks upon his honour and reputation. Everyone has the right to the protection of the law against such interference or attacks.

Article 13

1. Everyone has the right to freedom of movement and residence within the borders of each State.

2. Everyone has the right to leave any country, including his own, and to return to his country.

Article 14

1. Everyone has the right to seek and to enjoy in other countries asylum from persecution.

2. This right may not be invoked in the case of prosecutions genuinely arising from non-political crimes or from acts contrary to the purposes and principles of the United Nations.

Article 15

1. Everyone has the right to a nationality.

2. No one shall be arbitrarily deprived of his nationality nor denied the right to change his nationality.

Article 16

1. Men and women of full age, without any limitation due to race, nationality or religion, have the right to marry and to found a family. They are entitled to equal rights as to marriage, during marriage and at its dissolution.

2. Marriage shall be entered into only with the free and full consent of the intending spouses.

3. The family is the natural and fundamental group unit of society and is entitled to protection by society and the State.

Article 17

1. Everyone has the right to own property alone as well as in association with others.

2. No one shall be arbitrarily deprived of his property.

Article 18

Everyone has the right to freedom of thought, conscience and religion; this right includes freedom to change his religion or belief, and freedom, either alone or in community with others and in public or private, to manifest his religion or belief in teaching, practice, worship and observance.

Article 19

Everyone has the right to freedom of opinion and expression; this right includes freedom to hold opinions without interference and to seek, receive and impart information and ideas through any media and regardless of frontiers.

Article 20

1. Everyone has the right to freedom of peaceful assembly and association.

2. No one may be compelled to belong to an association.

Article 21

1. Everyone has the right to take part in the government of his country, directly or through freely chosen representatives.

2. Everyone has the right to equal access to public service in his country.

3. The will of the people shall be the basis of the authority of government; this will shall be expressed in periodic and genuine elections which shall be by universal and equal suffrage and shall be held by secret vote or by equivalent free voting procedures.

Article 22

Everyone, as a member of society, has the right to social security and is entitled to realization, through national effort and international co-operation and in accordance with the organization and resources of each State, of the economic, social and cultural rights indispensable for his dignity and the free development of his personality.

Article 23

1. Everyone has the right to work, to free choice of employment, to just and favourable conditions of work and to protection against unemployment.

2. Everyone, without any discrimination, has the right to equal pay for equal work.

3. Everyone who works has the right to just and favourable remuneration ensuring for himself and his family an existence worthy of human dignity, and supplemented, if necessary, by other means of social protection.

4. Everyone has the right to form and to join trade unions for the protection of his interests.

Article 24

Everyone has the right to rest and leisure, including reasonable limitation of working hours and periodic holidays with pay.

Article 25

1. Everyone has the right to a standard of living adequate for the health and well-being of himself and of his family, including food, clothing, housing and medical care and necessary social services, and the right to security in the event of unemployment, sickness, disability, widowhood, old age or other lack of livelihood in circumstances beyond his control.

2. Motherhood and childhood are entitled to special care and assistance. All children, whether born in or out of wedlock, shall enjoy the same social protection.

Article 26

1. Everyone has the right to education. Education shall be free, at least in the elementary and fundamental stages. Elementary education shall be compulsory. Technical and professional education shall be made generally available and higher education shall be equally accessible to all on the basis of merit.

2. Education shall be directed to the full development of the human personality and to the strengthening of respect for

human rights and fundamental freedoms. It shall promote understanding, tolerance and friendship among all nations, racial or religious groups, and shall further the activities of the United Nations for the maintenance of peace.

3. Parents have a prior right to choose the kind of education that shall be given to their children.

Article 27

1. Everyone has the right freely to participate in the cultural life of the community, to enjoy the arts and to share in scientific advancement and its benefits.

2. Everyone has the right to the protection of the moral and material interests resulting from any scientific, literary or artistic production of which he is the author.

Article 28

Everyone is entitled to a social and international order in which the rights and freedoms set forth in this Declaration can be fully realized.

Article 29

1. Everyone has duties to the community in which alone the free and full development of his personality is possible.

2. In the exercise of his rights and freedoms, everyone shall be subject only to such limitations as are determined by law solely for the purpose of securing due recognition and respect for the rights and freedoms of others and of meeting the just requirements of morality, public order and the general welfare in a democratic society.

3. These rights and freedoms may in no case be exercised contrary to the purposes and principles of the United Nations.

Article 30

Nothing in this Declaration may be interpreted as implying for any State, group or person any right to engage in any activity or to perform any act aimed at the destruction of any of the rights and freedoms set forth herein.

International Covenant on Economic, Social and Cultural Rights

G.A. res. 2200A (XXI), 21 U.N.GAOR Supp. (No. 16) at 49,
U.N. Doc. A/6316 (1966), 993 U.N.T.S. 3,
entered into force Jan. 3, 1976.

PREAMBLE

The States Parties to the present Covenant,

Considering that, in accordance with the principles proclaimed in the Charter of the United Nations, recognition of the inherent dignity and of the equal and inalienable rights of all members of the human family is the foundation of freedom, justice and peace in the world,

Recognizing that these rights derive from the inherent dignity of the human person,

Recognizing that, in accordance with the Universal Declaration of Human Rights, the ideal of free human beings enjoying freedom from fear and want can only be achieved if conditions are created whereby everyone may enjoy his economic, social and cultural rights, as well as his civil and political rights,

Considering the obligation of States under the Charter of the United Nations to promote universal respect for, and observance of, human rights and freedoms,

Realizing that the individual, having duties to other individuals and to the community to which he belongs, is under a responsibility to strive for the promotion and observance of the rights recognized in the present Covenant,

Agree upon the following articles:

PART I

Article 1

1. All peoples have the right of self-determination. By virtue of that right they freely determine their political status and freely pursue their economic, social and cultural development.

2. All peoples may, for their own ends, freely dispose of their natural wealth and resources without prejudice to any obligations arising out of international economic co-operation, based upon the principle of mutual benefit, and international law. In no case may a people be deprived of its own means of subsistence.

3. The States Parties to the present Covenant, including those having responsibility for the administration of Non-Self-Governing and Trust Territories, shall promote the realization of the right of self-determination, and shall respect that right, in conformity with the provisions of the Charter of the United Nations.

PART II

Article 2

1. Each State Party to the present Covenant undertakes to take steps, individually and through international assistance and co-operation, especially economic and technical, to the maximum of its available resources, with a view to achieving progressively the full realization of the rights recognized in the present Covenant by all appropriate means, including particularly the adoption of legislative measures.

2. The States Parties to the present Covenant undertake to guarantee that the rights enunciated in the present Covenant will be exercised without discrimination of any kind as to race, colour, sex, language, religion, political or other opinion, national or social origin, property, birth or other status.

3. Developing countries, with due regard to human rights and their national economy, may determine to what extent they would guarantee the economic rights recognized in the present Covenant to non-nationals.

Article 3

The States Parties to the present Covenant undertake to ensure the equal right of men and women to the enjoyment of all economic, social and cultural rights set forth in the present Covenant.

Article 4

The States Parties to the present Covenant recognize that, in the enjoyment of those rights provided by the State in conformity with the present Covenant, the State may subject such rights only to such limitations as are determined by law only in so far as this may be compatible with the nature of these rights and solely for the purpose of promoting the general welfare in a democratic society.

Article 5

1. Nothing in the present Covenant may be interpreted as implying for any State, group or person any right to engage in any activity or to perform any act aimed at the destruction of any of the rights or freedoms recognized herein, or at their limitation to a greater extent than is provided for in the present Covenant.

2. No restriction upon or derogation from any of the fundamental human rights recognized or existing in any country in virtue of law, conventions, regulations or custom shall be admitted on the pretext that the present Covenant does not recognize such rights or that it recognizes them to a lesser extent.

PART III

Article 6

1. The States Parties to the present Covenant recognize the right to work, which includes the right of everyone to the opportunity to gain his living by work which he freely chooses or accepts, and will take appropriate steps to safeguard this right.

2. The steps to be taken by a State Party to the present Covenant to achieve the full realization of this right shall include technical and vocational guidance and training programmes, policies and techniques to achieve steady economic, social and cultural development and full and productive employment under conditions safeguarding fundamental political and economic freedoms to the individual.

Article 7

The States Parties to the present Covenant recognize the right of everyone to the enjoyment of just and favourable conditions of work which ensure, in particular:

(a) Remuneration which provides all workers, as a minimum, with:

(i) Fair wages and equal remuneration for work of equal value without distinction of any kind, in particular women being guaranteed conditions of work not inferior to those enjoyed by men, with equal pay for equal work;

(ii) A decent living for themselves and their families in accordance with the provisions of the present Covenant;

(b) Safe and healthy working conditions;

(c) Equal opportunity for everyone to be promoted in his employment to an appropriate higher level, subject to no considerations other than those of seniority and competence;

(d) Rest, leisure and reasonable limitation of working hours and periodic holidays with pay, as well as remuneration for public holidays.

Article 8

1. The States Parties to the present Covenant undertake to ensure:

(a) The right of everyone to form trade unions and join the trade union of his choice, subject only to the rules of the organization concerned, for the promotion and protection of his economic and social interests. No restrictions may be placed on the exercise of this right other than those prescribed by law and which are necessary in a democratic society in the interests of national security or public order or for the protection of the rights and freedoms of others;

(b) The right of trade unions to establish national federations or confederations and the right of the latter to form or join international trade-union organizations;

(c) The right of trade unions to function freely subject to no limitations other than those prescribed by law and which are necessary in a democratic society in the interests of national security or public order or for the protection of the rights and freedoms of others;

(d) The right to strike, provided that it is exercised in conformity with the laws of the particular country.

2. This article shall not prevent the imposition of lawful restrictions on the exercise of these rights by members of the armed forces or of the police or of the administration of the State.

3. Nothing in this article shall authorize States Parties to the International Labour Organisation Convention of 1948 concerning Freedom of Association and Protection of the Right to Organize to take legislative measures which would prejudice, or apply the law in such a manner as would prejudice, the guarantees provided for in that Convention.

Article 9

The States Parties to the present Covenant recognize the right of everyone to social security, including social insurance.

Article 10

The States Parties to the present Covenant recognize that:

1. The widest possible protection and assistance should be accorded to the family, which is the natural and fundamental group unit of society, particularly for its establishment and while it is responsible for the care and education of dependent children. Marriage must be entered into with the free consent of the intending spouses.

2. Special protection should be accorded to mothers during a reasonable period before and after childbirth. During such period working mothers should be accorded paid leave or leave with adequate social security benefits.

3. Special measures of protection and assistance should be taken on behalf of all children and young persons without any discrimination for reasons of parentage or other conditions. Children and young persons should be protected from economic and social exploitation. Their employment in work harmful to their morals or health or dangerous to life or likely to hamper their normal development should be punishable by law. States should also set age limits below which the paid employment of child labour should be prohibited and punishable by law.

Article 11

1. The States Parties to the present Covenant recognize the right of everyone to an adequate standard of living for himself and his family, including adequate food, clothing and housing, and to the continuous improvement of living conditions. The States Parties will take appropriate steps to ensure the realization of this right, recognizing to this effect the essential importance of international co-operation based on free consent.

2. The States Parties to the present Covenant, recognizing the fundamental right of everyone to be free from hunger, shall take, individually and through international co-operation, the measures, including specific programmes, which are needed:

(a) To improve methods of production, conservation and distribution of food by making full use of technical and scientific knowledge, by disseminating knowledge of the principles of nutrition and by developing or reforming agrarian systems in such a way as to achieve the most efficient development and utilization of natural resources;

(b) Taking into account the problems of both food-importing and food-exporting countries, to ensure an equitable distribution of world food supplies in relation to need.

Article 12

1. The States Parties to the present Covenant recognize the right of everyone to the enjoyment of the highest attainable standard of physical and mental health.

2. The steps to be taken by the States Parties to the present Covenant to achieve the full realization of this right shall include those necessary for:

(a) The provision for the reduction of the stillbirth-rate and of infant mortality and for the healthy development of the child;

(b) The improvement of all aspects of environmental and industrial hygiene;

(c) The prevention, treatment and control of epidemic, endemic, occupational and other diseases;

(d) The creation of conditions which would assure to all medical service and medical attention in the event of sickness.

Article 13

1. The States Parties to the present Covenant recognize the right of everyone to education. They agree that education shall be directed to the full development of the human personality and the sense of its dignity, and shall strengthen the respect for human rights and fundamental freedoms. They further agree that education shall enable all persons to participate effectively in a free society, promote understanding, tolerance and friendship among all nations and all racial, ethnic or religious groups, and further the activities of the United Nations for the maintenance of peace.

2. The States Parties to the present Covenant recognize that, with a view to achieving the full realization of this right:

(a) Primary education shall be compulsory and available free to all;

(b) Secondary education in its different forms, including technical and vocational secondary education, shall be made generally available and accessible to all by every appropriate means, and in particular by the progressive introduction of free education;

(c) Higher education shall be made equally accessible to all, on the basis of capacity, by every appropriate means, and in particular by the progressive introduction of free education;

(d) Fundamental education shall be encouraged or intensified as far as possible for those persons who have not received or completed the whole period of their primary education;

(e) The development of a system of schools at all levels shall be actively pursued, an adequate fellowship system shall be established, and the material conditions of teaching staff shall be continuously improved.

3. The States Parties to the present Covenant undertake to have respect for the liberty of parents and, when applicable, legal guardians to choose for their children schools, other than those established by the public authorities, which conform to such minimum educational standards as may be laid down or approved by the State and to ensure the religious and moral education of their children in conformity with their own convictions.

4. No part of this article shall be construed so as to interfere with the liberty of individuals and bodies to establish and direct educational institutions, subject always to the observance of the principles set forth in paragraph 1 of this article and to the requirement that the education given in such institutions shall conform to such minimum standards as may be laid down by the State.

Article 14

Each State Party to the present Covenant which, at the time of becoming a Party, has not been able to secure in its metropolitan territory or other territories under its jurisdiction compulsory primary education, free of charge, undertakes, within two years, to work out and adopt a detailed plan of action for the progressive implementation, within a reasonable number of years, to be fixed in the plan, of the principle of compulsory education free of charge for all.

Article 15

1. The States Parties to the present Covenant recognize the right of everyone:

(a) To take part in cultural life;

(b) To enjoy the benefits of scientific progress and its application;

(c) To benefit from the protection of the moral and material interests resulting from any scientific, literary or artistic production of which he is the author.

2. The steps to be taken by the States Parties to the present Covenant to achieve the full realization of this right shall include those necessary for the conservation, the development and the diffusion of science and culture.

3. The States Parties to the present Covenant undertake to respect the freedom indispensable for scientific research and creative activity.

4. The States Parties to the present Covenant recognize the benefits to be derived from the encouragement and development of international contacts and co-operation in the scientific and cultural fields.

PART IV

Article 16

1. The States Parties to the present Covenant undertake to submit in conformity with this part of the Covenant reports on the measures which they have adopted and the progress made in achieving the observance of the rights recognized herein.

2. (a) All reports shall be submitted to the Secretary-General of the United Nations, who shall transmit copies to the Economic and Social Council for consideration in accordance with the provisions of the present Covenant;

(b) The Secretary-General of the United Nations shall also transmit to the specialized agencies copies of the reports, or any relevant parts therefrom, from States Parties to the present Covenant which are also members of these specialized agencies in so far as these reports, or parts therefrom, relate to any matters which fall within the responsibilities of the said agencies in accordance with their constitutional instruments.

Article 17

1. The States Parties to the present Covenant shall furnish their reports in stages, in accordance with a programme to be established by the Economic and Social council within one year of the entry into force of the present Covenant after consultation with the States Parties and the specialized agencies concerned.

2. Reports may indicate factors and difficulties affecting the degree of fulfilment of obligations under the present Covenant.

3. Where relevant information has previously been furnished to the United Nations or to any specialized agency by any State Party to the present Covenant, it will not be necessary

to reproduce that information, but a precise reference to the information so furnished will suffice.

Article 18

Pursuant to its responsibilities under the Charter of the United Nations in the field of human rights and fundamental freedoms, the Economic and Social Council may make arrangements with the specialized agencies in respect of their reporting to it on the progress made in achieving the observance of the provisions of the present Covenant falling within the scope of their activities. These reports may include particulars of decisions and recommendations on such implementation adopted by their competent organs.

Article 19

The Economic and Social Council may transmit to the Commission on Human Rights for study and general recommendation or, as appropriate, for information the reports concerning human rights submitted by States in accordance with articles 16 and 17, and those concerning human rights submitted by the specialized agencies in accordance with article 18.

Article 20

The States Parties to the present Covenant and the specialized agencies concerned may submit comments to the Economic and Social Council on any general recommendation under article 19 or reference to such general recommendation in any report of the Commission on Human Rights or any documentation referred to therein.

Article 21

The Economic and Social Council may submit from time to time to the General Assembly reports with recommendations of a general nature and a summary of the information received from the States Parties to the present Covenant and the specialized agencies on the measures taken and the progress made in achieving general observance of the rights recognized in the present Covenant.

Article 22

The Economic and Social Council may bring to the attention of other organs of the United Nations, their subsidiary organs and specialized agencies concerned with furnishing technical assistance any matters arising out of the reports referred to in this part of the present Covenant which may assist such bodies in deciding, each within its field of competence, on the advisability of international measures likely to contribute to the effective progressive implementation of the present Covenant.

Article 23

The States Parties to the present Covenant agree that international action for the achievement of the rights recognized in the present Covenant includes such methods as the conclusion of conventions, the adoption of recommendations, the furnishing of technical assistance and the holding of regional meetings and technical meetings for the purpose of consultation and study organized in conjunction with the Governments concerned.

Article 24

Nothing in the present Covenant shall be interpreted as impairing the provisions of the Charter of the United Nations and of the constitutions of the specialized agencies which define the respective responsibilities of the various organs of the United Nations and of the specialized agencies in regard to the matters dealt with in the present Covenant.

Article 25

Nothing in the present Covenant shall be interpreted as impairing the inherent right of all peoples to enjoy and utilize fully and freely their natural wealth and resources.

PART V

Article 26

1. The present Covenant is open for signature by any State Member of the United Nations or member of any of its specialized agencies, by any State Party to the Statute of the International Court of Justice, and by any other State which has been invited by the General Assembly of the United Nations to become a party to the present Covenant.

2. The present Covenant is subject to ratification.

Instruments of ratification shall be deposited with the Secretary-General of the United Nations.

3. The Present Covenant shall be open to accession by any State referred to in paragraph 1 of this article.

4. Accession shall be effected by the deposit of any instrument of accession with the Secretary-General of the United Nations.

5. The Secretary-General of the United Nations shall inform all States which have signed the present Covenant or accede to it of the deposit of each instrument of ratification or accession.

Article 27

1. The present Covenant shall enter into force three months after the date of the deposit with the Secretary-General of the United Nations of the thirty-fifth instrument of ratification or instrument of accession.

2. For each State ratifying the present Covenant or acceding to it after the deposit of the thirty-fifth instrument of ratification or instrument of accession, the present Covenant shall enter into force three months after the date of the deposit of its own instrument of ratification or instrument of accession.

Article 28

The provisions of the present Covenant shall extend to all parts of federal States without any limitations or exceptions.

Article 29

1. Any State Party to the present Covenant may propose an amendment and file it with the Secretary-General of the United Nations. The Secretary-General shall thereupon communicate any proposed amendments to the States Parties to the present Covenant with a request that they notify him whether they favour a conference of States Parties for the purpose of considering and voting upon the proposals. In the event that at least one third of the States Parties favours such a conference, the Secretary-General shall convene the conference under the auspices of the United Nations. Any amendment adopted by a majority of the States Parties present and voting at the conference shall be submitted to the General Assembly of the United Nations for approval.

2. Amendments shall come into force when they have been approved by the General Assembly of the United Nations and

accepted by a two-thirds majority of the States Parties to the present Covenant in accordance with their respective constitutional processes.

3. When amendments come into force they shall be binding on those States Parties which have accepted them, other State Parties still being bound by the provisions of the present Covenant and any earlier amendment which they have accepted.

Article 30

Irrespective of the notification made under article 26, paragraph 5, the Secretary-General of the United Nations shall inform all States referred to in paragraph 1 of the same article of the following particulars:

(a) Signatures, ratification and accessions under article 26;

(b) The date of the entry into force of the present Covenant under article 27 and the date of the entry into force of any amendments under article 29.

Article 31

1. The present Covenant, of which the Chinese, English, French, Russian and Spanish texts are equally authentic, shall be deposited in the archives of the United Nations.

2. The Secretary-General of the United Nations shall transmit certified copies of the present Covenant to all States referred to in article 26.

International Covenant on Civil and Political Rights

G.A. res. 2200A (XXI), 21 U.N. GAOR Supp. (No. 16) at 52, U.N. Doc. A/6316 (1966), 999 U.N.T.S. 171, entered into force Mar. 23, 1976.

PREAMBLE

The States Parties to the present Covenant,

Considering that, in accordance with the principles proclaimed in the Charter of the United Nations, recognition of the inherent dignity and of the equal and inalienable rights of all members of the human family is the foundation of freedom, justice and peace in the world,

Recognizing that these rights derive from the inherent dignity of the human person,

Recognizing that, in accordance with the Universal Declaration of Human Rights, the ideal of free human beings enjoying civil and political freedom and freedom from fear and want can only be achieved if conditions are created whereby everyone may enjoy his civil and political rights, as well as his economic, social and cultural rights,

Considering the obligation of States under the Charter of the United Nations to promote universal respect for, and observance of, human rights and freedoms,

Realizing that the individual, having duties to other individuals and to the community to which he belongs, is under a responsibility to strive for the promotion and observance of the rights recognized in the present Covenant,

Agree upon the following articles:

PART I

Article 1

1. All peoples have the right of self-determination. By virtue of that right they freely determine their political status and freely pursue their economic, social and cultural development.

2. All peoples may, for their own ends, freely dispose of their natural wealth and resources without prejudice to any obligations arising out of international economic co-operation, based upon the principle of mutual benefit, and international law. In no case may a people be deprived of its own means of subsistence.

3. The States Parties to the present Covenant, including those having responsibility for the administration of Non-Self-Governing and Trust Territories, shall promote the realization of the right of self-determination, and shall respect that right, in conformity with the provisions of the Charter of the United Nations.

PART II

Article 2

1. Each State Party to the present Covenant undertakes to respect and to ensure to all individuals within its territory and

subject to its jurisdiction the rights recognized in the present Covenant, without distinction of any kind, such as race, colour, sex, language, religion, political or other opinion, national or social origin, property, birth or other status.

2. Where not already provided for by existing legislative or other measures, each State Party to the present Covenant undertakes to take the necessary steps, in accordance with its constitutional processes and with the provisions of the present Covenant, to adopt such other measures as may be necessary to give effect to the rights recognized in the present Covenant.

3. Each State Party to the present Covenant undertakes:

(a) To ensure that any person whose rights or freedoms as herein recognized are violated shall have an effective remedy, notwithstanding that the violation has been committed by persons acting in an official capacity;

(b) To ensure that any person claiming such a remedy shall have his right thereto determined by competent judicial, administrative or legislative authorities, or by any other competent authority provided for by the legal system of the State, and to develop the possibilities of judicial remedy;

(c) To ensure that the competent authorities shall enforce such remedies when granted.

Article 3

The States Parties to the present Covenant undertake to ensure the equal right of men and women to the enjoyment of all civil and political rights set forth in the present Covenant.

Article 4

1. In time of public emergency which threatens the life of the nation and the existence of which is officially proclaimed, the States Parties to the present Covenant may take measures derogating from their obligations under the present Covenant to the extent strictly required by the exigencies of the situation, provided that such measures are not inconsistent with their other obligations under international law and do not involve discrimination solely on the ground of race, colour, sex, language, religion or social origin.

2. No derogation from articles 6, 7, 8 (paragraphs I and 2), 11, 15, 16 and 18 may be made under this provision.

3. Any State Party to the present Covenant availing itself of the right of derogation shall immediately inform the other

States Parties to the present Covenant, through the intermediary of the Secretary-General of the United Nations, of the provisions from which it has derogated and of the reasons by which it was actuated. A further communication shall be made, through the same intermediary, on the date on which it terminates such derogation.

Article 5

1. Nothing in the present Covenant may be interpreted as implying for any State, group or person any right to engage in any activity or perform any act aimed at the destruction of any of the rights and freedoms recognized herein or at their limitation to a greater extent than is provided for in the present Covenant.

2. There shall be no restriction upon or derogation from any of the fundamental human rights recognized or existing in any State Party to the present Covenant pursuant to law, conventions, regulations or custom on the pretext that the present Covenant does not recognize such rights or that it recognizes them to a lesser extent.

PART III

Article 6

1. Every human being has the inherent right to life. This right shall be protected by law. No one shall be arbitrarily deprived of his life.

2. In countries which have not abolished the death penalty, sentence of death may be imposed only for the most serious crimes in accordance with the law in force at the time of the commission of the crime and not contrary to the provisions of the present Covenant and to the Convention on the Prevention and Punishment of the Crime of Genocide. This penalty can only be carried out pursuant to a final judgement rendered by a competent court.

3. When deprivation of life constitutes the crime of genocide, it is understood that nothing in this article shall authorize any State Party to the present Covenant to derogate in any way from any obligation assumed under the provisions of the Convention of the Prevention and Punishment of the Crime of Genocide.

4. Anyone sentenced to death shall have the right to seek pardon or commutation of the sentence. Amnesty, pardon or commutation of the sentence of death may be granted in all cases.

5. Sentence of death shall not be imposed for crimes committed by persons below eighteen years of age and shall not be carried out on pregnant women.

6. Nothing in this article shall be invoked to delay or to prevent the abolition of capital punishment by any State Party to the present Covenant.

Article 7

No one shall be subjected to torture or to cruel, inhuman or degrading treatment or punishment. In particular, no one shall be subjected without his free consent to medical or scientific experimentation.

Article 8

1. No one shall be held in slavery; slavery and the slave-trade in all their forms shall be prohibited.

2. No one shall be held in servitude.

3. (a) No one shall be required to perform forced or compulsory labour;

(b) Paragraph 3 (a) shall not be held to preclude, in countries where imprisonment with hard labour may be imposed as a punishment for a crime, the performance of hard labour in pursuance of a sentence to such punishment by a competent court;

(c) For the purpose of this paragraph the term "forced or compulsory labour" shall not include:

(i) Any work or service, not referred to in subparagraph (b), normally required of a person who is under detention in consequence of a lawful order of a court, or of a person during conditional release from such detention;

(ii) Any service of a military character and, in countries where conscientious objection is recognized, any national service required by law of conscientious objectors;

(iii) Any service exacted in cases of emergency or calamity threatening the life or well-being of the community;

(iv) Any work or service which forms part of normal civil obligations.

Article 9

1. Everyone has the right to liberty and security of person. No one shall be subjected to arbitrary arrest or detention. No one shall be deprived of his liberty except on

such grounds and in accordance with such procedure as are established by law.

2. Anyone who is arrested shall be informed, at the time of arrest, of the reasons for his arrest and shall be promptly informed of any charges against him.

3. Anyone arrested or detained on a criminal charge shall be brought promptly before a judge or other officer authorized by law to exercise judicial power and shall be entitled to trial within a reasonable time or to release. It shall not be the general rule that persons awaiting trial shall be detained in custody, but release may be subject to guarantees to appear for trial, at any other stage of the judicial proceedings, and, should occasion arise, for execution of the judgement.

4. Anyone who is deprived of his liberty by arrest or detention shall be entitled to take proceedings before a court, in order that court may decide without delay on the lawfulness of his detention and order his release if the detention is not lawful.

5. Anyone who has been the victim of unlawful arrest or detention shall have an enforceable right to compensation.

Article 10

1. All persons deprived of their liberty shall be treated with humanity and with respect for the inherent dignity of the human person.

2. (a) Accused persons shall, save in exceptional circumstances, be segregated from convicted persons and shall be subject to separate treatment appropriate to their status as unconvicted persons;

(b) Accused juvenile persons shall be separated from adults and brought as speedily as possible for adjudication.

3. The penitentiary system shall comprise treatment of prisoners the essential aim of which shall be their reformation and social rehabilitation. Juvenile offenders shall be segregated from adults and be accorded treatment appropriate to their age and legal status.

Article 11

No one shall be imprisoned merely on the ground of inability to fulfil a contractual obligation.

Article 12

1. Everyone lawfully within the territory of a State shall,

within that territory, have the right to liberty of movement and freedom to choose his residence.

2. Everyone shall be free to leave any country, including his own.

3. The above-mentioned rights shall not be subject to any restrictions except those which are provided by law, are necessary to protect national security, public order (*ordre public*), public health or morals or the rights and freedoms of others, and are consistent with the other rights recognized in the present Covenant.

4. No one shall be arbitrarily deprived of the right to enter his own country.

Article 13

An alien lawfully in the territory of a State Party to the present Covenant may be expelled therefrom only in pursuance of a decision reached in accordance with law and shall, except where compelling reasons of national security otherwise require, be allowed to submit the reasons against his expulsion and to have his case reviewed by, and be represented for the purpose before, the competent authority or a person or persons especially designated by the competent authority.

Article 14

1. All persons shall be equal before the courts and tribunals. In the determination of any criminal charge against him, or of his rights and obligations in a suit at law, everyone shall be entitled to a fair and public hearing by a competent, independent and impartial tribunal established by law. The press and the public may be excluded from all or part of a trial for reasons of morals, public order (*ordre public*) or national security in a democratic society, or when the interest of the private lives of the parties so requires, or to the extent strictly necessary in the opinion of the court in special circumstances where publicity would prejudice the interests of justice; but any judgement rendered in a criminal case or in a suit at law shall be made public except where the interest of juvenile persons otherwise requires or the proceedings concern matrimonial disputes or the guardianship of children.

2. Everyone charged with a criminal offence shall have the right to be presumed innocent until proved guilty according to law.

3. In the determination of any criminal charge against him, everyone shall be entitled to the following minimum guarantees, in full equality:

(a) To be informed promptly and in detail in a language which he understands of the nature and cause of the charge against him;

(b) To have adequate time and facilities for the preparation of his defence and to communicate with counsel of his own choosing;

(c) To be tried without undue delay;

(d) To be tried in his presence, and to defend himself in person or through legal assistance of his own choosing; to be informed, if he does not have legal assistance, of this right; and to have legal assistance assigned to him, in any case where the interests of justice so require, and without payment by him in any such case if he does not have sufficient means to pay for it;

(e) To examine, or have examined, the witnesses against him and to obtain the attendance and examination of witnesses on his behalf under the same conditions as witnesses against him;

(f) To have the free assistance of an interpreter if he cannot understand or speak the language used in court;

(g) Not to be compelled to testify against himself or to confess guilt.

4. In the case of juvenile persons, the procedure shall be such as will take account of their age and the desirability of promoting their rehabilitation.

5. Everyone convicted of a crime shall have the right to his conviction and sentence being reviewed by a higher tribunal according to law.

6. When a person has by a final decision been convicted of a criminal offence and when subsequently his conviction has been reversed or he has been pardoned on the ground that a new or newly discovered fact shows conclusively that there has been a miscarriage of justice, the person who has suffered punishment as a result of such conviction shall be compensated according to law, unless it is proved that the non-disclosure of the unknown fact in time is wholly or partly attributable to him.

7. No one shall be liable to be tried or punished again for an offence for which he has already been finally convicted or acquitted in accordance with the law and penal procedure of each country.

Article 15

1. No one shall be held guilty of any criminal offence on account of any act or omission which did not constitute a criminal offence, under national or international law, at the time when it was committed. Nor shall a heavier penalty be imposed than the one that was applicable at the time when the criminal offence was committed. If, subsequent to the commission of the offence, provision is made by law for the imposition of the lighter penalty, the offender shall benefit thereby.

2. Nothing in this article shall prejudice the trial and punishment of any person for any act or omission which, at the time when it was committed, was criminal according to the general principles of law recognized by the community of nations.

Article 16

Everyone shall have the right to recognition everywhere as a person before the law.

Article 17

1. No one shall be subjected to arbitrary or unlawful interference with his privacy, family, home or correspondence, nor to unlawful attacks on his honour and reputation.

2. Everyone has the right to the protection of the law against such interference or attacks.

Article 18

1. Everyone shall have the right to freedom of thought, conscience and religion. This right shall include freedom to have or to adopt a religion or belief of his choice, and freedom, either individually or in community with others and in public or private, to manifest his religion or belief in worship, observance, practice and teaching.

2. No one shall be subject to coercion which would impair his freedom to have or to adopt a religion or belief of his choice.

3. Freedom to manifest one's religion or beliefs may be subject only to such limitations as are prescribed by law and are necessary to protect public safety, order, health, or morals or the fundamental rights and freedoms of others.

4. The States Parties to the present Covenant undertake to have respect for the liberty of parents and, when applicable,

legal guardians to ensure the religious and moral education of their children in conformity with their own convictions.

Article 19

1. Everyone shall have the right to hold opinions without interference.

2. Everyone shall have the right to freedom of expression; this right shall include freedom to seek, receive and impart information and ideas of all kinds, regardless of frontiers, either orally, in writing or in print, in the form of art, or through any other media of his choice.

3. The exercise of the rights provided for in paragraph 2 of this article carries with it special duties and responsibilities. It may therefore be subject to certain restrictions, but these shall only be such as are provided by law and are necessary:

(a) For respect of the rights or reputations of others;

(b) For the protection of national security or of public order (*ordre public*), or of public health or morals.

Article 20

1. Any propaganda for war shall be prohibited by law.

2. Any advocacy of national, racial or religious hatred that constitutes incitement to discrimination, hostility or violence shall be prohibited by law.

Article 21

The right of peaceful assembly shall be recognized. No restrictions may be placed on the exercise of this right other than those imposed in conformity with the law and which are necessary in a democratic society in the interests of national security or public safety, public order (*ordre public*), the protection of public health or morals or the protection of the rights and freedoms of others.

Article 22

1. Everyone shall have the right to freedom of association with others, including the right to form and join trade unions for the protection of his interests.

2. No restrictions may be placed on the exercise of this right other than those which are prescribed by law and which are necessary in a democratic society in the interests of

national security or public safety, public order (*ordre public*), the protection of public health or morals or the protection of the rights and freedoms of others. This article shall not prevent the imposition of lawful restrictions on members of the armed forces and of the police in their exercise of this right.

3. Nothing in this article shall authorize States Parties to the International Labour Organisation Convention of 1948 concerning Freedom of Association and Protection of the Right to Organize to take legislative measures which would prejudice, or to apply the law in such a manner as to prejudice, the guarantees provided for in that Convention.

Article 23

1. The family is the natural and fundamental group unit of society and is entitled to protection by society and the State.

2. The right of men and women of marriageable age to marry and to found a family shall be recognized.

3. No marriage shall be entered into without the free and full consent of the intending spouses.

4. States Parties to the present Covenant shall take appropriate steps to ensure equality of rights and responsibilities of spouses as to marriage, during marriage and at its dissolution. In the case of dissolution, provision shall be made for the necessary protection of any children.

Article 24

1. Every child shall have, without any discrimination as to race, colour, sex, language, religion, national or social origin, property or birth, the right to such measures of protection as are required by his status as a minor, on the part of his family, society and the State.

2. Every child shall be registered immediately after birth and shall have a name.

3. Every child has the right to acquire a nationality.

Article 25

Every citizen shall have the right and the opportunity, without any of the distinctions mentioned in article 2 and without unreasonable restrictions:

(a) To take part in the conduct of public affairs, directly or through freely chosen representatives;

(b) To vote and to be elected at genuine periodic elections which shall be by universal and equal suffrage and shall be held by secret ballot, guaranteeing the free expression of the will of the electors;

(c) To have access, on general terms of equality, to public service in his country.

Article 26

All persons are equal before the law and are entitled without any discrimination to the equal protection of the law. In this respect, the law shall prohibit any discrimination and guarantee to all persons equal and effective protection against discrimination on any ground such as race, colour, sex, language, religion, political or other opinion, national or social origin, property, birth or other status.

Article 27

In those States in which ethnic, religious or linguistic minorities exist, persons belonging to such minorities shall not be denied the right, in community with the other members of their group, to enjoy their own culture, to profess and practise their own religion, or to use their own language.

PART IV

Article 28

1. There shall be established a Human Rights Committee (hereafter referred to in the present Covenant as the Committee). It shall consist of eighteen members and shall carry out the functions hereinafter provided.

2. The Committee shall be composed of nationals of the States Parties to the present Covenant who shall be persons of high moral character and recognized competence in the field of human rights, consideration being given to the usefulness of the participation of some persons having legal experience.

3. The members of the Committee shall be elected and shall serve in their personal capacity.

Article 29

1 . The members of the Committee shall be elected by secret ballot from a list of persons possessing the qualifications

prescribed in article 28 and nominated for the purpose by the States Parties to the present Covenant.

2. Each State Party to the present Covenant may nominate not more than two persons. These persons shall be nationals of the nominating State.

3. A person shall be eligible for renomination.

Article 30

1. The initial election shall be held no later than six months after the date of the entry into force of the present Covenant.

2. At least four months before the date of each election to the Committee, other than an election to fill a vacancy declared in accordance with article 34, the Secretary-General of the United Nations shall address a written invitation to the States Parties to the present Covenant to submit their nominations for membership of the Committee within three months.

3. The Secretary-General of the United Nations shall prepare a list in alphabetical order of all the persons thus nominated, with an indication of the States Parties which have nominated them, and shall submit it to the States Parties to the present Covenant no later than one month before the date of each election.

4. Elections of the members of the Committee shall be held at a meeting of the States Parties to the present Covenant convened by the Secretary General of the United Nations at the Headquarters of the United Nations. At that meeting, for which two thirds of the States Parties to the present Covenant shall constitute a quorum, the persons elected to the Committee shall be those nominees who obtain the largest number of votes and an absolute majority of the votes of the representatives of States Parties present and voting.

Article 31

1. The Committee may not include more than one national of the same State.

2. In the election of the Committee, consideration shall be given to equitable geographical distribution of membership and to the representation of the different forms of civilization and of the principal legal systems.

Article 32

1. The members of the Committee shall be elected for a

term of four years. They shall be eligible for re-election if renominated. However, the terms of nine of the members elected at the first election shall expire at the end of two years; immediately after the first election, the names of these nine members shall be chosen by lot by the Chairman of the meeting referred to in article 30, paragraph 4.

2. Elections at the expiry of office shall be held in accordance with the preceding articles of this part of the present Covenant.

Article 33

1. If, in the unanimous opinion of the other members, a member of the Committee has ceased to carry out his functions for any cause other than absence of a temporary character, the Chairman of the Committee shall notify the Secretary-General of the United Nations, who shall then declare the seat of that member to be vacant.

2. In the event of the death or the resignation of a member of the Committee, the Chairman shall immediately notify the Secretary-General of the United Nations, who shall declare the seat vacant from the date of death or the date on which the resignation takes effect.

Article 34

1. When a vacancy is declared in accordance with article 33 and if the term of office of the member to be replaced does not expire within six months of the declaration of the vacancy, the Secretary-General of the United Nations shall notify each of the States Parties to the present Covenant, which may within two months submit nominations in accordance with article 29 for the purpose of filling the vacancy.

2. The Secretary-General of the United Nations shall prepare a list in alphabetical order of the persons thus nominated and shall submit it to the States Parties to the present Covenant. The election to fill the vacancy shall then take place in accordance with the relevant provisions of this part of the present Covenant.

3. A member of the Committee elected to fill a vacancy declared in accordance with article 33 shall hold office for the remainder of the term of the member who vacated the seat on the Committee under the provisions of that article.

Article 35

The members of the Committee shall, with the approval of

the General Assembly of the United Nations, receive emoluments from United Nations resources on such terms and conditions as the General Assembly may decide, having regard to the importance of the Committee's responsibilities.

Article 36

The Secretary-General of the United Nations shall provide the necessary staff and facilities for the effective performance of the functions of the Committee under the present Covenant.

Article 37

1. The Secretary-General of the United Nations shall convene the initial meeting of the Committee at the Headquarters of the United Nations.

2. After its initial meeting, the Committee shall meet at such times as shall be provided in its rules of procedure.

3. The Committee shall normally meet at the Headquarters of the United Nations or at the United Nations Office at Geneva.

Article 38

Every member of the Committee shall, before taking up his duties, make a solemn declaration in open committee that he will perform his functions impartially and conscientiously.

Article 39

1. The Committee shall elect its officers for a term of two years. They may be re-elected.

2. The Committee shall establish its own rules of procedure, but these rules shall provide, *inter alia,* that:

(a) Twelve members shall constitute a quorum;

(b) Decisions of the Committee shall be made by a majority vote of the members present.

Article 40

1. The States Parties to the present Covenant undertake to submit reports on the measures they have adopted which give effect to the rights recognized herein and on the progress made in the enjoyment of those rights:

(a) Within one year of the entry into force of the present Covenant for the States Parties concerned;

(b) Thereafter whenever the Committee so requests.

2. All reports shall be submitted to the Secretary-General of the United Nations, who shall transmit them to the Committee for consideration. Reports shall indicate the factors and difficulties, if any, affecting the implementation of the present Covenant.

3. The Secretary-General of the United Nations may, after consultation with the Committee, transmit to the specialized agencies concerned copies of such parts of the reports as may fall within their field of competence.

4. The Committee shall study the reports submitted by the States Parties to the present Covenant. It shall transmit its reports, and such general comments as it may consider appropriate, to the States Parties. The Committee may also transmit to the Economic and Social Council these comments along with the copies of the reports it has received from States Parties to the present Covenant.

5. The States Parties to the present Covenant may submit to the Committee observations on any comments that may be made in accordance with paragraph 4 of this article.

Article 41

1. A State Party to the present Covenant may at any time declare under this article that it recognizes the competence of the Committee to receive and consider communications to the effect that a State Party claims that another State Party is not fulfilling its obligations under the present Covenant. Communications under this article may be received and considered only if submitted by a State Party which has made a declaration recognizing in regard to itself the competence of the Committee. No communication shall be received by the Committee if it concerns a State Party which has not made such a declaration. Communications received under this article shall be dealt with in accordance with the following procedure:

(a) If a State Party to the present Covenant considers that another State Party is not giving effect to the provisions of the present Covenant, it may, by written communication, bring the matter to the attention of that State Party. Within three months after the receipt of the communication the receiving State shall afford the State which sent the communication an explanation, or any other statement in writing clarifying the matter which should include, to the extent possible and pertinent, reference to domestic procedures and remedies taken, pending, or available in the matter;

(b) If the matter is not adjusted to the satisfaction of both States Parties concerned within six months after the receipt by the receiving State of the initial communication, either State shall have the right to refer the matter to the Committee, by notice given to the Committee and to the other State;

(c) The Committee shall deal with a matter referred to it only after it has ascertained that all available domestic remedies have been invoked and exhausted in the matter, in conformity with the generally recognized principles of international law. This shall not be the rule where the application of the remedies is unreasonably prolonged;

(d) The Committee shall hold closed meetings when examining communications under this article;

(e) Subject to the provisions of subparagraph (c), the Committee shall make available its good offices to the States Parties concerned with a view to a friendly solution of the matter on the basis of respect for human rights and fundamental freedoms as recognized in the present Covenant;

(f) In any matter referred to it, the Committee may call upon the States Parties concerned, referred to in subparagraph (b), to supply any relevant information;

(g) The States Parties concerned, referred to in subparagraph (b), shall have the right to be represented when the matter is being considered in the Committee and to make submissions orally and/or in writing;

(h) The Committee shall, within twelve months after the date of receipt of notice under subparagraph (b), submit a report:

(i) If a solution within the terms of subparagraph (e) is reached, the Committee shall confine its report to a brief statement of the facts and of the solution reached;

(ii) If a solution within the terms of subparagraph (e) is not reached, the Committee shall confine its report to a brief statement of the facts; the written submissions and record of the oral submissions made by the States Parties concerned shall be attached to the report.

In every matter, the report shall be communicated to the States Parties concerned.

2. The provisions of this article shall come into force when ten States Parties to the present Covenant have made declarations under paragraph I of this article. Such declarations shall be deposited by the States Parties with the Secretary-General of the United Nations, who shall transmit copies thereof to the other States Parties. A declaration may be

withdrawn at any time by notification to the Secretary-General. Such a withdrawal shall not prejudice the consideration of any matter which is the subject of a communication already transmitted under this article; no further communication by any State Party shall be received after the notification of withdrawal of the declaration has been received by the Secretary-General, unless the State Party concerned has made a new declaration.

Article 42

1. (a) If a matter referred to the Committee in accordance with article 41 is not resolved to the satisfaction of the States Parties concerned, the Committee may, with the prior consent of the States Parties concerned, appoint an *ad hoc* Conciliation Commission (hereinafter referred to as the Commission). The good offices of the Commission shall be made available to the States Parties concerned with a view to an amicable solution of the matter on the basis of respect for the present Covenant;

(b) The Commission shall consist of five persons acceptable to the States Parties concerned. If the States Parties concerned fail to reach agreement within three months on all or part of the composition of the Commission, the members of the Commission concerning whom no agreement has been reached shall be elected by secret ballot by a two-thirds majority vote of the Committee from among its members.

2. The members of the Commission shall serve in their personal capacity. They shall not be nationals of the States Parties concerned, or of a State not Party to the present Covenant, or of a State Party which has not made a declaration under article 41.

3. The Commission shall elect its own Chairman and adopt its own rules of procedure.

4. The meetings of the Commission shall normally be held at the Headquarters of the United Nations or at the United Nations Office at Geneva. However, they may be held at such other convenient places as the Commission may determine in consultation with the Secretary-General of the United Nations and the States Parties concerned.

5. The secretariat provided in accordance with article 36 shall also service the commissions appointed under this article.

6. The information received and collated by the Committee shall be made available to the Commission and the Commission may call upon the States Parties concerned to supply any other relevant information.

7. When the Commission has fully considered the matter, but in any event not later than twelve months after having been seized of the matter, it shall submit to the Chairman of the Committee a report for communication to the States Parties concerned:

(a) If the Commission is unable to complete its consideration of the matter within twelve months, it shall confine its report to a brief statement of the status of its consideration of the matter;

(b) If an amicable solution to the matter on tie basis of respect for human rights as recognized in the present Covenant is reached, the Commission shall confine its report to a brief statement of the facts and of the solution reached;

(c) If a solution within the terms of subparagraph (b) is not reached, the Commission's report shall embody its findings on all questions of fact relevant to the issues between the States Parties concerned, and its views on the possibilities of an amicable solution of the matter. This report shall also contain the written submissions and a record of the oral submissions made by the States Parties concerned;

(d) If the Commission's report is submitted under subparagraph (c), the States Parties concerned shall, within three months of the receipt of the report, notify the Chairman of the Committee whether or not they accept the contents of the report of the Commission.

8. The provisions of this article are without prejudice to the responsibilities of the Committee under article 41.

9. The States Parties concerned shall share equally all the expenses of the members of the Commission in accordance with estimates to be provided by the Secretary-General of the United Nations.

10. The Secretary-General of the United Nations shall be empowered to pay the expenses of the members of the Commission, if necessary, before reimbursement by the States Parties concerned, in accordance with paragraph 9 of this article.

Article 43

The members of the Committee, and of the *ad hoc* conciliation commissions which may be appointed under article 42, shall be entitled to the facilities, privileges and immunities of experts on mission for the United Nations as laid down in the relevant sections of the Convention on the Privileges and Immunities of the United Nations.

Article 44

The provisions for the implementation of the present Covenant shall apply without prejudice to the procedures prescribed in the field of human rights by or under the constituent instruments and the conventions of the United Nations and of the specialized agencies and shall not prevent the States Parties to the present Covenant from having recourse to other procedures for settling a dispute in accordance with general or special international agreements in force between them.

Article 45

The Committee shall submit to the General Assembly of the United Nations, through the Economic and Social Council, an annual report on its activities.

PART V

Article 46

Nothing in the present Covenant shall be interpreted as impairing the provisions of the Charter of the United Nations and of the constitutions of the specialized agencies which define the respective responsibilities of the various organs of the United Nations and of the specialized agencies in regard to the matters dealt with in the present Covenant.

Article 47

Nothing in the present Covenant shall be interpreted as impairing the inherent right of all peoples to enjoy and utilize fully and freely their natural wealth and resources.

PART VI

Article 48

1. The present Covenant is open for signature by any State Member of the United Nations or member of any of its specialized agencies, by any State Party to the Statute of the International Court of Justice, and by any other State which has been invited by the General Assembly of the United Nations to become a Party to the present Covenant.

2. The present Covenant is subject to ratification. Instruments of ratification shall be deposited with the Secretary-General of the United Nations.

3. The present Covenant shall be open to accession by any State referred to in paragraph 1 of this article.

4. Accession shall be effected by the deposit of an instrument of accession with the Secretary-General of the United Nations.

5. The Secretary-General of the United Nations shall inform all States which have signed this Covenant or acceded to it of the deposit of each instrument of ratification or accession.

Article 49

1. The present Covenant shall enter into force three months after the date of the deposit with the Secretary-General of the United Nations of the thirty-fifth instrument of ratification or instrument of accession.

2. For each State ratifying the present Covenant or acceding to it after the deposit of the thirty-fifth instrument of ratification or instrument of accession, the present Covenant shall enter into force three months after the date of the deposit of its own instrument of ratification or instrument of accession.

Article 50

The provisions of the present Covenant shall extend to all parts of federal States without any limitations or exceptions.

Article 51

1. Any State Party to the present Covenant may propose an amendment and file it with the Secretary-General of the United Nations. The Secretary-General of the United Nations shall thereupon communicate any proposed amendments to the States Parties to the present Covenant with a request that they notify him whether they favour a conference of States Parties for the purpose of considering and voting upon the proposals. In the event that at least one third of the States Parties favours such a conference, the Secretary-General shall convene the conference under the auspices of the United Nations. Any amendment adopted by a majority of the States Parties present and voting at the conference shall be submitted to the General Assembly of the United Nations for approval.

2. Amendments shall come into force when they have been

approved by the General Assembly of the United Nations and accepted by a two-thirds majority of the States Parties to the present Covenant in accordance with their respective constitutional processes.

3. When amendments come into force, they shall be binding on those States Parties which have accepted them, other States Parties still being bound by the provisions of the present Covenant and any earlier amendment which they have accepted.

Article 52

Irrespective of the notifications made under article 48, paragraph 5, the Secretary-General of the United Nations shall inform all States referred to in paragraph I of the same article of the following particulars:

(a) Signatures, ratifications and accessions under article 48;

(b) The date of the entry into force of the present Covenant under article 49 and the date of the entry into force of any amendments under article 51.

Article 53

1. The present Covenant, of which the Chinese, English, French, Russian and Spanish texts are equally authentic, shall be deposited in the archives of the United Nations.

2. The Secretary-General of the United Nations shall transmit certified copies of the present Covenant to all States referred to in article 48.

Optional Protocol to the International Covenant on Civil and Political Rights

G.A. res. 2200A (XXI), 21 U.N. GAOR Supp. (No. 16) at 59, U.N. Doc. A/6316 (1966), 999 U.N.T.S. 302, entered into force March 23, 1976.

The States Parties to the present Protocol,

Considering that in order further to achieve the purposes of the International Covenant on Civil and Political Rights (hereinafter referred to as the Covenant) and the implementation of its provisions it would be appropriate to enable the Human Rights Committee set up in part IV of the Covenant (hereinafter referred to as the Committee) to receive and consider, as provided in the present Protocol, communications from individuals claiming to be victims of violations of any of the rights set forth in the Covenant.

Have agreed as follows:

Article 1

A State Party to the Covenant that becomes a Party to the present Protocol recognizes the competence of the Committee to receive and consider communications from individuals subject to its jurisdiction who claim to be victims of a violation by that State Party of any of the rights set forth in the Covenant. No communication shall be received by the Committee if it concerns a State Party to the Covenant which is not a Party to the present Protocol.

Article 2

Subject to the provisions of article 1, individuals who claim that any of their rights enumerated in the Covenant have been violated and who have exhausted all available domestic remedies may submit a written communication to the Committee for consideration.

Article 3

The Committee shall consider inadmissible any communication under the present Protocol which is anonymous, or which it considers to be an abuse of the right of submission of such communications or to be incompatible with the provisions of the Covenant.

Article 4

1. Subject to the provisions of article 3, the Committee shall bring any communications submitted to it under the present Protocol to the attention of the State Party to the present Protocol alleged to be violating any provision of the Covenant.

2. Within six months, the receiving State shall submit to the Committee written explanations or statements clarifying the matter and the remedy, if any, that may have been taken by that State.

Article 5

1. The Committee shall consider communications received under the present Protocol in the light of all written information made available to it by the individual and by the State Party concerned.

2. The Committee shall not consider any communication from an individual unless it has ascertained that:

(a) The same matter is not being examined under another procedure of international investigation or settlement;

(b) The individual has exhausted all available domestic remedies. This shall not be the rule where the application of the remedies is unreasonably prolonged.

3. The Committee shall hold closed meetings when examining communications under the present Protocol.

4. The Committee shall forward its views to the State Party concerned and to the individual.

Article 6

The Committee shall include in its annual report under article 45 of the Covenant a summary of its activities under the present Protocol.

Article 7

Pending the achievement of the objectives of resolution 1514(XV) adopted by the General Assembly of the United Nations on 14 December 1960 concerning the Declaration on the Granting of Independence to Colonial Countries and Peoples, the provisions of the present Protocol shall in no way limit the right of petition granted to these peoples by the Charter of the United Nations and other international conventions and instruments under the United Nations and its specialized agencies.

Article 8

1. The present Protocol is open for signature by any State which has signed the Covenant.

2. The present Protocol is subject to ratification by any State which has ratified or acceded to the Covenant. Instruments of ratification shall be deposited with the Secretary-General of the United Nations.

3. The present Protocol shall be open to accession by any State which has ratified or acceded to the Covenant.

4. Accession shall be effected by the deposit of an instrument of accession with the Secretary-General of the United Nations.

5. The Secretary-General of the United Nations shall inform all States which have signed the present Protocol or acceded to it of the deposit of each instrument of ratification or accession.

Article 9

1. Subject to the entry into force of the Covenant, the present Protocol shall enter into force three months after the date of the deposit with the Secretary-General of the United Nations of the tenth instrument of ratification or instrument of accession.

2. For each State ratifying the present Protocol or acceding to it after the deposit of the tenth instrument of ratification or instrument of accession, the present Protocol shall enter into force three months after the date of the deposit of its own instrument of ratification or instrument of accession.

Article 10

The provisions of the present Protocol shall extend to all parts of federal States without any limitations or exceptions.

Article 11

1. Any State Party to the present Protocol may propose an amendment and file it with the Secretary-General of the United Nations. The Secretary-General shall thereupon communicate any proposed amendments to the States Parties to the present Protocol with a request that they notify him whether they favour a conference of States Parties for the purpose of considering and voting upon the proposal. In the event that at least one third of the States Parties favours such a conference, the Secretary-General shall convene the conference under the auspices of the United Nations. Any amendment adopted by a majority of the States Parties present and voting at the conference shall be submitted to the General Assembly of the United Nations for approval.

2. Amendments shall come into force when they have been approved by the General Assembly of the United Nations and accepted by a two-thirds majority of the States Parties to the present Protocol in accordance with their respective constitutional processes.

3. When amendments come into force, they shall be binding on those States Parties which have accepted them, other States Parties still being bound by the provisions of the present Protocol and any earlier amendment which they have accepted.

Article 12

1. Any State Party may denounce the present Protocol at any time by written notification addressed to the Secretary-General of the United Nations. Denunciation shall take effect three months after the date of receipt of the notification by the Secretary-General.

2. Denunciation shall be without prejudice to the continued application of the provisions of the present Protocol to any communication submitted under article 2 before the effective date of denunciation.

Article 13

Irrespective of the notifications made under article 8, paragraph 5, of the present Protocol, the Secretary-General of the United Nations shall inform all States referred to in article 48, paragraph I, of the Covenant of the following particulars:

(a) Signatures, ratifications and accessions under article 8;

(b) The date of the entry into force of the present Protocol under article 9 and the date of the entry into force of any amendments under article 11;

(c) Denunciations under article 12.

Article 14

1. The present Protocol, of which the Chinese, English, French, Russian and Spanish texts are equally authentic, shall be deposited in the archives of the United Nations.

2. The Secretary-General of the United Nations shall transmit certified copies of the present Protocol to all States referred to in article 48 of the Covenant.

Second Optional Protocol to the International Covenant on Civil and Political Rights, aiming at the abolition of the death penalty

G.A. res. 44/128, annex, 44 U.N. GAOR Supp. (No. 49) at 207, U.N. Doc. A/44/49 (1989), entered into force July 11, 1991.

The States Parties to the present Protocol,
Believing that abolition of the death penalty contributes to

enhancement of human dignity and progressive development of human rights,

Recalling article 3 of the Universal Declaration of Human Rights, adopted on 10 December 1948, and article 6 of the International Covenant on Civil and Political Rights, adopted on 16 December 1966,

Noting that article 6 of the International Covenant on Civil and Political Rights refers to abolition of the death penalty in terms that strongly suggest that abolition is desirable,

Convinced that all measures of abolition of the death penalty should be considered as progress in the enjoyment of the right to life,

Desirous to undertake hereby an international commitment to abolish the death penalty,

Have agreed as follows:

Article 1

1. No one within the jurisdiction of a State Party to the present Protocol shall be executed.

2. Each State Party shall take all necessary measures to abolish the death penalty within its jurisdiction.

Article 2

1. No reservation is admissible to the present Protocol, except for a reservation made at the time of ratification or accession that provides for the application of the death penalty in time of war pursuant to a conviction for a most serious crime of a military nature committed during wartime.

2. The State Party making such a reservation shall at the time of ratification or accession communicate to the Secretary-General of the United Nations the relevant provisions of its national legislation applicable during wartime.

3. The State Party having made such a reservation shall notify the Secretary-General of the United Nations of any beginning or ending of a state of war applicable to its territory.

Article 3

The States Parties to the present Protocol shall include in the reports they submit to the Human Rights Committee, in accordance with article 40 of the Covenant, information on the measures that they have adopted to give effect to the present Protocol.

Article 4

With respect to the States Parties to the Covenant that have made a declaration under article 41, the competence of the Human Rights Committee to receive and consider communications when a State Party claims that another State Party is not fulfilling its obligations shall extend to the provisions of the present Protocol, unless the State Party concerned has made a statement to the contrary at the moment of ratification or accession.

Article 5

With respect to the States Parties to the first Optional Protocol to the International Covenant on Civil and Political Rights adopted on 16 December 1966, the competence of the Human Rights Committee to receive and consider communications from individuals subject to its jurisdiction shall extend to the provisions of the present Protocol, unless the State Party concerned has made a statement to the contrary at the moment of ratification or accession.

Article 6

1. The provisions of the present Protocol shall apply as additional provisions to the Covenant.

2. Without prejudice to the possibility of a reservation under article 2 of the present Protocol, the right guaranteed in article 1, paragraph 1, of the present Protocol shall not be subject to any derogation under article 4 of the Covenant.

Article 7

1. The present Protocol is open for signature by any State that has signed the Covenant.

2. The present Protocol is subject to ratification by any State that has ratified the Covenant or acceded to it. Instruments of ratification shall be deposited with the Secretary-General of the United Nations.

3. The present Protocol shall be open to accession by any State that has ratified the Covenant or acceded to it.

4. Accession shall be effected by the deposit of an instrument of accession with the Secretary-General of the United Nations.

5. The Secretary-General of the United Nations shall inform

all States that have signed the present Protocol or acceded to it of the deposit of each instrument of ratification or accession.

Article 8

1. The present Protocol shall enter into force three months after the date of the deposit with the Secretary-General of the United Nations of the tenth instrument of ratification or accession.

2. For each State ratifying the present Protocol or acceding to it after the deposit of the tenth instrument of ratification or accession, the present Protocol shall enter into force three months after the date of the deposit of its own instrument of ratification or accession.

Article 9

The provisions of the present Protocol shall extend to all parts of federal States without any limitations or exceptions.

Article 10

The Secretary-General of the United Nations shall inform all States referred to in article 48, paragraph 1, of the Covenant of the following particulars:

(a) Reservations, communications and notifications under article 2 of the present Protocol;

(b) Statements made under articles 4 or 5 of the present Protocol;

(c) Signatures, ratifications and accessions under article 7 of the present Protocol:

(d) The date of the entry into force of the present Protocol under article 8 thereof.

Article 11

1. The present Protocol, of which the Arabic, Chinese, English, French, Russian and Spanish texts are equally authentic, shall be deposited in the archives of the United Nations.

2. The Secretary-General of the United Nations shall transmit certified copies of the present Protocol to all States referred to in article 48 of the Covenant.

Convention on the Elimination of All Forms of Discrimination against Women

G.A. res. 34/180, 34 U.N. GAOR Supp. (No. 46) at 193,
U.N. Doc. A/34/46,
entered into force Sept. 3, 1981.

The States Parties to the present Convention,

Noting that the Charter of the United Nations reaffirms faith in fundamental human rights, in the dignity and worth of the human person and in the equal rights of men and women,

Noting that the Universal Declaration of Human Rights affirms the principle of the inadmissibility of discrimination and proclaims that all human beings are born free and equal in dignity and rights and that everyone is entitled to all the rights and freedoms set forth therein, without distinction of any kind, including distinction based on sex,

Noting that the States Parties to the International Covenants on Human Rights have the obligation to ensure the equal rights of men and women to enjoy all economic, social, cultural, civil and political rights,

Considering the international conventions concluded under the auspices of the United Nations and the specialized agencies promoting equality of rights of men and women,

Noting also the resolutions, declarations and recommendations adopted by the United Nations and the specialized agencies promoting equality of rights of men and women,

Concerned, however, that despite these various instruments extensive discrimination against women continues to exist,

Recalling that discrimination against women violates the principles of equality of rights and respect for human dignity, is an obstacle to the participation of women, on equal terms with men, in the political, social, economic and cultural life of their countries, hampers the growth of the prosperity of society and the family and makes more difficult the full development of the potentialities of women in the service of their countries and of humanity,

Concerned that in situations of poverty women have the least access to food, health, education, training and opportunities for employment and other needs,

Convinced that the establishment of the new international economic order based on equity and justice will contribute significantly towards the promotion of equality between men and women,

Emphasizing that the eradication of apartheid, all forms of racism, racial discrimination, colonialism, neo-colonialism, aggression, foreign occupation and domination and interference in the internal affairs of States is essential to the full enjoyment of the rights of men and women,

Affirming that the strengthening of international peace and security, the relaxation of international tension, mutual co-operation among all States irrespective of their social and economic systems, general and complete disarmament, in particular nuclear disarmament under strict and effective international control, the affirmation of the principles of justice, equality and mutual benefit in relations among countries and the realization of the right of peoples under alien and colonial domination and foreign occupation to self-determination and independence, as well as respect for national sovereignty and territorial integrity, will promote social progress and development and as a consequence will contribute to the attainment of full equality between men and women,

Convinced that the full and complete development of a country, the welfare of the world and the cause of peace require the maximum participation of women on equal terms with men in all fields,

Bearing in mind the great contribution of women to the welfare of the family and to the development of society, so far not fully recognized, the social significance of maternity and the role of both parents in the family and in the upbringing of children, and aware that the role of women in procreation should not be a basis for discrimination but that the upbringing of children requires a sharing of responsibility between men and women and society as a whole,

Aware that a change in the traditional role of men as well as the role of women in society and in the family is needed to achieve full equality between men and women,

Determined to implement the principles set forth in the Declaration on the Elimination of Discrimination against Women and, for that purpose, to adopt the measures required for the elimination of such discrimination in all its forms and manifestations,

Have agreed on the following:

PART I

Article 1

For the purposes of the present Convention, the term "discrimination against women" shall mean any distinction, exclusion or restriction made on the basis of sex which has the effect or purpose of impairing or nullifying the recognition, enjoyment or exercise by women, irrespective of their marital status, on a basis of equality of men and women, of human rights and fundamental freedoms in the political, economic, social, cultural, civil or any other field.

Article 2

States Parties condemn discrimination against women in all its forms, agree to pursue by all appropriate means and without delay a policy of eliminating discrimination against women and, to this end, undertake:

(a) To embody the principle of the equality of men and women in their national constitutions or other appropriate legislation if not yet incorporated therein and to ensure, through law and other appropriate means, the practical realization of this principle;

(b) To adopt appropriate legislative and other measures, including sanctions where appropriate, prohibiting all discrimination against women;

(c) To establish legal protection of the rights of women on an equal basis with men and to ensure through competent national tribunals and other public institutions the effective protection of women against any act of discrimination;

(d) To refrain from engaging in any act or practice of discrimination against women and to ensure that public authorities and institutions shall act in conformity with this obligation;

(e) To take all appropriate measures to eliminate discrimination against women by any person, organization or enterprise;

(f) To take all appropriate measures, including legislation, to modify or abolish existing laws, regulations, customs and practices which constitute discrimination against women;

(g) To repeal all national penal provisions which constitute discrimination against women.

Article 3

States Parties shall take in all fields, in particular in the political, social, economic and cultural fields, all appropriate measures, including legislation, to ensure the full development and advancement of women, for the purpose of guaranteeing them the exercise and enjoyment of human rights and fundamental freedoms on a basis of equality with men.

Article 4

1. Adoption by States Parties of temporary special measures aimed at accelerating *de facto* equality between men and women shall not be considered discrimination as defined in the present Convention, but shall in no way entail as a consequence the maintenance of unequal or separate standards; these measures shall be discontinued when the objectives of equality of opportunity and treatment have been achieved.

2. Adoption by States Parties of special measures, including those measures contained in the present Convention, aimed at protecting maternity shall not be considered discriminatory.

Article 5

States Parties shall take all appropriate measures:

(a) To modify the social and cultural patterns of conduct of men and women, with a view to achieving the elimination of prejudices and customary and all other practices which are based on the idea of the inferiority or the superiority of either of the sexes or on stereotyped roles for men and women;

(b) To ensure that family education includes a proper understanding of maternity as a social function and the recognition of the common responsibility of men and women in the upbringing and development of their children, it being understood that the interest of the children is the primordial consideration in all cases.

Article 6

States Parties shall take all appropriate measures, including legislation, to suppress all forms of traffic in women and exploitation of prostitution of women.

PART II

Article 7

States Parties shall take all appropriate measures to eliminate discrimination against women in the political and public life of the country and, in particular, shall ensure to women, on equal terms with men, the right:

(a) To vote in all elections and public referenda and to be eligible for election to all publicly elected bodies;

(b) To participate in the formulation of government policy and the implementation thereof and to hold public office and perform all public functions at all levels of government;

(c) To participate in non-governmental organizations and associations concerned with the public and political life of the country.

Article 8

States Parties shall take all appropriate measures to ensure to women, on equal terms with men and without any discrimination, the opportunity to represent their Governments at the international level and to participate in the work of international organizations.

Article 9

1. States Parties shall grant women equal rights with men to acquire, change or retain their nationality. They shall ensure in particular that neither marriage to an alien nor change of nationality by the husband during marriage shall automatically change the nationality of the wife, render her stateless or force upon her the nationality of the husband.

2. States Parties shall grant women equal rights with men with respect to the nationality of their children.

PART III

Article 10

States Parties shall take all appropriate measures to eliminate discrimination against women in order to ensure to them equal rights with men in the field of education and in particular to ensure, on a basis of equality of men and women:

(a) The same conditions for career and vocational guidance, for access to studies and for the achievement of diplomas in educational establishments of all categories in rural as well as in urban areas; this equality shall be ensured in pre-school, general, technical, professional and higher technical education, as well as in all types of vocational training;

(b) Access to the same curricula, the same examinations, teaching staff with qualifications of the same standard and school premises and equipment of the same quality;

(c) The elimination of any stereotyped concept of the roles of men and women at all levels and in all forms of education by encouraging coeducation and other types of education which will help to achieve this aim and, in particular, by the revision of textbooks and school programmes and the adaptation of teaching methods;

(d) The same opportunities to benefit from scholarships and other study grants;

(e) The same opportunities for access to programmes of continuing education, including adult and functional literacy programmes, particularly those aimed at reducing, at the earliest possible time, any gap in education existing between men and women;

(f) The reduction of female student drop-out rates and the organization of programmes for girls and women who have left school prematurely;

(g) The same opportunities to participate actively in sports and physical education;

(h) Access to specific educational information to help to ensure the health and well-being of families, including information and advice on family planning.

Article 11

1. States Parties shall take all appropriate measures to eliminate discrimination against women in the field of employment in order to ensure, on a basis of equality of men and women, the same rights, in particular:

(a) The right to work as an inalienable right of all human beings;

(b) The right to the same employment opportunities, including the application of the same criteria for selection in matters of employment;

(c) The right to free choice of profession and employment, the right to promotion, job security and all benefits and conditions of service and the right to receive vocational training and retraining, including apprenticeships, advanced vocational training and recurrent training;

(d) The right to equal remuneration, including benefits, and to equal treatment in respect of work of equal value, as well as equality of treatment in the evaluation of the quality of work;

(e) The right to social security, particularly in cases of retirement, unemployment, sickness, invalidity and old age and other incapacity to work, as well as the right to paid leave;

(f) The right to protection of health and to safety in working conditions, including the safeguarding of the function of reproduction.

2. In order to prevent discrimination against women on the grounds of marriage or maternity and to ensure their effective right to work, States Parties shall take appropriate measures:

(a) To prohibit, subject to the imposition of sanctions, dismissal on the grounds of pregnancy or of maternity leave and discrimination in dismissals on the basis of marital status;

(b) To introduce maternity leave with pay or with comparable social benefits without loss of former employment, seniority or social allowances;

(c) To encourage the provision of the necessary supporting social services to enable parents to combine family obligations with work responsibilities and participation in public life, in particular through promoting the establishment and development of a network of child-care facilities;

(d) To provide special protection to women during pregnancy in types of work proved to be harmful to them.

3. Protective legislation relating to matters covered in this article shall be reviewed periodically in the light of scientific and technological knowledge and shall be revised, repealed or extended as necessary.

Article 12

1. States Parties shall take all appropriate measures to eliminate discrimination against women in the field of health care in order to ensure, on a basis of equality of men and women, access to health care services, including those related to family planning.

2. Notwithstanding the provisions of paragraph I of this article, States Parties shall ensure to women appropriate services in connection with pregnancy, confinement and the post-natal period, granting free services where

necessary, as well as adequate nutrition during pregnancy and lactation.

Article 13

States Parties shall take all appropriate measures to eliminate discrimination against women in other areas of economic and social life in order to ensure, on a basis of equality of men and women, the same rights, in particular:

(a) The right to family benefits;

(b) The right to bank loans, mortgages and other forms of financial credit;

(c) The right to participate in recreational activities, sports and all aspects of cultural life.

Article 14

1. States Parties shall take into account the particular problems faced by rural women and the significant roles which rural women play in the economic survival of their families, including their work in the non-monetized sectors of the economy, and shall take all appropriate measures to ensure the application of the provisions of the present Convention to women in rural areas.

2. States Parties shall take all appropriate measures to eliminate discrimination against women in rural areas in order to ensure, on a basis of equality of men and women, that they participate in and benefit from rural development and, in particular, shall ensure to such women the right:

(a) To participate in the elaboration and implementation of development planning at all levels;

(b) To have access to adequate health care facilities, including information, counselling and services in family planning;

(c) To benefit directly from social security programmes;

(d) To obtain all types of training and education, formal and non-formal, including that relating to functional literacy, as well as, *inter alia*, the benefit of all community and extension services, in order to increase their technical proficiency;

(e) To organize self-help groups and co-operatives in order to obtain equal access to economic opportunities through employment or self employment;

(f) To participate in all community activities;

(g) To have access to agricultural credit and loans,

marketing facilities, appropriate technology and equal treatment in land and agrarian reform as well as in land resettlement schemes;

(h) To enjoy adequate living conditions, particularly in relation to housing, sanitation, electricity and water supply, transport and communications.

PART IV

Article 15

1. States Parties shall accord to women equality with men before the law.

2. States Parties shall accord to women, in civil matters, a legal capacity identical to that of men and the same opportunities to exercise that capacity. In particular, they shall give women equal rights to conclude contracts and to administer property and shall treat them equally in all stages of procedure in courts and tribunals.

3. States Parties agree that all contracts and all other private instruments of any kind with a legal effect which is directed at restricting the legal capacity of women shall be deemed null and void.

4. States Parties shall accord to men and women the same rights with regard to the law relating to the movement of persons and the freedom to choose their residence and domicile.

Article 16

1. States Parties shall take all appropriate measures to eliminate discrimination against women in all matters relating to marriage and family relations and in particular shall ensure, on a basis of equality of men and women:

(a) The same right to enter into marriage;

(b) The same right freely to choose a spouse and to enter into marriage only with their free and full consent;

(c) The same rights and responsibilities during marriage and at its dissolution;

(d) The same rights and responsibilities as parents, irrespective of their marital status, in matters relating to their children; in all cases the interests of the children shall be paramount;

(e) The same rights to decide freely and responsibly on the

number and spacing of their children and to have access to the information, education and means to enable them to exercise these rights;

(f) The same rights and responsibilities with regard to guardianship, wardship, trusteeship and adoption of children, or similar institutions where these concepts exist in national legislation; in all cases the interests of the children shall be paramount;

(g) The same personal rights as husband and wife, including the right to choose a family name, a profession and an occupation;

(h) The same rights for both spouses in respect of the ownership, acquisition, management, administration, enjoyment and disposition of property, whether free of charge or for a valuable consideration.

2. The betrothal and the marriage of a child shall have no legal effect, and all necessary action, including legislation, shall be taken to specify a minimum age for marriage and to make the registration of marriages in an official registry compulsory.

PART V

Article 17

1. For the purpose of considering the progress made in the implementation of the present Convention, there shall be established a Committee on the Elimination of Discrimination against Women (hereinafter referred to as the Committee) consisting, at the time of entry into force of the Convention, of eighteen and, after ratification of or accession to the Convention by the thirty-fifth State Party, of twenty-three experts of high moral standing and competence in the field covered by the Convention. The experts shall be elected by States Parties from among their nationals and shall serve in their personal capacity, consideration being given to equitable geographical distribution and to the representation of the different forms of civilization as well as the principal legal systems.

2. The members of the Committee shall be elected by secret ballot from a list of persons nominated by States Parties. Each State Party may nominate one person from among its own nationals.

3. The initial election shall be held six months after the date of the entry into force of the present Convention. At least three

months before the date of each election the Secretary-General of the United Nations shall address a letter to the States Parties inviting them to submit their nominations within two months. The Secretary-General shall prepare a list in alphabetical order of all persons thus nominated, indicating the States Parties which have nominated them, and shall submit it to the States Parties.

4. Elections of the members of the Committee shall be held at a meeting of States Parties convened by the Secretary-General at United Nations Headquarters. At that meeting, for which two thirds of the States Parties shall constitute a quorum, the persons elected to the Committee shall be those nominees who obtain the largest number of votes and an absolute majority of the votes of the representatives of States Parties present and voting.

5. The members of the Committee shall be elected for a term of four years. However, the terms of nine of the members elected at the first election shall expire at the end of two years; immediately after the first election the names of these nine members shall be chosen by lot by the Chairman of the Committee.

6. The election of the five additional members of the Committee shall be held in accordance with the provisions of paragraphs 2, 3 and 4 of this article, following the thirty-fifth ratification or accession. The terms of two of the additional members elected on this occasion shall expire at the end of two years, the names of these two members having been chosen by lot by the Chairman of the Committee.

7. For the filling of casual vacancies, the State Party whose expert has ceased to function as a member of the Committee shall appoint another expert from among its nationals, subject to the approval of the Committee.

8. The members of the Committee shall, with the approval of the General Assembly, receive emoluments from United Nations resources on such terms and conditions as the Assembly may decide, having regard to the importance of the Committee's responsibilities.

9. The Secretary-General of the United Nations shall provide the necessary staff and facilities for the effective performance of the functions of the Committee under the present Convention.

Article 18

1. States Parties undertake to submit to the Secretary-

General of the United Nations, for consideration by the Committee, a report on the legislative, judicial, administrative or other measures which they have adopted to give effect to the provisions of the present Convention and on the progress made in this respect:

(a) Within one year after the entry into force for the State concerned;

(b) Thereafter at least every four years and further whenever the Committee so requests.

2. Reports may indicate factors and difficulties affecting the degree of fulfilment of obligations under the present Convention.

Article 19

1. The Committee shall adopt its own rules of procedure.

2. The Committee shall elect its officers for a term of two years.

Article 20

1. The Committee shall normally meet for a period of not more than two weeks annually in order to consider the reports submitted in accordance with article 18 of the present Convention.

2. The meetings of the Committee shall normally be held at United Nations Headquarters or at any other convenient place as determined by the Committee.

Article 21

1. The Committee shall, through the Economic and Social Council, report annually to the General Assembly of the United Nations on its activities and may make suggestions and general recommendations based on the examination of reports and information received from the States Parties. Such suggestions and general recommendations shall be included in the report of the Committee together with comments, if any, from States Parties.

2. The Secretary-General of the United Nations shall transmit the reports of the Committee to the Commission on the Status of Women for its information.

Article 22

The specialized agencies shall be entitled to be represented at the consideration of the implementation of such provisions of the present Convention as fall within the scope of their activities. The Committee may invite the specialized agencies to submit reports on the implementation of the Convention in areas falling within the scope of their activities.

PART VI

Article 23

Nothing in the present Convention shall affect any provisions that are more conducive to the achievement of equality between men and women which may be contained:

(a) In the legislation of a State Party; or

(b) In any other international convention, treaty or agreement in force for that State.

Article 24

States Parties undertake to adopt all necessary measures at the national level aimed at achieving the full realization of the rights recognized in the present Convention.

Article 25

1. The present Convention shall be open for signature by all States.

2. The Secretary-General of the United Nations is designated as the depositary of the present Convention.

3. The present Convention is subject to ratification. Instruments of ratification shall be deposited with the Secretary General of the United Nations.

4. The present Convention shall be open to accession by all States. Accession shall be effected by the deposit of an instrument of accession with the Secretary-General of the United Nations.

Article 26

1. A request for the revision of the present Convention may be made at any time by any State Party by means of a notification in writing addressed to the Secretary-General of the United Nations.

2. The General Assembly of the United Nations shall decide upon the steps, if any, to be taken in respect of such a request.

Article 27

1. The present Convention shall enter into force on the thirtieth day after the date of deposit with the Secretary-General of the United Nations of the twentieth instrument of ratification or accession.

2. For each State ratifying the present Convention or acceding to it after the deposit of the twentieth instrument of ratification or accession, the Convention shall enter into force on the thirtieth day after the date of the deposit of its own instrument of ratification or accession.

Article 28

1. The Secretary-General of the United Nations shall receive and circulate to all States the text of reservations made by States at the time of ratification or accession.

2. A reservation incompatible with the object and purpose of the present Convention shall not be permitted.

3. Reservations may be withdrawn at any time by notification to this effect addressed to the Secretary-General of the United Nations, who shall then inform all States thereof. Such notification shall take effect on the date on which it is received.

Article 29

1. Any dispute between two or more States Parties concerning the interpretation or application of the present Convention which is not settled by negotiation shall, at the request of one of them, be submitted to arbitration. If within six months from the date of the request for arbitration the parties are unable to agree on the organization of the arbitration, any one of those parties may refer the dispute to the International Court of Justice by request in conformity with the Statute of the Court.

2. Each State Party may at the time of signature or ratification of the present Convention or accession thereto declare that it does not consider itself bound by paragraph I of this article. The other States Parties shall not be bound by that paragraph with respect to any State Party which has made such a reservation.

3. Any State Party which has made a reservation in accordance with paragraph 2 of this article may at any time withdraw that reservation by notification to the Secretary-General of the United Nations.

Article 30

The present Convention, the Arabic, Chinese, English, French, Russian and Spanish texts of which are equally authentic, shall be deposited with the Secretary-General of the United Nations.

IN WITNESS WHEREOF the undersigned, duly authorized, have signed the present Convention.

International Convention on the Elimination of All Forms of Racial Discrimination

660 U.N.T.S. 195, entered into force Jan. 4, 1969.

The States Parties to this Convention,

Considering that the Charter of the United Nations is based on the principles of the dignity and equality inherent in all human beings, and that all Member States have pledged themselves to take joint and separate action, in co-operation with the Organization, for the achievement of one of the purposes of the United Nations which is to promote and encourage universal respect for and observance of human rights and fundamental freedoms for all, without distinction as to race, sex, language or religion,

Considering that the Universal Declaration of Human Rights proclaims that all human beings are born free and equal in dignity and rights and that everyone is entitled to all the rights and freedoms set out therein, without distinction of any kind, in particular as to race, colour or national origin,

Considering that all human beings are equal before the law and are entitled to equal protection of the law against any discrimination and against any incitement to discrimination,

Considering that the United Nations has condemned colonialism and all practices of segregation and discrimination associated therewith, in whatever form and wherever they exist, and that the Declaration on the Granting of Independence to Colonial Countries and Peoples of 14 December 1960 (General Assembly resolution 1514 (XV)) has affirmed and solemnly proclaimed the necessity of bringing them to a speedy and unconditional end,

Considering that the United Nations Declaration on the Elimination of All Forms of Racial Discrimination of 20 November 1963 (General Assembly resolution 1904 (XVIII))

solemnly affirms the necessity of speedily eliminating racial discrimination throughout the world in all its forms and manifestations and of securing understanding of and respect for the dignity of the human person,

Convinced that any doctrine of superiority based on racial differentiation is scientifically false, morally condemnable, socially unjust and dangerous, and that there is no justification for racial discrimination, in theory or in practice, anywhere,

Reaffirming that discrimination between human beings on the grounds of race, colour or ethnic origin is an obstacle to friendly and peaceful relations among nations and is capable of disturbing peace and security among peoples and the harmony of persons living side by side even within one and the same State,

Convinced that the existence of racial barriers is repugnant to the ideals of any human society,

Alarmed by manifestations of racial discrimination still in evidence in some areas of the world and by governmental policies based on racial superiority or hatred, such as policies of apartheid, segregation or separation,

Resolved to adopt all necessary measures for speedily eliminating racial discrimination in all its forms and manifestations, and to prevent and combat racist doctrines and practices in order to promote understanding between races and to build an international community free from all forms of racial segregation and racial discrimination,

Bearing in mind the Convention concerning Discrimination in respect of Employment and Occupation adopted by the International Labour Organisation in 1958, and the Convention against Discrimination in Education adopted by the United Nations Educational, Scientific and Cultural Organization in 1960,

Desiring to implement the principles embodied in the United Nations Declaration on the Elimination of All Forms of Racial Discrimination and to secure the earliest adoption of practical measures to that end,

Have agreed as follows:

PART I

Article 1

1. In this Convention, the term "racial discrimination" shall mean any distinction, exclusion, restriction or preference based on race, colour, descent, or national or ethnic origin which has

the purpose or effect of nullifying or impairing the recognition, enjoyment or exercise, on an equal footing, of human rights and fundamental freedoms in the political, economic, social, cultural or any other field of public life.

2. This Convention shall not apply to distinctions, exclusions, restrictions or preferences made by a State Party to this Convention between citizens and non-citizens.

3. Nothing in this Convention may be interpreted as affecting in any way the legal provisions of States Parties concerning nationality, citizenship or naturalization, provided that such provisions do not discriminate against any particular nationality.

4. Special measures taken for the sole purpose of securing adequate advancement of certain racial or ethnic groups or individuals requiring such protection as may be necessary in order to ensure such groups or individuals equal enjoyment or exercise of human rights and fundamental freedoms shall not be deemed racial discrimination, provided, however, that such measures do not, as a consequence, lead to the maintenance of separate rights for different racial groups and that they shall not be continued after the objectives for which they were taken have been achieved.

Article 2

1. States Parties condemn racial discrimination and undertake to pursue by all appropriate means and without delay a policy of eliminating racial discrimination in all its forms and promoting understanding among all races, and, to this end:

(a) Each State Party undertakes to engage in no act or practice of racial discrimination against persons, groups of persons or institutions and to ensure that all public authorities and public institutions, national and local, shall act in conformity with this obligation;

(b) Each State Party undertakes not to sponsor, defend or support racial discrimination by any persons or organizations;

(c) Each State Party shall take effective measures to review governmental, national and local policies, and to amend, rescind or nullify any laws and regulations which have the effect of creating or perpetuating racial discrimination wherever it exists;

(d) Each State Party shall prohibit and bring to an end, by all appropriate means, including legislation as required by circumstances, racial discrimination by any persons, group or organization;

(e) Each State Party undertakes to encourage, where appropriate, integrationist multiracial organizations and movements and other means of eliminating barriers between races, and to discourage anything which tends to strengthen racial division.

2. States Parties shall, when the circumstances so warrant, take, in the social, economic, cultural and other fields, special and concrete measures to ensure the adequate development and protection of certain racial groups or individuals belonging to them, for the purpose of guaranteeing them the full and equal enjoyment of human rights and fundamental freedoms. These measures shall in no case entail as a consequence the maintenance of unequal or separate rights for different racial groups after the objectives for which they were taken have been achieved.

Article 3

States Parties particularly condemn racial segregation and apartheid and undertake to prevent, prohibit and eradicate all practices of this nature in territories under their jurisdiction.

Article 4

States Parties condemn all propaganda and all organizations which are based on ideas or theories of superiority of one race or group of persons of one colour or ethnic origin, or which attempt to justify or promote racial hatred and discrimination in any form, and undertake to adopt immediate and positive measures designed to eradicate all incitement to, or acts of, such discrimination and, to this end, with due regard to the principles embodied in the Universal Declaration of Human Rights and the rights expressly set forth in article 5 of this Convention, *inter alia:*

(a) Shall declare an offence punishable by law all dissemination of ideas based on racial superiority or hatred, incitement to racial discrimination, as well as all acts of violence or incitement to such acts against any race or group of persons of another colour or ethnic origin, and also the provision of any assistance to racist activities, including the financing thereof;

(b) Shall declare illegal and prohibit organizations, and also organized and all other propaganda activities, which promote and incite racial discrimination, and shall recognize participation in such organizations or activities as an offence punishable by law;

(c) Shall not permit public authorities or public institutions, national or local, to promote or incite racial discrimination.

Article 5

In compliance with the fundamental obligations laid down in article 2 of this Convention, States Parties undertake to prohibit and to eliminate racial discrimination in all its forms and to guarantee the right of everyone, without distinction as to race, colour, or national or ethnic origin, to equality before the law, notably in the enjoyment of the following rights:

(a) The right to equal treatment before the tribunals and all other organs administering justice;

(b) The right to security of person and protection by the State against violence or bodily harm, whether inflicted by government officials or by any individual group or institution;

(c) Political rights, in particular the right to participate in elections—to vote and to stand for election—on the basis of universal and equal suffrage, to take part in the Government as well as in the conduct of public affairs at any level and to have equal access to public service;

(d) Other civil rights, in particular:

(i) The right to freedom of movement and residence within the border of the State;

(ii) The right to leave any country, including one's own, and to return to one's country;

(iii) The right to nationality;

(iv) The right to marriage and choice of spouse;

(v) The right to own property alone as well as in association with others;

(vi) The right to inherit;

(vii) The right to freedom of thought, conscience and religion;

(viii) The right to freedom of opinion and expression;

(ix) The right to freedom of peaceful assembly and association;

(e) Economic, social and cultural rights, in particular:

(i) The rights to work, to free choice of employment, to just and favourable conditions of work, to protection against unemployment, to equal pay for equal work, to just and favourable remuneration;

(ii) The right to form and join trade unions;

(iii) The right to housing;

(iv) The right to public health, medical care, social security and social services;

(v) The right to education and training;

(vi) The right to equal participation in cultural activities;

(f) The right of access to any place or service intended for use by the general public, such as transport hotels, restaurants, cafes, theatres and parks.

Article 6

States Parties shall assure to everyone within their jurisdiction effective protection and remedies, through the competent national tribunals and other State institutions, against any acts of racial discrimination which violate his human rights and fundamental freedoms contrary to this Convention, as well as the right to seek from such tribunals just and adequate reparation or satisfaction for any damage suffered as a result of such discrimination.

Article 7

States Parties undertake to adopt immediate and effective measures, particularly in the fields of teaching, education, culture and information, with a view to combating prejudices which lead to racial discrimination and to promoting understanding, tolerance and friendship among nations and racial or ethnical groups, as well as to propagating the purposes and principles of the Charter of the United Nations, the Universal Declaration of Human Rights, the United Nations Declaration on the Elimination of All Forms of Racial Discrimination, and this Convention.

PART II

Article 8

1. There shall be established a Committee on the Elimination of Racial Discrimination (hereinafter referred to as the Committee) consisting of eighteen experts of high moral standing and acknowledged impartiality elected by States Parties from among their nationals, who shall serve in their personal capacity, consideration being given to equitable geographical distribution and to the representation of the different forms of civilization as well as of the principal legal systems.

2. The members of the Committee shall be elected by secret ballot from a list of persons nominated by the States Parties.

Each State Party may nominate one person from among its own nationals.

3. The initial election shall be held six months after the date of the entry into force of this Convention. At least three months before the date of each election the Secretary-General of the United Nations shall address a letter to the States Parties inviting them to submit their nominations within two months. The Secretary-General shall prepare a list in alphabetical order of all persons thus nominated, indicating the States Parties which have nominated them, and shall submit it to the States Parties.

4. Elections of the members of the Committee shall be held at a meeting of States Parties convened by the Secretary-General at United Nations Headquarters. At that meeting, for which two thirds of the States Parties shall constitute a quorum, the persons elected to the Committee shall be nominees who obtain the largest number of votes and an absolute majority of the votes of the representatives of States Parties present and voting.

5. (a) The members of the Committee shall be elected for a term of four years. However, the terms of nine of the members elected at the first election shall expire at the end of two years; immediately after the first election the names of these nine members shall be chosen by lot by the Chairman of the Committee;

(b) For the filling of casual vacancies, the State Party whose expert has ceased to function as a member of the Committee shall appoint another expert from among its nationals, subject to the approval of the Committee.

6. States Parties shall be responsible for the expenses of the members of the Committee while they are in performance of Committee duties.

Article 9

1. States Parties undertake to submit to the Secretary-General of the United Nations, for consideration by the Committee, a report on the legislative, judicial, administrative or other measures which they have adopted and which give effect to the provisions of this Convention:

(a) within one year after the entry into force of the Convention for the State concerned; and

(b) thereafter every two years and whenever the Committee so requests. The Committee may request further information from the States Parties.

2. The Committee shall report annually, through the Secretary General, to the General Assembly of the United Nations on its activities and may make suggestions and general recommendations based on the examination of the reports and information received from the States Parties. Such suggestions and general recommendations shall be reported to the General Assembly together with comments, if any, from States Parties.

Article 10

1. The Committee shall adopt its own rules of procedure.

2. The Committee shall elect its officers for a term of two years.

3. The secretariat of the Committee shall be provided by the Secretary General of the United Nations.

4. The meetings of the Committee shall normally be held at United Nations Headquarters.

Article 11

1. If a State Party considers that another State Party is not giving effect to the provisions of this Convention, it may bring the matter to the attention of the Committee. The Committee shall then transmit the communication to the State Party concerned. Within three months, the receiving State shall submit to the Committee written explanations or statements clarifying the matter and the remedy, if any, that may have been taken by that State.

2. If the matter is not adjusted to the satisfaction of both parties, either by bilateral negotiations or by any other procedure open to them, within six months after the receipt by the receiving State of the initial communication, either State shall have the right to refer the matter again to the Committee by notifying the Committee and also the other State.

3. The Committee shall deal with a matter referred to it in accordance with paragraph 2 of this article after it has ascertained that all available domestic remedies have been invoked and exhausted in the case, in conformity with the generally recognized principles of international law. This shall not be the rule where the application of the remedies is unreasonably prolonged.

4. In any matter referred to it, the Committee may call upon the States Parties concerned to supply any other relevant information.

5. When any matter arising out of this article is being considered by the Committee, the States Parties concerned shall be entitled to send a representative to take part in the proceedings of the Committee, without voting rights, while the matter is under consideration.

Article 12

1. (a) After the Committee has obtained and collated all the information it deems necessary, the Chairman shall appoint an *ad hoc* Conciliation Commission (hereinafter referred to as the Commission) comprising five persons who may or may not be members of the Committee. The members of the Commission shall be appointed with the unanimous consent of the parties to the dispute, and its good offices shall be made available to the States concerned with a view to an amicable solution of the matter on the basis of respect for this Convention;

(b) If the States parties to the dispute fail to reach agreement within three months on all or part of the composition of the Commission, the members of the Commission not agreed upon by the States parties to the dispute shall be elected by secret ballot by a two thirds majority vote of the Committee from among its own members.

2. The members of the Commission shall serve in their personal capacity. They shall not be nationals of the States parties to the dispute or of a State not Party to this Convention.

3. The Commission shall elect its own Chairman and adopt its own rules of procedure.

4. The meetings of the Commission shall normally be held at United Nations Headquarters or at any other convenient place as determined by the Commission.

5. The secretariat provided in accordance with article 10, paragraph 3, of this Convention shall also service the Commission whenever a dispute among States Parties brings the Commission into being.

6. The States parties to the dispute shall share equally all the expenses of the members of the Commission in accordance with estimates to be provided by the Secretary-General of the United Nations.

7. The Secretary-General shall be empowered to pay the expenses of the members of the Commission, if necessary, before reimbursement by the States parties to the dispute in accordance with paragraph 6 of this article.

8. The information obtained and collated by the Committee

shall be made available to the Commission, and the Commission may call upon the States concerned to supply any other relevant information.

Article 13

1. When the Commission has fully considered the matter, it shall prepare and submit to the Chairman of the Committee a report embodying its findings on all questions of fact relevant to the issue between the parties and containing such recommendations as it may think proper for the amicable solution of the dispute.

2. The Chairman of the Committee shall communicate the report of the Commission to each of the States parties to the dispute. These States shall, within three months, inform the Chairman of the Committee whether or not they accept the recommendations contained in the report of the Commission.

3. After the period provided for in paragraph 2 of this article, the Chairman of the Committee shall communicate the report of the Commission and the declarations of the States Parties concerned to the other States Parties to this Convention.

Article 14

1. A State Party may at any time declare that it recognizes the competence of the Committee to receive and consider communications from individuals or groups of individuals within its jurisdiction claiming to be victims of a violation by that State Party of any of the rights set forth in this Convention. No communication shall be received by the Committee if it concerns a State Party which has not made such a declaration.

2. Any State Party which makes a declaration as provided for in paragraph I of this article may establish or indicate a body within its national legal order which shall be competent to receive and consider petitions from individuals and groups of individuals within its jurisdiction who claim to be victims of a violation of any of the rights set forth in this Convention and who have exhausted other available local remedies.

3. A declaration made in accordance with paragraph 1 of this article and the name of any body established or indicated in accordance with paragraph 2 of this article shall be deposited by the State Party concerned with the Secretary-General of the United Nations, who shall transmit copies thereof to the other States Parties. A declaration may be withdrawn at any time by

notification to the Secretary-General, but such a withdrawal shall not affect communications pending before the Committee.

4. A register of petitions shall be kept by the body established or indicated in accordance with paragraph 2 of this article, and certified copies of the register shall be filed annually through appropriate channels with the Secretary-General on the understanding that the contents shall not be publicly disclosed.

5. In the event of failure to obtain satisfaction from the body established or indicated in accordance with paragraph 2 of this article, the petitioner shall have the right to communicate the matter to the Committee within six months.

6. (a) The Committee shall confidentially bring any communication referred to it to the attention of the State Party alleged to be violating any provision of this Convention, but the identity of the individual or groups of individuals concerned shall not be revealed without his or their express consent. The Committee shall not receive anonymous communications;

(b) Within three months, the receiving State shall submit to the Committee written explanations or statements clarifying the matter and the remedy, if any, that may have been taken by that State.

7. (a) The Committee shall consider communications in the light of all information made available to it by the State Party concerned and by the petitioner. The Committee shall not consider any communication from a petitioner unless it has ascertained that the petitioner has exhausted all available domestic remedies. However, this shall not be the rule where the application of the remedies is unreasonably prolonged;

(b) The Committee shall forward its suggestions and recommendations, if any, to the State Party concerned and to the petitioner.

8. The Committee shall include in its annual report a summary of such communications and, where appropriate, a summary of the explanations and statements of the States Parties concerned and of its own suggestions and recommendations.

9. The Committee shall be competent to exercise the functions provided for in this article only when at least ten States Parties to this Convention are bound by declarations in accordance with paragraph I of this article.

Article 15

1. Pending the achievement of the objectives of the Declaration on the Granting of Independence to Colonial

Countries and Peoples, contained in General Assembly resolution 1514 (XV) of 14 December 1960, the provisions of this Convention shall in no way limit the right of petition granted to these peoples by other international instruments or by the United Nations and its specialized agencies.

2. (a) The Committee established under article 8, paragraph 1, of this Convention shall receive copies of the petitions from, and submit expressions of opinion and recommendations on these petitions to, the bodies of the United Nations which deal with matters directly related to the principles and objectives of this Convention in their consideration of petitions from the inhabitants of Trust and Non-Self-Governing Territories and all other territories to which General Assembly resolution 1514 (XV) applies, relating to matters covered by this Convention which are before these bodies;

(b) The Committee shall receive from the competent bodies of the United Nations copies of the reports concerning the legislative, judicial, administrative or other measures directly related to the principles and objectives of this Convention applied by the administering Powers within the Territories mentioned in subparagraph (a) of this paragraph, and shall express opinions and make recommendations to these bodies.

3. The Committee shall include in its report to the General Assembly a summary of the petitions and reports it has received from United Nations bodies, and the expressions of opinion and recommendations of the Committee relating to the said petitions and reports.

4. The Committee shall request from the Secretary-General of the United Nations all information relevant to the objectives of this Convention and available to him regarding the Territories mentioned in paragraph 2 (a) of this article.

Article 16

The provisions of this Convention concerning the settlement of disputes or complaints shall be applied without prejudice to other procedures for settling disputes or complaints in the field of discrimination laid down in the constituent instruments of, or conventions adopted by, the United Nations and its specialized agencies, and shall not prevent the States Parties from having recourse to other procedures for settling a dispute in accordance with general or special international agreements in force between them.

PART III

Article 17

1. This Convention is open for signature by any State Member of the United Nations or member of any of its specialized agencies, by any State Party to the Statute of the International Court of Justice, and by any other State which has been invited by the General Assembly of the United Nations to become a Party to this Convention.

2. This Convention is subject to ratification. Instruments of ratification shall be deposited with the Secretary-General of the United Nations.

Article 18

1. This Convention shall be open to accession by any State referred to in article 17, paragraph 1, of the Convention.

2. Accession shall be effected by the deposit of an instrument of accession with the Secretary-General of the United Nations.

Article 19

1. This Convention shall enter into force on the thirtieth day after the date of the deposit with the Secretary-General of the United Nations of the twenty-seventh instrument of ratification or instrument of accession.

2. For each State ratifying this Convention or acceding to it after the deposit of the twenty-seventh instrument of ratification or instrument of accession, the Convention shall enter into force on the thirtieth day after the date of the deposit of its own instrument of ratification or instrument of accession.

Article 20

1. The Secretary-General of the United Nations shall receive and circulate to all States which are or may become Parties to this Convention reservations made by States at the time of ratification or accession. Any State which objects to the reservation shall, within a period of ninety days from the date of the said communication, notify the Secretary-General that it does not accept it.

2. A reservation incompatible with the object and purpose of this Convention shall not be permitted, nor shall a

reservation the effect of which would inhibit the operation of any of the bodies established by this Convention be allowed. A reservation shall be considered incompatible or inhibitive if at least two thirds of the States Parties to this Convention object to it.

3. Reservations may be withdrawn at any time by notification to this effect addressed to the Secretary-General. Such notification shall take effect on the date on which it is received.

Article 21

A State Party may denounce this Convention by written notification to the Secretary-General of the United Nations. Denunciation shall take effect one year after the date of receipt of the notification by the Secretary General.

Article 22

Any dispute between two or more States Parties with respect to the interpretation or application of this Convention, which is not settled by negotiation or by the procedures expressly provided for in this Convention, shall, at the request of any of the parties to the dispute, be referred to the International Court of Justice for decision, unless the disputants agree to another mode of settlement.

Article 23

1. A request for the revision of this Convention may be made at any time by any State Party by means of a notification in writing addressed to the Secretary-General of the United Nations.

2. The General Assembly of the United Nations shall decide upon the steps, if any, to be taken in respect of such a request.

Article 24

The Secretary-General of the United Nations shall inform all States referred to in article 17, paragraph 1, of this Convention of the following particulars:

(a) Signatures, ratifications and accessions under articles 17 and 18;

(b) The date of entry into force of this Convention under article 19;

(c) Communications and declarations received under articles 14, 20 and 23;

(d) Denunciations under article 21.

Article 25

1. This Convention, of which the Chinese, English, French, Russian and Spanish texts are equally authentic, shall be deposited in the archives of the United Nations.

2. The Secretary-General of the United Nations shall transmit certified copies of this Convention to all States belonging to any of the categories mentioned in article 17, paragraph 1, of the Convention.

Standard Minimum Rules for the Treatment of Prisoners

Adopted Aug. 30, 1955, by the First United Nations Congress on the Prevention of Crime and the Treatment of Offenders, U.N. Doc. A/CONF/611, annex I, E.S.C. res. 663C, 24 U.N. ESCOR Supp. (No. 1) at 11, U.N. Doc. E/3048 (1957), amended E.S.C. res. 2076, 62 U.N. ESCOR Supp. (No. 1) at 35, U.N. Doc. E/5988 (1977).

PRELIMINARY OBSERVATIONS

1. The following rules are not intended to describe in detail a model system of penal institutions.

They seek only, on the basis of the general consensus of contemporary thought and the essential elements of the most adequate systems of today, to set out what is generally accepted as being good principle and practice in the treatment of prisoners and the management of institutions.

2. In view of the great variety of legal, social, economic and geographical conditions of the world, it is evident that not all of the rules are capable of application in all places and at all times. They should, however, serve to stimulate a constant endeavour to overcome practical difficulties in the way of their application, in the knowledge that they represent, as a whole, the minimum conditions which are accepted as suitable by the United Nations.

3. On the other hand, the rules cover a field in which thought is constantly developing. They are not intended to preclude experiment and practices, provided these are in harmony with the principles and seek to further the purposes

which derive from the text of the rules as a whole. It will always be justifiable for the central prison administration to authorize departures from the rules in this spirit.

4. (1) Part I of the rules covers the general management of institutions, and is applicable to all categories of prisoners, criminal or civil, untried or convicted, including prisoners subject to "security measures" or corrective measures ordered by the judge.

(2) Part II contains rules applicable only to the special categories dealt with in each section. Nevertheless, the rules under section A, applicable to prisoners under sentence, shall be equally applicable to categories of prisoners dealt with in sections B, C and D, provided they do not conflict with the rules governing those categories and are for their benefit.

5. (1) The rules do not seek to regulate the management of institutions set aside for young persons such as Borstal institutions or correctional schools, but in general part I would be equally applicable in such institutions.

(2) The category of young prisoners should include at least all young persons who come within the jurisdiction of juvenile courts. As a rule, such young persons should not be sentenced to imprisonment.

PART I

RULES OF GENERAL APPLICATION

Basic principle

6. (1) The following rules shall be applied impartially. There shall be no discrimination on grounds of race, colour, sex, language, religion, political or other opinion, national or social origin, property, birth or other status.

(2) On the other hand, it is necessary to respect the religious beliefs and moral precepts of the group to which a prisoner belongs.

Register

7. (1) In every place where persons are imprisoned there shall be kept a bound registration book with numbered pages in which shall be entered in respect of each prisoner received:

(a) Information concerning his identity;

(b) The reasons for his commitment and the authority therefor;

(c) The day and hour of his admission and release.

(2) No person shall be received in an institution without a valid commitment order of which the details shall have been previously entered in the register.

Separation of categories

8. The different categories of prisoners shall be kept in separate institutions or parts of institutions taking account of their sex, age, criminal record, the legal reason for their detention and the necessities of their treatment. Thus,

(a) Men and women shall so far as possible be detained in separate institutions; in an institution which receives both men and women the whole of the premises allocated to women shall be entirely separate;

(b) Untried prisoners shall be kept separate from convicted prisoners;

(c) Persons imprisoned for debt and other civil prisoners shall be kept separate from persons imprisoned by reason of a criminal offence;

(d) Young prisoners shall be kept separate from adults.

Accommodation

9. (1) Where sleeping accommodation is in individual cells or rooms, each prisoner shall occupy by night a cell or room by himself. If for special reasons, such as temporary overcrowding, it becomes necessary for the central prison administration to make an exception to this rule, it is not desirable to have two prisoners in a cell or room.

(2) Where dormitories are used, they shall be occupied by prisoners carefully selected as being suitable to associate with one another in those conditions. There shall be regular supervision by night, in keeping with the nature of the institution.

10. All accommodation provided for the use of prisoners and in particular all sleeping accommodation shall meet all requirements of health, due regard being paid to climatic conditions and particularly to cubic content of air, minimum floor space, lighting, heating and ventilation.

11. In all places where prisoners are required to live or work,

(a) The windows shall be large enough to enable the prisoners to read or work by natural light, and shall be so constructed that they can allow the entrance of fresh air whether or not there is artificial ventilation;

(b) Artificial light shall be provided sufficient for the prisoners to read or work without injury to eyesight.

12. The sanitary installations shall be adequate to enable every prisoner to comply with the needs of nature when necessary and in a clean and decent manner.

13. Adequate bathing and shower installations shall be provided so that every prisoner may be enabled and required to have a bath or shower, at a temperature suitable to the climate, as frequently as necessary for general hygiene according to season and geographical region, but at least once a week in a temperate climate.

14. All pans of an institution regularly used by prisoners shall be properly maintained and kept scrupulously clean at all times.

Personal hygiene

15. Prisoners shall be required to keep their persons clean, and to this end they shall be provided with water and with such toilet articles as are necessary for health and cleanliness.

16. In order that prisoners may maintain a good appearance compatible with their self-respect, facilities shall be provided for the proper care of the hair and beard, and men shall be enabled to shave regularly.

Clothing and bedding

17. (1) Every prisoner who is not allowed to wear his own clothing shall be provided with an outfit of clothing suitable for the climate and adequate to keep him in good health. Such clothing shall in no manner be degrading or humiliating.

(2) All clothing shall be clean and kept in proper condition. Underclothing shall be changed and washed as often as necessary for the maintenance of hygiene.

(3) In exceptional circumstances, whenever a prisoner is removed outside the institution for an authorized purpose, he shall be allowed to wear his own clothing or other inconspicuous clothing.

18. If prisoners are allowed to wear their own clothing, arrangements shall be made on their admission to the institution to ensure that it shall be clean and fit for use.

19. Every prisoner shall, in accordance with local or national standards, be provided with a separate bed, and with separate and sufficient bedding which shall be clean when issued, kept in good order and changed often enough to ensure its cleanliness.

Food

20. (1) Every prisoner shall be provided by the administration at the usual hours with food of nutritional value adequate for health and strength, of wholesome quality and well prepared and served.

(2) Drinking water shall be available to every prisoner whenever he needs it.

Exercise and sport

21. (1) Every prisoner who is not employed in outdoor work shall have at least one hour of suitable exercise in the open air daily if the weather permits.

(2) Young prisoners, and others of suitable age and physique, shall receive physical and recreational training during the period of exercise. To this end space, installations and equipment should be provided.

Medical services

22. (1) At every institution there shall be available the services of at least one qualified medical officer who should have some knowledge of psychiatry. The medical services should be organized in close relationship to the general health administration of the community or nation. They shall include a psychiatric service for the diagnosis and, in proper cases, the treatment of states of mental abnormality.

(2) Sick prisoners who require specialist treatment shall be transferred to specialized institutions or to civil hospitals. Where hospital facilities are provided in an institution, their equipment, furnishings and pharmaceutical supplies shall be proper for the medical care and treatment of sick prisoners, and there shall be a staff of suitable trained officers.

(3) The services of a qualified dental officer shall be available to every prisoner.

23. (1) In women's institutions there shall be special accommodation for all necessary pre-natal and post-natal care and treatment. Arrangements shall be made wherever

practicable for children to be born in a hospital outside the institution. If a child is born in prison, this fact shall not be mentioned in the birth certificate.

(2) Where nursing infants are allowed to remain in the institution with their mothers, provision shall be made for a nursery staffed by qualified persons, where the infants shall be placed when they are not in the care of their mothers.

24. The medical officer shall see and examine every prisoner as soon as possible after his admission and thereafter as necessary, with a view particularly to the discovery of physical or mental illness and the taking of all necessary measures; the segregation of prisoners suspected of infectious or contagious conditions; the noting of physical or mental defects which might hamper rehabilitation; and the determination of the physical capacity of every prisoner for work.

25. (1) The medical officer shall have the care of the physical and mental health of the prisoners and should daily see all sick prisoners, all who complain of illness, and any prisoner to whom his attention is specially directed.

(2) The medical officer shall report to the director whenever he considers that a prisoner's physical or mental health has been or will be injuriously affected by continued imprisonment or by any condition of imprisonment.

26. (1) The medical officer shall regularly inspect and advise the director upon:

(a) The quantity, quality, preparation and service of food;

(b) The hygiene and cleanliness of the institution and the prisoners;

(c) The sanitation, heating, lighting and ventilation of the institution;

(d) The suitability and cleanliness of the prisoners' clothing and bedding;

(e) The observance of the rules concerning physical education and sports, in cases where there is no technical personnel in charge of these activities.

(2) The director shall take into consideration the reports and advice that the medical officer submits according to rules 25 (2) and 26 and, in case he concurs with the recommendations made, shall take immediate steps to give effect to those recommendations; if they are not within his competence or if he does not concur with them, he shall immediately submit his own report and the advice of the medical officer to higher authority.

Discipline and punishment

27. Discipline and order shall be maintained with firmness, but with no more restriction than is necessary for safe custody and well-ordered community life.

28. (1) No prisoner shall be employed, in the service of the institution, in any disciplinary capacity.

(2) This rule shall not, however, impede the proper functioning of systems based on self-government, under which specified social, educational or sports activities or responsibilities are entrusted, under supervision, to prisoners who are formed into groups for the purposes of treatment.

29. The following shall always be determined by the law or by the regulation of the competent administrative authority:

(a) Conduct constituting a disciplinary offence;

(b) The types and duration of punishment which may be inflicted;

(c) The authority competent to impose such punishment.

30. (1) No prisoner shall be punished except in accordance with the terms of such law or regulation, and never twice for the same offence.

(2) No prisoner shall be punished unless he has been informed of the offence alleged against him and given a proper opportunity of presenting his defence. The competent authority shall conduct a thorough examination of the case.

(3) Where necessary and practicable the prisoner shall be allowed to make his defence through an interpreter.

31. Corporal punishment, punishment by placing in a dark cell, and all cruel, inhuman or degrading punishments shall be completely prohibited as punishments for disciplinary offences.

32. (1) Punishment by close confinement or reduction of diet shall never be inflicted unless the medical officer has examined the prisoner and certified in writing that he is fit to sustain it.

(2) The same shall apply to any other punishment that may be prejudicial to the physical or mental health of a prisoner. In no case may such punishment be contrary to or depart from the principle stated in rule 31.

(3) The medical officer shall visit daily prisoners undergoing such punishments and shall advise the director if he considers the termination or alteration of the punishment necessary on grounds of physical or mental health.

Instruments of restraint

33. Instruments of restraint, such as handcuffs, chains, irons and strait-jacket, shall never be applied as a punishment. Furthermore, chains or irons shall not be used as restraints. Other instruments of restraint shall not be used except in the following circumstances:

(a) As a precaution against escape during a transfer, provided that they shall be removed when the prisoner appears before a judicial or administrative authority;

(b) On medical grounds by direction of the medical officer;

(c) By order of the director, if other methods of control fail, in order to prevent a prisoner from injuring himself or others or from damaging property; in such instances the director shall at once consult the medical officer and report to the higher administrative authority.

34. The patterns and manner of use of instruments of restraint shall be decided by the central prison administration. Such instruments must not be applied for any longer time than is strictly necessary.

Information to and complaints by prisoners

35. (1) Every prisoner on admission shall be provided with written information about the regulations governing the treatment of prisoners of his category, the disciplinary requirements of the institution, the authorized methods of seeking information and making complaints, and all such other matters as are necessary to enable him to understand both his rights and his obligations and to adapt himself to the life of the institution.

(2) If a prisoner is illiterate, the aforesaid information shall be conveyed to him orally.

36. (1) Every prisoner shall have the opportunity each week day of making requests or complaints to the director of the institution or the officer authorized to represent him.

(2) It shall be possible to make requests or complaints to the inspector of prisons during his inspection. The prisoner shall have the opportunity to talk to the inspector or to any other inspecting officer without the director or other members of the staff being present.

(3) Every prisoner shall be allowed to make a request or complaint, without censorship as to substance but in proper form, to the central prison administration, the judicial authority or other proper authorities through approved channels.

(4) Unless it is evidently frivolous or groundless, every request or complaint shall be promptly dealt with and replied to without undue delay.

Contact with the outside world

37. Prisoners shall be allowed under necessary supervision to communicate with their family and reputable friends at regular intervals, both by correspondence and by receiving visits.

38. (1) Prisoners who are foreign nationals shall be allowed reasonable facilities to communicate with the diplomatic and consular representatives of the State to which they belong.

(2) Prisoners who are nationals of States without diplomatic or consular representation in the country and refugees or stateless persons shall be allowed similar facilities to communicate with the diplomatic representative of the State which takes charge of their interests or any national or international authority whose task it is to protect such persons.

39. Prisoners shall be kept informed regularly of the more important items of news by the reading of newspapers, periodicals or special institutional publications, by hearing wireless transmissions, by lectures or by any similar means as authorized or controlled by the administration.

Books

40. Every institution shall have a library for the use of all categories of prisoners, adequately stocked with both recreational and instructional books, and prisoners shall be encouraged to make full use of it.

Religion

41. (1) If the institution contains a sufficient number of prisoners of the same religion, a qualified representative of that religion shall be appointed or approved. If the number of prisoners justifies it and conditions permit, the arrangement should be on a full-time basis.

(2) A qualified representative appointed or approved under paragraph (1) shall be allowed to hold regular services and to pay pastoral visits in private to prisoners of his religion at proper times.

(3) Access to a qualified representative of any religion shall not be refused to any prisoner. On the other hand, if any prisoner should object to a visit of any religious representative, his attitude shall be fully respected.

42. So far as practicable, every prisoner shall be allowed to satisfy the needs of his religious life by attending the services provided in the institution and having in his possession the books of religious observance and instruction of his denomination.

Retention of prisoners' property

43. (1) All money, valuables, clothing and other effects belonging to a prisoner which under the regulations of the institution he is not allowed to retain shall on his admission to the institution be placed in safe custody. An inventory thereof shall be signed by the prisoner. Steps shall be taken to keep them in good condition.

(2) On the release of the prisoner all such articles and money shall be returned to him except in so far as he has been authorized to spend money or send any such property out of the institution, or it has been found necessary on hygienic grounds to destroy any article of clothing. The prisoner shall sign a receipt for the articles and money returned to him.

(3) Any money or effects received for a prisoner from outside shall be treated in the same way.

(4) If a prisoner brings in any drugs or medicine, the medical officer shall decide what use shall be made of them.

Notification of death, illness, transfer, etc.

44. (1) Upon the death or serious illness of, or serious injury to a prisoner, or his removal to an institution for the treatment of mental affections, the director shall at once inform the spouse, if the prisoner is married, or the nearest relative and shall in any event inform any other person previously designated by the prisoner.

(2) A prisoner shall be informed at once of the death or serious illness of any near relative. In case of the critical illness of a near relative, the prisoner should be authorized, whenever circumstances allow, to go to his bedside either under escort or alone.

(3) Every prisoner shall have the right to inform at once his family of his imprisonment or his transfer to another institution.

Removal of prisoners

45. (1) When the prisoners are being removed to or from an institution, they shall be exposed to public view as little as

possible, and proper safeguards shall be adopted to protect them from insult, curiosity and publicity in any form.

(2) The transport of prisoners in conveyances with inadequate ventilation or light, or in any way which would subject them to unnecessary physical hardship, shall be prohibited.

(3) The transport of prisoners shall be carried out at the expense of the administration and equal conditions shall obtain for all of them.

Institutional personnel

46. (1) The prison administration, shall provide for the careful selection of every grade of the personnel, since it is on their integrity, humanity, professional capacity and personal suitability for the work that the proper administration of the institutions depends.

(2) The prison administration shall constantly seek to awaken and maintain in the minds both of the personnel and of the public the conviction that this work is a social service of great importance, and to this end all appropriate means of informing the public should be used.

(3) To secure the foregoing ends, personnel shall be appointed on a full-time basis as professional prison officers and have civil service status with security of tenure subject only to good conduct, efficiency and physical fitness. Salaries shall be adequate to attract and retain suitable men and women; employment benefits and conditions of service shall be favourable in view of the exacting nature of the work.

47. (1) The personnel shall possess an adequate standard of education and intelligence.

(2) Before entering on duty, the personnel shall be given a course of training in their general and specific duties and be required to pass theoretical and practical tests.

(3) After entering on duty and during their career, the personnel shall maintain and improve their knowledge and professional capacity by attending courses of in-service training to be organized at suitable intervals.

48. All members of the personnel shall at all times so conduct themselves and perform their duties as to influence the prisoners for good by their example and to command their respect.

49. (1) So far as possible, the personnel shall include a sufficient number of specialists such as psychiatrists, psychologists, social workers, teachers and trade instructors.

(2) The services of social workers, teachers and trade instructors shall be secured on a permanent basis, without thereby excluding part-time or voluntary workers.

50. (1) The director of an institution should be adequately qualified for his task by character, administrative ability, suitable training and experience.

(2) He shall devote his entire time to his official duties and shall not be appointed on a part-time basis.

(3) He shall reside on the premises of the institution or in its immediate vicinity.

(4) When two or more institutions are under the authority of one director, he shall visit each of them at frequent intervals. A responsible resident official shall be in charge of each of these institutions.

51. (1) The director, his deputy, and the majority of the other personnel of the institution shall be able to speak the language of the greatest number of prisoners, or a language understood by the greatest number of them.

(2) Whenever necessary, the services of an interpreter shall be used.

52. (1) In institutions which are large enough to require the services of one or more full-time medical officers, at least one of them shall reside on the premises of the institution or in its immediate vicinity.

(2) In other institutions the medical officer shall visit daily and shall reside near enough to be able to attend without delay in cases of urgency.

53. (1) In an institution for both men and women, the part of the institution set aside for women shall be under the authority of a responsible woman officer who shall have the custody of the keys of all that part of the institution.

(2) No male member of the staff shall enter the part of the institution set aside for women unless accompanied by a woman officer.

(3) Women prisoners shall be attended and supervised only by women officers. This does not, however, preclude male members of the staff, particularly doctors and teachers, from carrying out their professional duties in institutions or parts of institutions set aside for women.

54. (1) Officers of the institutions shall not, in their relations with the prisoners, use force except in self-defence or in cases of attempted escape, or active or passive physical resistance to an order based on law or regulations. Officers who have recourse to

force must use no more than is strictly necessary and must report the incident immediately to the director of the institution.

(2) Prison officers shall be given special physical training to enable them to restrain aggressive prisoners.

(3) Except in special circumstances, staff performing duties which bring them into direct contact with prisoners should not be armed. Furthermore, staff should in no circumstances be provided with arms unless they have been trained in their use.

Inspection

55. There shall be a regular inspection of penal institutions and services by qualified and experienced inspectors appointed by a competent authority. Their task shall be in particular to ensure that these institutions are administered in accordance with existing laws and regulations and with a view to bringing about the objectives of penal and correctional

PART II

RULES APPLICABLE TO SPECIAL CATEGORIES

A. Prisoners under Sentence

Guiding principles

56. The guiding principles hereafter are intended to show the spirit in which penal institutions should be administered and the purposes at which they should aim, in accordance with the declaration made under Preliminary Observation I of the present text.

57. Imprisonment and other measures which result in cutting off an offender from the outside world are afflictive by the very fact of taking from the person the right of self-determination by depriving him of his liberty. Therefore the prison system shall not, except as incidental to justifiable segregation or the maintenance of discipline, aggravate the suffering inherent in such a situation.

58. The purpose and justification of a sentence of imprisonment or a similar measure deprivative of liberty is ultimately to protect society against crime. This end can only be achieved if the period of imprisonment is used to ensure, so far as possible, that upon his return to society the offender is not only willing but able to lead a law-abiding and self-supporting life.

59. To this end, the institution should utilize all the remedial, educational, moral, spiritual and other forces and forms of assistance which are appropriate and available, and should seek to apply them according to the individual treatment needs of the prisoners.

60. (1) The regime of the institution should seek to minimize any differences between prison life and life at liberty which tend to lessen the responsibility of the prisoners or the respect due to their dignity as human beings.

(2) Before the completion of the sentence, it is desirable that the necessary steps be taken to ensure for the prisoner a gradual return to life in society. This aim may be achieved, depending on the case, by a pre-release regime organized in the same institution or in another appropriate institution, or by release on trial under some kind of supervision which must not be entrusted to the police but should be combined with effective social aid.

61. The treatment of prisoners should emphasize not their exclusion from the community, but their continuing part in it. Community agencies should, therefore, be enlisted wherever possible to assist the staff of the institution in the task of social rehabilitation of the prisoners. There should be in connection with every institution social workers charged with the duty of maintaining and improving all desirable relations of a prisoner with his family and with valuable social agencies. Steps should be taken to safeguard, to the maximum extent compatible with the law and the sentence, the rights relating to civil interests, social security rights and other social benefits of prisoners.

62. The medical services of the institution shall seek to detect and shall treat any physical or mental illnesses or defects which may hamper a prisoner's rehabilitation. All necessary medical, surgical and psychiatric services shall be provided to that end.

63. (1) The fulfilment of these principles requires individualization of treatment and for this purpose a flexible system of classifying prisoners in groups; it is therefore desirable that such groups should be distributed in separate institutions suitable for the treatment of each group.

(2) These institutions need not provide the same degree of security for every group. It is desirable to provide varying degrees of security according to the needs of different groups. Open institutions, by the very fact that they provide no physical security against escape but rely on the self-discipline of the

inmates, provide the conditions most favourable to rehabilitation for carefully selected prisoners.

(3) It is desirable that the number of prisoners in closed institutions should not be so large that the individualization of treatment is hindered. In some countries it is considered that the population of such institutions should not exceed five hundred. In open institutions the population should be as small as possible.

(4) On the other hand, it is undesirable to maintain prisons which are so small that proper facilities cannot be provided.

64. The duty of society does not end with a prisoner's release. There should, therefore, be governmental or private agencies capable of lending the released prisoner efficient after-care directed towards the lessening of prejudice against him and towards his social rehabilitation.

Treatment

65. The treatment of persons sentenced to imprisonment or a similar measure shall have as its purpose, so far as the length of the sentence permits, to establish in them the will to lead law abiding and self-supporting lives after their release and to fit them to do so. The treatment shall be such as will encourage their self-respect and develop their sense of responsibility.

66. (1) To these ends, all appropriate means shall be used, including religious care in the countries where this is possible, education, vocational guidance and training, social casework, employment counselling, physical development and strengthening of moral character, in accordance with the individual needs of each prisoner, taking account of his social and criminal history, his physical and mental capacities and aptitudes, his personal temperament, the length of his sentence and his prospects after release.

(2) For every prisoner with a sentence of suitable length, the director shall receive, as soon as possible after his admission, full reports on all the matters referred to in the foregoing paragraph. Such reports shall always include a report by a medical officer, wherever possible qualified in psychiatry, on the physical and mental condition of the prisoner.

(3) The reports and other relevant documents shall be placed in an individual file. This file shall be kept up to date and classified in such a way that it can be consulted by the responsible personnel whenever the need arises.

Classification and individualization

67. The purposes of classification shall be:

(a) To separate from others those prisoners who, by reason of their criminal records or bad characters, are likely to exercise a bad influence;

(b) To divide the prisoners into classes in order to facilitate their treatment with a view to their social rehabilitation.

68. So far as possible separate institutions or separate sections of an institution shall be used for the treatment of the different classes of prisoners.

69. As soon as possible after admission and after a study of the personality of each prisoner with a sentence of suitable length, a programme of treatment shall be prepared for him in the light of the knowledge obtained about his individual needs, his capacities and dispositions.

Privileges

70. Systems of privileges appropriate for the different classes of prisoners and the different methods of treatment shall be established at every institution, in order to encourage good conduct, develop a sense of responsibility and secure the interest and co-operation of the prisoners in their treatment.

Work

71. (1) Prison labour must not be of an afflictive nature.

(2) All prisoners under sentence shall be required to work, subject to their physical and mental fitness as determined by the medical officer.

(3) Sufficient work of a useful nature shall be provided to keep prisoners actively employed for a normal working day.

(4) So far as possible the work provided shall be such as will maintain or increase the prisoners, ability to earn an honest living after release.

(5) Vocational training in useful trades shall be provided for prisoners able to profit thereby and especially for young prisoners.

(6) Within the limits compatible with proper vocational selection and with the requirements of institutional administration and discipline, the prisoners shall be able to choose the type of work they wish to perform.

72. (1) The organization and methods of work in the institutions shall resemble as closely as possible those of similar

work outside institutions, so as to prepare prisoners for the conditions of normal occupational life.

(2) The interests of the prisoners and of their vocational training, however, must not be subordinated to the purpose of making a financial profit from an industry in the institution.

73. (1) Preferably institutional industries and farms should be operated directly by the administration and not by private contractors.

(2) Where prisoners are employed in work not controlled by the administration, they shall always be under the supervision of the institution's personnel. Unless the work is for other departments of the government the full normal wages for such work shall be paid to the administration by the persons to whom the labour is supplied, account being taken of the output of the prisoners.

74. (1) The precautions laid down to protect the safety and health of free workmen shall be equally observed in institutions.

(2) Provision shall be made to indemnify prisoners against industrial injury, including occupational disease, on terms not less favourable than those extended by law to free workmen.

75. (1) The maximum daily and weekly working hours of the prisoners shall be fixed by law or by administrative regulation, taking into account local rules or custom in regard to the employment of free workmen.

(2) The hours so fixed shall leave one rest day a week and sufficient time for education and other activities required as part of the treatment and rehabilitation of the prisoners.

76. (1) There shall be a system of equitable remuneration of the work of prisoners.

(2) Under the system prisoners shall be allowed to spend at least a part of their earnings on approved articles for their own use and to send a part of their earnings to their family.

(3) The system should also provide that a part of the earnings should be set aside by the administration so as to constitute a savings fund to be handed over to the prisoner on his release.

Education and recreation

77. (1) Provision shall be made for the further education of all prisoners capable of profiting thereby, including religious instruction in the countries where this is possible. The education of illiterates and young prisoners shall be compulsory and special attention shall be paid to it by the administration.

(2) So far as practicable, the education of prisoners shall be integrated with the educational system of the country so that after their release they may continue their education without difficulty.

78. Recreational and cultural activities shall be provided in all institutions for the benefit of the mental and physical health of prisoners.

Social relations and after-care

79. Special attention shall be paid to the maintenance and improvement of such relations between a prisoner and his family as are desirable in the best interests of both.

80. From the beginning of a prisoner's sentence consideration shall be given to his future after release and he shall be encouraged and assisted to maintain or establish such relations with persons or agencies outside the institution as may promote the best interests of his family and his own social rehabilitation.

81. (1) Services and agencies, governmental or otherwise, which assist released prisoners to re-establish themselves in society shall ensure, so far as is possible and necessary, that released prisoners be provided with appropriate documents and identification papers, have suitable homes and work to go to, are suitably and adequately clothed having regard to the climate and season, and have sufficient means to reach their destination and maintain themselves in the period immediately following their release.

(2) The approved representatives of such agencies shall have all necessary access to the institution and to prisoners and shall be taken into consultation as to the future of a prisoner from the beginning of his sentence.

(3) It is desirable that the activities of such agencies shall be centralized or co-ordinated as far as possible in order to secure the best use of their efforts.

B. Insane and Mentally Abnormal Prisoners

82. (1) Persons who are found to be insane shall not be detained in prisons and arrangements shall be made to remove them to mental institutions as soon as possible.

(2) Prisoners who suffer from other mental diseases or abnormalities shall be observed and treated in specialized institutions under medical management.

(3) During their stay in a prison, such prisoners shall be placed under the special supervision of a medical officer.

(4) The medical or psychiatric service of the penal institutions shall provide for the psychiatric treatment of all other prisoners who are in need of such treatment.

83. It is desirable that steps should be taken, by arrangement with the appropriate agencies, to ensure if necessary the continuation of psychiatric treatment after release and the provision of social-psychiatric after-care.

C. Prisoners under Arrest or Awaiting Trial

84. (1) Persons arrested or imprisoned by reason of a criminal charge against them, who are detained either in police custody or in prison custody (jail) but have not yet been tried and sentenced, will be referred to as "untried prisoners,' hereinafter in these rules.

(2) Unconvicted prisoners are presumed to be innocent and shall be treated as such.

(3) Without prejudice to legal rules for the protection of individual liberty or prescribing the procedure to be observed in respect of untried prisoners, these prisoners shall benefit by a special regime which is described in the following rules in its essential requirements only.

85. (1) Untried prisoners shall be kept separate from convicted prisoners.

(2) Young untried prisoners shall be kept separate from adults and shall in principle be detained in separate institutions.

86. Untried prisoners shall sleep singly in separate rooms, with the reservation of different local custom in respect of the climate.

87. Within the limits compatible with the good order of the institution, untried prisoners may, if they so desire, have their food procured at their own expense from the outside, either through the administration or through their family or friends. Otherwise, the administration shall provide their food.

88. (1) An untried prisoner shall be allowed to wear his own clothing if it is clean and suitable.

(2) If he wears prison dress, it shall be different from that supplied to convicted prisoners.

89. An untried prisoner shall always be offered opportunity to work, but shall not be required to work. If he chooses to work, he shall be paid for it.

90. An untried prisoner shall be allowed to procure at his own expense or at the expense of a third party such books, newspapers, writing materials and other means of occupation as are compatible with the interests of the administration of justice and the security and good order of the institution.

91. An untried prisoner shall be allowed to be visited and treated by his own doctor or dentist if there is reasonable ground for his application and he is able to pay any expenses incurred.

92. An untried prisoner shall be allowed to inform immediately his family of his detention and shall be given all reasonable facilities for communicating with his family and friends, and for receiving visits from them, subject only to restrictions and supervision as are necessary in the interests of the administration of justice and of the security and good order of the institution.

93. For the purposes of his defence, an untried prisoner shall be allowed to apply for free legal aid where such aid is available, and to receive visits from his legal adviser with a view to his defence and to prepare and hand to him confidential instructions. For these purposes, he shall if he so desires be supplied with writing material. Interviews between the prisoner and his legal adviser may be within sight but not within the hearing of a police or institution official.

D. Civil Prisoners

94. In countries where the law permits imprisonment for debt, or by order of a court under any other non-criminal process, persons so imprisoned shall not be subjected to any greater restriction or severity than is necessary to ensure safe custody and good order. Their treatment shall be not less favourable than that of untried prisoners, with the reservation, however, that they may possibly be required to work.

E. Persons Arrested or Detained Without Charge

95. Without prejudice to the provisions of article 9 of the International Covenant on Civil and Political Rights, persons arrested or imprisoned without charge shall be accorded the same protection as that accorded under part I and part II, section C. Relevant provisions of part II, section A, shall likewise be applicable where their application may be conducive to the benefit of this special group of persons in

custody, provided that no measures shall be taken implying that re-education or rehabilitation is in any way appropriate to persons not convicted of any criminal offence.

Freedom of Association and Protection of the Right to Organise Convention

(ILO No. 87), 68 U.N.T.S. 17, entered into force July 4, 1950.

The General Conference of the International Labour Organisation,

Having been convened at San Francisco by the Governing Body of the International Labour Office, and having met in its thirty-first session on 17 June 1948,

Having decided to adopt, in the form of a Convention, certain proposals concerning freedom of association and protection of the right to organise which is the seventh item on the agenda of the session,

Considering that the Preamble to the Constitution of the International Labour Organisation declares "recognition of the principle of freedom of association" to be a means of improving conditions of labour and of establishing peace,

Considering that the Declaration of Philadelphia reaffirms that "freedom of expression and of association are essential to sustained progress,"

Considering that the International Labour Conference, at its thirtieth session, unanimously adopted the principles which should form the basis for international regulation,

Considering that the General Assembly of the United Nations, at its second session, endorsed these principles and requested the International Labour Organisation to continue every effort in order that it may be possible to adopt one or several international Conventions,

Adopts this ninth day of July of the year one thousand nine hundred and forty-eight the following Convention, which may be cited as the Freedom of Association and Protection of the Right to Organise Convention, 1948:

PART I

FREEDOM OF ASSOCIATION

Article 1

Each Member of the International Labour Organisation for which this Convention is in force undertakes to give effect to the following provisions.

Article 2

Workers and employers, without distinction whatsoever, shall have the right to establish and, subject only to the rules of the organisation concerned, to join organisations of their own choosing without previous authorisation.

Article 3

1. Workers' and employers' organisations shall have the right to draw up their constitutions and rules, to elect their representatives in full freedom, to organise their administration and activities and to formulate their programmes.

2. The public authorities shall refrain from any interference which would restrict this right or impede the lawful exercise thereof.

Article 4

Workers' and employers' organisations shall not be liable to be dissolved or suspended by administrative authority.

Article 5

Workers' and employers' organisations shall have the right to establish and join federations and confederations and any such organisation, federation or confederation shall have the right to affiliate with international organisations of workers and employers.

Article 6

The provisions of articles 2, 3 and 4 hereof apply to federations and confederations of workers' and employers' organisations.

Article 7

The acquisition of legal personality by workers' and employers' organisations, federations and confederations shall not be made subject to conditions of such a character as to restrict the application of the provisions of articles 2, 3 and 4 hereof.

Article 8

1. In exercising the rights provided for in this Convention workers and employers and their respective organisations, like

other persons or organised collectivities, shall respect the law of the land.

2. The law of the land shall not be such as to impair, nor shall it be so applied as to impair, the guarantees provided for in this Convention.

Article 9

1. The extent to which the guarantees provided for in this Convention shall apply to the armed forces and the police shall be determined by national laws or regulations.

2. In accordance with the principle set forth in paragraph 8 of article 19 of the Constitution of the International Labour Organisation, the ratification of this Convention by any Member shall not be deemed to affect any existing law, award, custom or agreement in virtue of which members of the armed forces or the police enjoy any right guaranteed by this Convention.

Article 10

In this Convention the term "organisation" means any organisation of workers or of employers for furthering and defending the interests of workers or of employers.

PART II

PROTECTION OF THE RIGHT TO ORGANISE

Article 11

Each Member of the International Labour Organisation for which this Convention is in force undertakes to take all necessary and appropriate measures to ensure that workers and employers may exercise freely the right to organise.

PART III

MISCELLANEOUS PROVISIONS

Article 12

1. In respect of the territories referred to in article 35 of the Constitution of the International Labour Organisation as amended by the Constitution of the International Labour

Organisation Instrument of Amendment, 1946, other than the territories referred to in paragraphs 4 and 5 of the said article as so amended, each Member of the Organisation which ratifies this Convention shall communicate to the Director-General of the International Labour Office with or as soon as possible after its ratification a declaration stating:

(a) The territories in respect of which it undertakes that the provisions of the Convention shall be applied without modification;

(b) The territories in respect of which it undertakes that the provisions of the Convention shall be applied subject to modifications, together with details of the said modifications;

(c) The territories in respect of which the Convention is inapplicable and in such cases the grounds on which it is inapplicable;

(d) The territories in respect of which it reserves its decision.

2. The undertakings referred to in subparagraphs (a) and (b) of paragraph I of this article shall be deemed to be an integral part of the ratification and shall have the force of ratification.

3. Any Member may at any time by a subsequent declaration cancel in whole or in part any reservations made in its original declaration in virtue of subparagraphs (b), (c) or (d) of paragraph I of this article.

4. Any Member may, at any time at which this Convention is subject to denunciation in accordance with the provisions of article 16, communicate to the Director-General a declaration modifying in any other respect the terms of any former declaration and stating the present position in respect of such territories as it may specify.

Article 13

1. Where the subject-matter of this Convention is within the self-governing powers of any non-metropolitan territory, the Member responsible for the international relations of that territory may, in agreement with the government of the territory, communicate to the Director-General of the International Labour Office a declaration accepting on behalf of the territory the obligations of this Convention.

2. A declaration accepting the obligations of this Convention may be communicated to the Director-General of the International Labour Office:

(a) By two or more Members of the Organisation in respect of any territory which is under their joint authority; or

(b) By any international authority responsible for the administration of any territory, in virtue of the Charter of the United Nations or otherwise, in respect of any such territory.

3. Declarations communicated to the Director-General of the International Labour Office in accordance with the preceding paragraphs of this article shall indicate whether the provisions of the Convention will be applied in the territory concerned without modification or subject to modifications; when the declaration indicates that the provisions of the Convention will be applied subject to modifications it shall give details of the said modifications.

4. The Member, Members or international authority concerned may at any time by a subsequent declaration renounce in whole or in part the right to have recourse to any modification indicated in any former declaration.

5. The Member, Members or international authority concerned may, at any time at which this Convention is subject to denunciation in accordance with the provisions of article 16, communicate to the Director-General of the International Labour Office a declaration modifying in any other respect the terms of any former declaration and stating the present position in respect of the application of the Convention.

PART IV

FINAL PROVISIONS

Article 14

The formal ratifications of this Convention shall be communicated to the Director-General of the International Labour Office for registration.

Article 15

1. This convention shall be binding only upon those Members of the International Labour Organisation whose ratifications have been registered with the Director-General.

2. It shall come into force twelve months after the date on which the ratifications of two Members have been registered with the Director-General.

3. Thereafter, this Convention shall come into force for any

Member twelve months after the date on which its ratification
has been registered.

Article 16

1. A Member which has ratified this Convention may
denounce it after the expiration of ten years from the date on
which the Convention first comes into force, by an act
communicated to the Director-General of the International
Labour Office for registration. Such denunciation shall not take
effect until one year after the date on which it is registered.

2. Each Member which has ratified this Convention and
which does not, within the year following the expiration of the
period of ten years mentioned in the preceding paragraph,
exercise the right of denunciation provided for in this article,
will be bound for another period of ten years and, thereafter,
may denounce this convention at the expiration of each period
of ten years under the terms provided for in this article.

Article 17

1. The Director-General of the International Labour Office
shall notify all Members of the International Labour
Organisation of the registration of all ratifications, declarations
and denunciations communicated to him by the Members of the
Organisation.

2. When notifying the Members of the Organisation of the
registration of the second ratification communicated to him, the
Director-General shall draw the attention of the Members of the
Organisation to the date upon which the convention will come
into force.

Article 18

The Director-General of the International Labour Office
shall communicate to the Secretary-General of the United
Nations for registration in accordance with Article 102 of the
Charter of the United Nations full particulars of all ratifications,
declarations and acts of denunciation registered by him in
accordance with the provisions of the preceding articles.

Article 19

At the expiration of each period of ten years after the
coming into force of this Convention, the Governing Body of

the International Labour Office shall present to the General Conference a report on the working of this Convention and shall consider the desirability of placing on the agenda of the Conference the question of its revision in whole or in part.

Article 20

1. Should the Conference adopt a new Convention revising this Convention in whole or in part, then, unless the new Convention otherwise provides:

(a) The ratification by a Member of the new revising Convention shall *ipso jure* involve the immediate denunciation of this Convention, notwithstanding the provisions of article 16 above, if and when the new revising Convention shall have come into force;

(b) As from the date when the new revising Convention comes into force this Convention shall cease to be open to ratification by the Members.

2. This Convention shall in any case remain in force in its actual form and content for those Members which have ratified it but have not ratified the revising Convention.

Article 21

The English and French version of the text of this Convention are equally authoritative.

The foregoing is the authentic text of the Convention duly adopted by the General Conference of the International Labour Organisation during its thirty-first session which was held at San Francisco and declared closed the tenth day of July 1948.

In faith whereof we have appended our signatures this thirty-first day of August 1948.

Declaration of the Rights of the Child

G.A. res. 1386 (XIV), 14 U.N. GAOR Supp. (No. 16) at 19, U.N. Doc. A/4354 (1959).

PREAMBLE

Whereas the peoples of the United Nations have, in the Charter, reaffirmed their faith in fundamental human rights and in the dignity and worth of the human person, and have determined to promote social progress and better standards of life in larger freedom,

Whereas the United Nations has, in the Universal Declaration of Human Rights, proclaimed that everyone is entitled to all the rights and freedoms set forth therein, without distinction of any kind, such as race, colour, sex, language, religion, political or other opinion, national or social origin, property, birth or other status,

Whereas the child, by reason of his physical and mental immaturity, needs special safeguards and care, including appropriate legal protection, before as well as after birth,

Whereas the need for such special safeguards has been stated in the Geneva Declaration of the Rights of the Child of 1924, and recognized in the Universal Declaration of Human Rights and in the statutes of specialized agencies and international organizations concerned with the welfare of children,

Whereas mankind owes to the child the best it has to give,

Now therefore,

The General Assembly

Proclaims this Declaration of the Rights of the Child to the end that he may have a happy childhood and enjoy for his own good and for the good of society the rights and freedoms herein set forth, and calls upon parents, upon men and women as individuals, and upon voluntary organizations, local authorities and national Governments to recognize these rights and strive for their observance by legislative and other measures progressively taken in accordance with the following principles:

Principle 1

The child shall enjoy all the rights set forth in this Declaration. Every child, without any exception whatsoever, shall be entitled to these rights, without distinction or discrimination on account of race, colour, sex, language, religion, political or other opinion, national or social origin, property, birth or other status, whether of himself or of his family.

Principle 2

The child shall enjoy special protection, and shall be given opportunities and facilities, by law and by other means, to enable him to develop physically, mentally, morally, spiritually and socially in a healthy and normal manner and in conditions of freedom and dignity. In the enactment of laws for this purpose, the best interests of the child shall be the paramount consideration.

Principle 3

The child shall be entitled from his birth to a name and a nationality.

Principle 4

The child shall enjoy the benefits of social security. He shall be entitled to grow and develop in health; to this end, special care and protection shall be provided both to him and to his mother, including adequate pre-natal and post-natal care. The child shall have the right to adequate nutrition, housing, recreation and medical services.

Principle 5

The child who is physically, mentally or socially handicapped shall be given the special treatment, education and care required by his particular condition.

Principle 6

The child, for the full and harmonious development of his personality, needs love and understanding. He shall, wherever possible, grow up in the care and under the responsibility of his parents, and, in any case, in an atmosphere of affection and of moral and material security; a child of tender years shall not, save in exceptional circumstances, be separated from his mother. Society and the public authorities shall have the duty to extend particular care to children without a family and to those without adequate means of support. Payment of State and other assistance towards the maintenance of children of large families is desirable.

Principle 7

The child is entitled to receive education, which shall be free and compulsory, at least in the elementary stages. He shall be given an education which will promote his general culture and enable him, on a basis of equal opportunity, to develop his abilities, his individual judgement, and his sense of moral and social responsibility, and to become a useful member of society.

The best interests of the child shall be the guiding principle of those responsible for his education and guidance; that responsibility lies in the first place with his parents.

The child shall have full opportunity for play and recreation, which should be directed to the same purposes as education; society and the public authorities shall endeavour to promote the enjoyment of this right.

Principle 8

The child shall in all circumstances be among the first to receive protection and relief.

Principle 9

The child shall be protected against all forms of neglect, cruelty and exploitation. He shall not be the subject of traffic, in any form.

The child shall not be admitted to employment before an appropriate minimum age; he shall in no case be caused or permitted to engage in any occupation or employment which would prejudice his health or education, or interfere with his physical, mental or moral development.

Principle 10

The child shall be protected from practices which may foster racial, religious and any other form of discrimination. He shall be brought up in a spirit of understanding, tolerance, friendship among peoples, peace and universal brotherhood, and in full consciousness that his energy and talents should be devoted to the service of his fellow men.

Convention on the Rights of the Child

G.A. res. 44/25, annex, 44 U.N. GAOR Supp. (No. 49) at 167, U.N. Doc. A/44/49 (1989).

PREAMBLE

The States Parties to the present Convention,

Considering that, in accordance with the principles proclaimed in the Charter of the United Nations, recognition of the inherent dignity and of the equal and inalienable rights of all members of the human family is the foundation of freedom, justice and peace in the world,

Bearing in mind that the peoples of the United Nations have, in the Charter, reaffirmed their faith in fundamental human rights and in the dignity and worth of the human person, and have determined to promote social progress and better standards of life in larger freedom,

Recognizing that the United Nations has, in the Universal Declaration of Human Rights and in the International Covenants on Human Rights, proclaimed and agreed that everyone is entitled to all the rights and freedoms set forth therein, without distinction of any kind, such as race, colour, sex, language, religion, political or other opinion, national or social origin, property, birth or other status,

Recalling that, in the Universal Declaration of Human Rights, the United Nations has proclaimed that childhood is entitled to special care and assistance,

Convinced that the family, as the fundamental group of society and the natural environment for the growth and well-being of all its members and particularly children, should be afforded the necessary protection and assistance so that it can fully assume its responsibilities within the community,

Recognizing that the child, for the full and harmonious development of his or her personality, should grow up in a family environment, in an atmosphere of happiness, love and understanding,

Considering that the child should be fully prepared to live an individual life in society, and brought up in the spirit of the ideals proclaimed in the Charter of the United Nations, and in particular in the spirit of peace, dignity, tolerance, freedom, equality and solidarity,

Bearing in mind that the need to extend particular care to the child has been stated in the Geneva Declaration of the Rights of the Child of 1924 and in the Declaration of the Rights of the Child adopted by the General Assembly on 20 November 1959 and recognized in the Universal Declaration of Human Rights, in the International Covenant on Civil and Political Rights (in particular in articles 23 and 24), in the International Covenant on Economic, Social and Cultural Rights (in particular in article 10) and in the statutes and relevant instruments of specialized agencies and international organizations concerned with the welfare of children,

Bearing in mind that, as indicated in the Declaration of the

Rights of the Child, "the child, by reason of his physical and mental immaturity, needs special safeguards and care, including appropriate legal protection, before as well as after birth,"

Recalling the provisions of the Declaration on Social and Legal Principles relating to the Protection and Welfare of Children, with Special Reference to Foster Placement and Adoption Nationally and Internationally; the United Nations Standard Minimum Rules for the Administration of Juvenile Justice (The Beijing Rules); and the Declaration on the Protection of Women and Children in Emergency and Armed Conflict,

Recognizing that, in all countries in the world, there are children living in exceptionally difficult conditions, and that such children need special consideration,

Taking due account of the importance of the traditions and cultural values of each people for the protection and harmonious development of the child,

Recognizing the importance of international co-operation for improving the living conditions of children in every country, in particular in the developing countries,

Have agreed as follows:

PART I

Article 1

For the purposes of the present Convention, a child means every human being below the age of eighteen years unless under the law applicable to the child, majority is attained earlier.

Article 2

1. States Parties shall respect and ensure the rights set forth in the present Convention to each child within their jurisdiction without discrimination of any kind, irrespective of the child's or his or her parent's or legal guardian's race, colour, sex, language, religion, political or other opinion, national, ethnic or social origin, property, disability, birth or other status.

2. States Parties shall take all appropriate measures to ensure that the child is protected against all forms of discrimination or punishment on the basis of the status, activities, expressed opinions, or beliefs of the child's parents, legal guardians, or family members.

Article 3

1. In all actions concerning children, whether undertaken by public or private social welfare institutions, courts of law, administrative authorities or legislative bodies, the best interests of the child shall be a primary consideration.

2. States Parties undertake to ensure the child such protection and care as is necessary for his or her well-being, taking into account the rights and duties of his or her parents, legal guardians, or other individuals legally responsible for him or her, and, to this end, shall take all appropriate legislative and administrative measures.

3. States Parties shall ensure that the institutions, services and facilities responsible for the care or protection of children shall conform with the standards established by competent authorities, particularly in the areas of safety, health, in the number and suitability of their staff, as well as competent supervision.

Article 4

States Parties shall undertake all appropriate legislative, administrative, and other measures for the implementation of the rights recognized in the present Convention. With regard to economic, social and cultural rights, States Parties shall undertake such measures to the maximum extent of their available resources and, where needed, within the framework of international co-operation.

Article 5

States Parties shall respect the responsibilities, rights and duties of parents or, where applicable, the members of the extended family or community as provided for by local custom, legal guardians or other persons legally responsible for the child, to provide, in a manner consistent with the evolving capacities of the child, appropriate direction and guidance in the exercise by the child of the rights recognized in the present Convention.

Article 6

1. States Parties recognize that every child has the inherent right to life.

2. States Parties shall ensure to the maximum extent possible the survival and development of the child.

Article 7

1. The child shall be registered immediately after birth and shall have the right from birth to a name, the right to acquire a nationality and, as far as possible, the right to know and be cared for by his or her parents.

2. States Parties shall ensure the implementation of these rights in accordance with their national law and their obligations under the relevant international instruments in this field, in particular where the child would otherwise be stateless.

Article 8

1. States Parties undertake to respect the right of the child to preserve his or her identity, including nationality, name and family relations as recognized by law without unlawful interference.

2. Where a child is illegally deprived of some or all of the elements of his or her identity, States Parties shall provide appropriate assistance and protection, with a view to re-establishing speedily his or her identity.

Article 9

1. States Parties shall ensure that a child shall not be separated from his or her parents against their will, except when competent authorities subject to judicial review determine, in accordance with applicable law and procedures, that such separation is necessary for the best interests of the child. Such determination may be necessary in a particular case such as one involving abuse or neglect of the child by the parents, or one where the parents are living separately and a decision must be made as to the child's place of residence.

2. In any proceedings pursuant to paragraph 1 of the present article, all interested parties shall be given an opportunity to participate in the proceedings and make their views known.

3. States Parties shall respect the right of the child who is separated from one or both parents to maintain personal relations and direct contact with both parents on a regular basis, except if it is contrary to the child's best interests.

4. Where such separation results from any action initiated by a State Party, such as the detention, imprisonment, exile, deportation or death (including death arising from any cause while the person is in the custody of the State) of one or both

parents or of the child, that State Party shall, upon request, provide the parents, the child or, if appropriate, another member of the family with the essential information concerning the whereabouts of the absent member(s) of the family unless the provision of the information would be detrimental to the well-being of the child. States Parties shall further ensure that the submission of such a request shall of itself entail no adverse consequences for the person(s) concerned.

Article 10

1. In accordance with the obligation of States Parties under article 9, paragraph 1, applications by a child or his or her parents to enter or leave a State Party for the purpose of family reunification shall be dealt with by States Parties in a positive, humane and expeditious manner. States Parties shall further ensure that the submission of such a request shall entail no adverse consequences for the applicants and for the members of their family.

2. A child whose parents reside in different States shall have the right to maintain on a regular basis, save in exceptional circumstances, personal relations and direct contacts with both parents. Towards that end and in accordance with the obligation of States Parties under article 9, paragraph 1, States Parties shall respect the right of the child and his or her parents to leave any country, including their own, and to enter their own country. The right to leave any country shall be subject only to such restrictions as are prescribed by law and which are necessary to protect the national security, public order (*ordre public*), public health or morals or the rights and freedoms of others and are consistent with the other rights recognized in the present Convention.

Article 11

1. States Parties shall take measures to combat the illicit transfer and non-return of children abroad.

2. To this end, States Parties shall promote the conclusion of bilateral or multilateral agreements or accession to existing agreements.

Article 12

1. States Parties shall assure to the child who is capable of forming his or her own views the right to express those views

freely in all matters affecting the child, the views of the child being given due weight in accordance with the age and maturity of the child.

2. For this purpose, the child shall in particular be provided the opportunity to be heard in any judicial and administrative proceedings affecting the child, either directly, or through a representative or an appropriate body, in a manner consistent with the procedural rules of national law.

Article 13

1. The child shall have the right to freedom of expression; this right shall include freedom to seek, receive and impart information and ideas of all kinds, regardless of frontiers, either orally, in writing or in print, in the form of art, or through any other media of the child's choice.

2. The exercise of this right may be subject to certain restrictions, but these shall only be such as are provided by law and are necessary:

(a) For respect of the rights or reputations of others; or

(b) For the protection of national security or of public order (*ordre public*), or of public health or morals.

Article 14

1. States Parties shall respect the right of the child to freedom of thought, conscience and religion.

2. States Parties shall respect the rights and duties of the parents and, when applicable, legal guardians, to provide direction to the child in the exercise of his or her right in a manner consistent with the evolving capacities of the child.

3. Freedom to manifest one's religion or beliefs may be subject only to such limitations as are prescribed by law and are necessary to protect public safety, order, health or morals, or the fundamental rights and freedoms of others.

Article 15

1. States Parties recognize the rights of the child to freedom of association and to freedom of peaceful assembly.

2. No restrictions may be placed on the exercise of these rights other than those imposed in conformity with the law and which are necessary in a democratic society in the interests of national security or public safety, public order (*ordre public*), the

protection of public health or morals or the protection of the rights and freedoms of others.

Article 16

1. No child shall be subjected to arbitrary or unlawful interference with his or her privacy, family, home or correspondence, nor to unlawful attacks on his or her honour and reputation.

2. The child has the right to the protection of the law against such interference or attacks.

Article 17

States Parties recognize the important function performed by the mass media and shall ensure that the child has access to information and material from a diversity of national and international sources, especially those aimed at the promotion of his or her social, spiritual and moral well-being and physical and mental health. To this end, States Parties shall:

(a) Encourage the mass media to disseminate information and material of social and cultural benefit to the child and in accordance with the spirit of article 29;

(b) Encourage international co-operation in the production, exchange and dissemination of such information and material from a diversity of cultural, national and international sources;

(c) Encourage the production and dissemination of children's books;

(d) Encourage the mass media to have particular regard to the linguistic needs of the child who belongs to a minority group or who is indigenous;

(e) Encourage the development of appropriate guidelines for the protection of the child from information and material injurious to his or her well-being, bearing in mind the provisions of articles 13 and 18.

Article 18

1. States Parties shall use their best efforts to ensure recognition of the principle that both parents have common responsibilities for the upbringing and development of the child. Parents or, as the case may be, legal guardians, have the primary responsibility for the upbringing and development of the child. The best interests of the child will be their basic concern.

2. For the purpose of guaranteeing and promoting the rights set forth in the present Convention, States Parties shall render appropriate assistance to parents and legal guardians in the performance of their child-rearing responsibilities and shall ensure the development of institutions, facilities and services for the care of children.

3. States Parties shall take all appropriate measures to ensure that children of working parents have the right to benefit from child-care services and facilities for which they are eligible.

Article 19

1. States Parties shall take all appropriate legislative, administrative, social and educational measures to protect the child from all forms of physical or mental violence, injury or abuse, neglect or negligent treatment, maltreatment or exploitation, including sexual abuse, while in the care of parent(s), legal guardian(s) or any other person who has the care of the child.

2. Such protective measures should, as appropriate, include effective procedures for the establishment of social programmes to provide necessary support for the child and for those who have the care of the child, as well as for other forms of prevention and for identification, reporting, referral, investigation, treatment and follow-up of instances of child maltreatment described heretofore, and, as appropriate, for judicial involvement.

Article 20

1. A child temporarily or permanently deprived of his or her family environment, or in whose own best interests cannot be allowed to remain in that environment, shall be entitled to special protection and assistance provided by the State.

2. States Parties shall in accordance with their national laws ensure alternative care for such a child.

3. Such care could include, *inter alia,* foster placement, kafalah of Islamic law, adoption or if necessary placement in suitable institutions for the care of children. When considering solutions, due regard shall be paid to the desirability of continuity in a child's upbringing and to the child's ethnic, religious, cultural and linguistic background.

Article 21

States Parties that recognize and/or permit the system of adoption shall ensure that the best interests of the child shall be the paramount consideration and they shall:

(a) Ensure that the adoption of a child is authorized only by competent authorities who determine, in accordance with applicable law and procedures and on the basis of all pertinent and reliable information, that the adoption is permissible in view of the child's status concerning parents, relatives and legal guardians and that, if required, the persons concerned have given their informed consent to the adoption on the basis of such counselling as may be necessary;

(b) Recognize that inter-country adoption may be considered as an alternative means of child's care, if the child cannot be placed in a foster or an adoptive family or cannot in any suitable manner be cared for in the child's country of origin;

(c) Ensure that the child concerned by inter-country adoption enjoys safeguards and standards equivalent to those existing in the case of national adoption;

(d) Take all appropriate measures to ensure that, in inter-country adoption, the placement does not result in improper financial gain for those involved in it;

(e) Promote, where appropriate, the objectives of the present article by concluding bilateral or multilateral arrangements or agreements, and endeavour, within this framework, to ensure that the placement of the child in another country is carried out by competent authorities or organs.

Article 22

1. States Parties shall take appropriate measures to ensure that a child who is seeking refugee status or who is considered a refugee in accordance with applicable international or domestic law and procedures shall, whether unaccompanied or accompanied by his or her parents or by any other person, receive appropriate protection and humanitarian assistance in the enjoyment of applicable rights set forth in the present Convention and in other international human rights or humanitarian instruments to which the said States are Parties.

2. For this purpose, States Parties shall provide, as they consider appropriate, co-operation in any efforts by the United Nations and other competent intergovernmental organizations or non-governmental organizations co-operating with the

United Nations to protect and assist such a child and to trace the parents or other members of the family of any refugee child in order to obtain information necessary for reunification with his or her family. In cases where no parents or other members of the family can be found, the child shall be accorded the same protection as any other child permanently or temporarily deprived of his or her family environment for any reason , as set forth in the present Convention.

Article 23

1. States Parties recognize that a mentally or physically disabled child should enjoy a full and decent life, in conditions which ensure dignity, promote self-reliance and facilitate the child's active participation in the community.

2. States Parties recognize the right of the disabled child to special care and shall encourage and ensure the extension, subject to available resources, to the eligible child and those responsible for his or her care, of assistance for which application is made and which is appropriate to the child's condition and to the circumstances of the parents or others caring for the child.

3. Recognizing the special needs of a disabled child, assistance extended in accordance with paragraph 2 of the present article shall be provided free of charge, whenever possible, taking into account the financial resources of the parents or others caring for the child, and shall be designed to ensure that the disabled child has effective access to and receives education, training, health care services, rehabilitation services, preparation for employment and recreation opportunities in a manner conducive to the child's achieving the fullest possible social integration and individual development, including his or her cultural and spiritual development

4. States Parties shall promote, in the spirit of international cooperation, the exchange of appropriate information in the field of preventive health care and of medical, psychological and functional treatment of disabled children, including dissemination of and access to information concerning methods of rehabilitation, education and vocational services, with the aim of enabling States Parties to improve their capabilities and skills and to widen their experience in these areas. In this regard, particular account shall be taken of the needs of developing countries.

Article 24

1. States Parties recognize the right of the child to the enjoyment of the highest attainable standard of health and to facilities for the treatment of illness and rehabilitation of health. States Parties shall strive to ensure that no child is deprived of his or her right of access to such health care services.

2. States Parties shall pursue full implementation of this right and, in particular, shall take appropriate measures:

(a) To diminish infant and child mortality;

(b) To ensure the provision of necessary medical assistance and health care to all children with emphasis on the development of primary health care;

(c) To combat disease and malnutrition, including within the framework of primary health care, through, *inter alia,* the application of readily available technology and through the provision of adequate nutritious foods and clean drinking-water, taking into consideration the dangers and risks of environmental pollution;

(d) To ensure appropriate pre-natal and post-natal health care for mothers;

(e) To ensure that all segments of society, in particular parents and children, are informed, have access to education and are supported in the use of basic knowledge of child health and nutrition, the advantages of breastfeeding, hygiene and environmental sanitation and the prevention of accidents;

(f) To develop preventive health care, guidance for parents and family planning education and services.

3. States Parties shall take all effective and appropriate measures with a view to abolishing traditional practices prejudicial to the health of children.

4. States Parties undertake to promote and encourage international co-operation with a view to achieving progressively the full realization of the right recognized in the present article. In this regard, particular account shall be taken of the needs of developing countries.

Article 25

States Parties recognize the right of a child who has been placed by the competent authorities for the purposes of care, protection or treatment of his or her physical or mental health, to a periodic review of the treatment provided to the child and all other circumstances relevant to his or her placement.

Article 26

1. States Parties shall recognize for every child the right to benefit from social security, including social insurance, and shall take the necessary measures to achieve the full realization of this right in accordance with their national law.

2. The benefits should, where appropriate, be granted, taking into account the resources and the circumstances of the child and persons having responsibility for the maintenance of the child, as well as any other consideration relevant to an application for benefits made by or on behalf of the child.

Article 27

1. States Parties recognize the right of every child to a standard of living adequate for the child's physical, mental, spiritual, moral and social development.

2. The parent(s) or others responsible for the child have the primary responsibility to secure, within their abilities and financial capacities, the conditions of living necessary for the child's development.

3. States Parties, in accordance with national conditions and within their means, shall take appropriate measures to assist parents and others responsible for the child to implement this right and shall in case of need provide material assistance and support programmes, particularly with regard to nutrition, clothing and housing.

4. States Parties shall take all appropriate measures to secure the recovery of maintenance for the child from the parents or other persons having financial responsibility for the child, both within the State Party and from abroad. In particular, where the person having financial responsibility for the child lives in a State different from that of the child, States Parties shall promote the accession to international agreements or the conclusion of such agreements, as well as the making of other appropriate arrangements.

Article 28

1. States Parties recognize the right of the child to education, and with a view to achieving this right progressively and on the basis of equal opportunity, they shall, in particular:

(a) Make primary education compulsory and available free to all;

(b) Encourage the development of different forms of

secondary education, including general and vocational education, make them available and accessible to every child, and take appropriate measures such as the introduction of free education and offering financial assistance in case of need;

(c) Make higher education accessible to all on the basis of capacity by every appropriate means;

(d) Make educational and vocational information and guidance available and accessible to all children;

(e) Take measures to encourage regular attendance at schools and the reduction of drop-out rates.

2. States Parties shall take all appropriate measures to ensure that school discipline is administered in a manner consistent with the child's human dignity and in conformity with the present Convention.

3. States Parties shall promote and encourage international cooperation in matters relating to education, in particular with a view to contributing to the elimination of ignorance and illiteracy throughout the world and facilitating access to scientific and technical knowledge and modern teaching methods. In this regard, particular account shall be taken of the needs of developing countries.

Article 29

1. States Parties agree that the education of the child shall be directed to:

(a) The development of the child's personality, talents and mental and physical abilities to their fullest potential;

(b) The development of respect for human rights and fundamental freedoms, and for the principles enshrined in the Charter of the United Nations;

(c) The development of respect for the child's parents, his or her own cultural identity, language and values, for the national values of the country in which the child is living, the country from which he or she may originate, and for civilizations different from his or her own;

(d) The preparation of the child for responsible life in a free society, in the spirit of understanding, peace, tolerance, equality of sexes, and friendship among all peoples, ethnic, national and religious groups and persons of indigenous origin;

(e) The development of respect for the natural environment.

2. No part of the present article or article 28 shall be construed so as to interfere with the liberty of individuals and

bodies to establish and direct educational institutions, subject always to the observance of the principle set forth in paragraph 1 of the present article and to the requirements that the education given in such institutions shall conform to such minimum standards as may be laid down by the State.

Article 30

In those States in which ethnic, religious or linguistic minorities or persons of indigenous origin exist, a child belonging to such a minority or who is indigenous shall not be denied the right, in community with other members of his or her group, to enjoy his or her own culture, to profess and practise his or her own religion, or to use his or her own language.

Article 31

1. States Parties recognize the right of the child to rest and leisure, to engage in play and recreational activities appropriate to the age of the child and to participate freely in cultural life and the arts.

2. States Parties shall respect and promote the right of the child to participate fully in cultural and artistic life and shall encourage the provision of appropriate and equal opportunities for cultural, artistic, recreational and leisure activity.

Article 32

1. States Parties recognize the right of the child to be protected from economic exploitation and from performing any work that is likely to be hazardous or to interfere with the child's education, or to be harmful to the child's health or physical, mental, spiritual, moral or social development.

2. States Parties shall take legislative, administrative, social and educational measures to ensure the implementation of the present article. To this end, and having regard to the relevant provisions of other international instruments, States Parties shall in particular:

(a) Provide for a minimum age or minimum ages for admission to employment;

(b) Provide for appropriate regulation of the hours and conditions of employment;

(c) Provide for appropriate penalties or other sanctions to ensure the effective enforcement of the present article.

Article 33

States Parties shall take all appropriate measures, including legislative, administrative, social and educational measures, to protect children from the illicit use of narcotic drugs and psychotropic substances as defined in the relevant international treaties, and to prevent the use of children in the illicit production and trafficking of such substances.

Article 34

States Parties undertake to protect the child from all forms of sexual exploitation and sexual abuse. For these purposes, States Parties shall in particular take all appropriate national, bilateral and multilateral measures to prevent:

(a) The inducement or coercion of a child to engage in any unlawful sexual activity;

(b) The exploitative use of children in prostitution or other unlawful sexual practices;

(c) The exploitative use of children in pornographic performances and materials.

Article 35

States Parties shall take all appropriate national, bilateral and multilateral measures to prevent the abduction of, the sale of or traffic in children for any purpose or in any form.

Article 36

States Parties shall protect the child against all other forms of exploitation prejudicial to any aspects of the child's welfare.

Article 37

States Parties shall ensure that:

(a) No child shall be subjected to torture or other cruel, inhuman or degrading treatment or punishment. Neither capital punishment nor life imprisonment without possibility of release shall be imposed for offences committed by persons below eighteen years of age;

(b) No child shall be deprived of his or her liberty unlawfully or arbitrarily. The arrest, detention or imprisonment of a child shall be in conformity with the law and shall be used only as a measure of last resort and for the shortest appropriate period of time;

(c) Every child deprived of liberty shall be treated with humanity and respect for the inherent dignity of the human person, and in a manner which takes into account the needs of persons of his or her age. In particular, every child deprived of liberty shall be separated from adults unless it is considered in the child's best interest not to do so and shall have the right to maintain contact with his or her family through correspondence and visits, save in exceptional circumstances;

(d) Every child deprived of his or her liberty shall have the right to prompt access to legal and other appropriate assistance, as well as the right to challenge the legality of the deprivation of his or her liberty before a court or other competent, independent and impartial authority, and to a prompt decision on any such action.

Article 38

1. States Parties undertake to respect and to ensure respect for rules of international humanitarian law applicable to them in armed conflicts which are relevant to the child.

2. States Parties shall take all feasible measures to ensure that persons who have not attained the age of fifteen years do not take a direct part in hostilities.

3. States Parties shall refrain from recruiting any person who has not attained the age of fifteen years into their armed forces. In recruiting among those persons who have attained the age of fifteen years but who have not attained the age of eighteen years, States Parties shall endeavour to give priority to those who are oldest.

4. In accordance with their obligations under international humanitarian law to protect the civilian population in armed conflicts, States Parties shall take all feasible measures to ensure protection and care of children who are affected by an armed conflict.

Article 39

States Parties shall take all appropriate measures to promote physical and psychological recovery and social reintegration of a child victim of: any form of neglect, exploitation, or abuse; torture or any other form of cruel, inhuman or degrading treatment or punishment; or armed conflicts. Such recovery and reintegration shall take place in an environment which fosters the health, self-respect and dignity of the child.

Article 40

1. States Parties recognize the right of every child alleged as, accused of, or recognized as having infringed the penal law to be treated in a manner consistent with the promotion of the child's sense of dignity and worth, which reinforces the child's respect for the human rights and fundamental freedoms of others and which takes into account the child's age and the desirability of promoting the child's reintegration and the child's assuming a constructive role in society.

2. To this end, and having regard to the relevant provisions of international instruments, States Parties shall, in particular, ensure that:

(a) No child shall be alleged as, be accused of, or recognized as having infringed the penal law by reason of acts or omissions that were not prohibited by national or international law at the time they were committed;

(b) Every child alleged as or accused of having infringed the penal law has at least the following guarantees:

(i) To be presumed innocent until proven guilty according to law;

(ii) To be informed promptly and directly of the charges against him or her, and, if appropriate, through his or her parents or legal guardians, and to have legal or other appropriate assistance in the preparation and presentation of his or her defence;

(iii) To have the matter determined without delay by a competent, independent and impartial authority or judicial body in a fair hearing according to law, in the presence of legal or other appropriate assistance and, unless it is considered not to be in the best interest of the child, in particular, taking into account his or her age or situation, his or her parents or legal guardians;

(iv) Not to be compelled to give testimony or to confess guilt; to examine or have examined adverse witnesses and to obtain the participation and examination of witnesses on his or her behalf under conditions of equality;

(v) If considered to have infringed the penal law, to have this decision and any measures imposed in consequence thereof reviewed by a higher competent, independent and impartial authority or judicial body according to law;

(vi) To have the free assistance of an interpreter if the child cannot understand or speak the language used;

(vii) To have his or her privacy fully respected at all stages of the proceedings.

3. States Parties shall seek to promote the establishment of laws, procedures, authorities and institutions specifically applicable to children alleged as, accused of, or recognized as having infringed the penal law, and, in particular:

(a) The establishment of a minimum age below which children shall be presumed not to have the capacity to infringe the penal law;

(b) Whenever appropriate and desirable, measures for dealing with such children without resorting to judicial proceedings, providing that human rights and legal safeguards are fully respected.

4. A variety of dispositions, such as care, guidance and supervision orders; counselling; probation; foster care; education and vocational training programmes and other alternatives to institutional care shall be available to ensure that children are dealt with in a manner appropriate to their well-being and proportionate both to their circumstances and the offence.

Article 41

Nothing in the present Convention shall affect any provisions which are more conducive to the realization of the rights of the child and which may be contained in:

(a) The law of a State party; or

(b) International law in force for that State.

PART II

Article 42

States Parties undertake to make the principles and provisions of the Convention widely known, by appropriate and active means, to adults and children alike.

Article 43

1. For the purpose of examining the progress made by States Parties in achieving the realization of the obligations undertaken in the present Convention, there shall be established a Committee on the Rights of the Child, which shall carry out the functions hereinafter provided.

2. The Committee shall consist of ten experts of high moral standing and recognized competence in the field covered by

this Convention. The members of the Committee shall be elected by States Parties from among their nationals and shall serve in their personal capacity, consideration being given to equitable geographical distribution, as well as to the principal legal systems.

3. The members of the Committee shall be elected by secret ballot from a list of persons nominated by States Parties. Each State Party may nominate one person from among its own nationals.

4. The initial election to the Committee shall be held no later than six months after the date of the entry into force of the present Convention and thereafter every second year. At least four months before the date of each election, the Secretary-General of the United Nations shall address a letter to States Parties inviting them to submit their nominations within two months. The Secretary-General shall subsequently prepare a list in alphabetical order of all persons thus nominated, indicating States Parties which have nominated them, and shall submit it to the States Parties to the present Convention.

5. The elections shall be held at meetings of States Parties convened by the Secretary-General at United Nations Headquarters. At those meetings, for which two thirds of States Parties shall constitute a quorum, the persons elected to the Committee shall be those who obtain the largest number of votes and an absolute majority of the votes of the representatives of States Parties present and voting.

6. The members of the Committee shall be elected for a term of four years. They shall be eligible for re-election if renominated. The term of five of the members elected at the first election shall expire at the end of two years; immediately after the first election, the names of these five members shall be chosen by lot by the Chairman of the meeting.

7. If a member of the Committee dies or resigns or declares that for any other cause he or she can no longer perform the duties of the Committee, the State Party which nominated the member shall appoint another expert from among its nationals to serve for the remainder of the term, subject to the approval of the Committee.

8. The Committee shall establish its own rules of procedure.

9. The Committee shall elect its officers for a period of two years.

10. The meetings of the Committee shall normally be held

at United Nations Headquarters or at any other convenient place as determined by the Committee. The Committee shall normally meet annually. The duration of the meetings of the Committee shall be determined, and reviewed, if necessary, by a meeting of the States Parties to the present Convention, subject to the approval of the General Assembly.

11. The Secretary-General of the United Nations shall provide the necessary staff and facilities for the effective performance of the functions of the Committee under the present Convention.

12. With the approval of the General Assembly, the members of the Committee established under the present Convention shall receive emoluments from United Nations resources on such terms and conditions as the Assembly may decide.

Article 44

1. States Parties undertake to submit to the Committee, through the Secretary-General of the United Nations, reports on the measures they have adopted which give effect to the rights recognized herein and on the progress made on the enjoyment of those rights:

(a) Within two years of the entry into force of the Convention for the State Party concerned;

(b) Thereafter every five years.

2. Reports made under the present article shall indicate factors and difficulties, if any, affecting the degree of fulfilment of the obligations under the present Convention. Reports shall also contain sufficient information to provide the Committee with a comprehensive understanding of the implementation of the Convention in the country concerned.

3. A State Party which has submitted a comprehensive initial report to the Committee need not, in its subsequent reports submitted in accordance with paragraph 1 (b) of the present article, repeat basic information previously provided.

4. The Committee may request from States Parties further information relevant to the implementation of the Convention.

5. The Committee shall submit to the General Assembly, through the Economic and Social Council, every two years, reports on its activities.

6. States Parties shall make their reports widely available to the public in their own countries.

Article 45

In order to foster the effective implementation of the Convention and to encourage international co-operation in the field covered by the Convention:

(a) The specialized agencies, the United Nations Children's Fund, and other United Nations organs shall be entitled to be represented at the consideration of the implementation of such provisions of the present Convention as fall within the scope of their mandate. The Committee may invite the specialized agencies, the United Nations Children's Fund and other competent bodies as it may consider appropriate to provide expert advice on the implementation of the Convention in areas falling within the scope of their respective mandates. The Committee may invite the specialized agencies, the United Nations Children's Fund, and other United Nations organs to submit reports on the implementation of the Convention in areas falling within the scope of their activities;

(b) The Committee shall transmit, as it may consider appropriate, to the specialized agencies, the United Nations Children's Fund and other competent bodies, any reports from States Parties that contain a request, or indicate a need, for technical advice or assistance, along with the Committee's observations and suggestions, if any, on these requests or indications;

(c) The Committee may recommend to the General Assembly to request the Secretary-General to undertake on its behalf studies on specific issues relating to the rights of the child;

(d) The Committee may make suggestions and general recommendations based on information received pursuant to articles 44 and 45 of the present Convention. Such suggestions and general recommendations shall be transmitted to any State Party concerned and reported to the General Assembly, together with comments, if any, from States Parties.

PART III

Article 46

The present Convention shall be open for signature by all States.

Article 47

The present Convention is subject to ratification. Instruments of ratification shall be deposited with the Secretary-General of the United Nations.

Article 48

The present Convention shall remain open for accession by any State. The instruments of accession shall be deposited with the Secretary-General of the United Nations.

Article 49

1. The present Convention shall enter into force on the thirtieth day following the date of deposit with the Secretary-General of the United Nations of the twentieth instrument of ratification or accession.

2. For each State ratifying or acceding to the Convention after the deposit of the twentieth instrument of ratification or accession, the Convention shall enter into force on the thirtieth day after the deposit by such State of its instrument of ratification or accession.

Article 50

1. Any State Party may propose an amendment and file it with the Secretary-General of the United Nations. The Secretary-General shall thereupon communicate the proposed amendment to States Parties, with a request that they indicate whether they favour a conference of States Parties for the purpose of considering and voting upon the proposals. In the event that, within four months from the date of such communication, at least one third of the States Parties favour such a conference, the Secretary-General shall convene the conference under the auspices of the United Nations. Any amendment adopted by a majority of States Parties present and voting at the conference shall be submitted to the General Assembly for approval.

2. An amendment adopted in accordance with paragraph 1 of the present article shall enter into force when it has been approved by the General Assembly of the United Nations and accepted by a two-thirds majority of States Parties.

3. When an amendment enters into force, it shall be binding on those States Parties which have accepted it, other States Parties

still being bound by the provisions of the present Convention and any earlier amendments which they have accepted.

Article 51

1. The Secretary-General of the United Nations shall receive and circulate to all States the text of reservations made by States at the time of ratification or accession.

2. A reservation incompatible with the object and purpose of the present Convention shall not be permitted.

3. Reservations may be withdrawn at any time by notification to that effect addressed to the Secretary-General of the United Nations, who shall then inform all States. Such notification shall take effect on the date on which it is received by the Secretary-General

Article 52

A State Party may denounce the present Convention by written notification to the Secretary-General of the United Nations. Denunciation becomes effective one year after the date of receipt of the notification by the Secretary-General.

Article 53

The Secretary-General of the United Nations is designated as the depositary of the present Convention.

Article 54

The original of the present Convention, of which the Arabic, Chinese, English, French, Russian and Spanish texts are equally authentic, shall be deposited with the Secretary-General of the United Nations.

In Witness Thereof the undersigned plenipotentiaries, being duly authorized thereto by their respective governments, have signed the present Convention.

Declaration on the Rights of Mentally Retarded Persons

G.A. res. 2856 (XXVI), 26 U.N. GAOR Supp. (No. 29) at 93, U.N. Doc. A/8429 (1971).

The General Assembly,
Mindful of the pledge of the States Members of the United Nations under the Charter to take joint and separate action in

co-operation with the Organization to promote higher standards of living, full employment and conditions of economic and social progress and development,

Reaffirming faith in human rights and fundamental freedoms and in the principles of peace, of the dignity and worth of the human person and of social justice proclaimed in the Charter,

Recalling the principles of the Universal Declaration of Human Rights, the International Covenants on Human Rights, the Declaration of the Rights of the Child and the standards already set for social progress in the constitutions, conventions, recommendations and resolutions of the International Labour Organisation, the United Nations Educational, Scientific and Cultural Organization, the World Health Organization, the United Nations Children's Fund and other organizations concerned,

Emphasizing that the Declaration on Social Progress and Development has proclaimed the necessity of protecting the rights and assuring the welfare and rehabilitation of the physically and mentally disadvantaged,

Bearing in mind the necessity of assisting mentally retarded persons to develop their abilities in various fields of activities and of promoting their integration as far as possible in normal life,

Aware that certain countries, at their present stage of development, can devote only limited efforts to this end,

Proclaims this Declaration on the Rights of Mentally Retarded Persons and calls for national and international action to ensure that it will be used as a common basis and frame of reference for the protection of these rights:

1. The mentally retarded person has, to the maximum degree of feasibility, the same rights as other human beings.

2. The mentally retarded person has a right to proper medical care and physical therapy and to such education, training, rehabilitation and guidance as will enable him to develop his ability and maximum potential.

3. The mentally retarded person has a right to economic security and to a decent standard of living. He has a right to perform productive work or to engage in any other meaningful occupation to the fullest possible extent of his capabilities.

4. Whenever possible, the mentally retarded person should live with his own family or with foster parents and participate in different forms of community life. The family with which he

lives should receive assistance. If care in an institution becomes necessary, it should be provided in surroundings and other circumstances as close as possible to those of normal life.

5. The mentally retarded person has a right to a qualified guardian when this is required to protect his personal well-being and interests.

6. The mentally retarded person has a right to protection from exploitation, abuse and degrading treatment. If prosecuted for any offence, he shall have a right to due process of law with full recognition being given to his degree of mental responsibility.

7. Whenever mentally retarded persons are unable, because of the severity of their handicap, to exercise all their rights in a meaningful way or it should become necessary to restrict or deny some or all of these rights, the procedure used for that restriction or denial of rights must contain proper legal safeguards against every form of abuse. This procedure must be based on an evaluation of the social capability of the mentally retarded person by qualified experts and must be subject to periodic review and to the right of appeal to higher authorities.

Declaration on the Rights of Disabled Persons

G.A. res. 3447 (XXX), 30 U.N. GAOR Supp. (No. 34) at 88,
U.N. Doc. A/10034 (1975).

The General Assembly,

Mindful of the pledge made by Member States, under the Charter of the United Nations to take joint and separate action in co-operation with the Organization to promote higher standards of living, full employment and conditions of economic and social progress and development,

Reaffirming its faith in human rights and fundamental freedoms and in the principles of peace, of the dignity and worth of the human person and of social justice proclaimed in the Charter,

Recalling the principles of the Universal Declaration of Human Rights, the International Covenants on Human Rights, the Declaration of the Rights of the Child and the Declaration on the Rights of Mentally Retarded Persons, as well as the standards already set for social progress in the constitutions, conventions, recommendations and resolutions of the International Labour Organisation, the United Nations Educational, Scientific and Cultural Organization, the World

Health Organization, the United Nations Children's Fund and other organizations concerned,

Recalling also Economic and Social Council resolution 1921 (LVIII) of 6 May 1975 on the prevention of disability and the rehabilitation of disabled persons,

Emphasizing that the Declaration on Social Progress and Development has proclaimed the necessity of protecting the rights and assuring the welfare and rehabilitation of the physically and mentally disadvantaged,

Bearing in mind the necessity of preventing physical and mental disabilities and of assisting disabled persons to develop their abilities in the most varied fields of activities and of promoting their integration as far as possible in normal life,

Aware that certain countries, at their present stage of development, can devote only limited efforts to this end,

Proclaims this Declaration on the Rights of Disabled Persons and calls for national and international action to ensure that it will be used as a common basis and frame of reference for the protection of these rights:

1. The term "disabled person" means any person unable to ensure by himself or herself, wholly or partly, the necessities of a normal individual and/or social life, as a result of deficiency, either congenital or not, in his or her physical or mental capabilities.

2. Disabled persons shall enjoy all the rights set forth in this Declaration. These rights shall be granted to all disabled persons without any exception whatsoever and without distinction or discrimination on the basis of race, colour, sex, language, religion, political or other opinions, national or social origin, state of wealth, birth or any other situation applying either to the disabled person himself or herself or to his or her family.

3. Disabled persons have the inherent right to respect for their human dignity. Disabled persons, whatever the origin, nature and seriousness of their handicaps and disabilities, have the same fundamental rights as their fellow-citizens of the same age, which implies first and foremost the right to enjoy a decent life, as normal and full as possible.

4. Disabled persons have the same civil and political rights as other human beings; paragraph 7 of the Declaration on the Rights of Mentally Retarded Persons applies to any possible limitation or suppression of those rights for mentally disabled persons.

5. Disabled persons are entitled to the measures designed to enable them to become as self-reliant as possible.

6. Disabled persons have the right to medical, psychological and functional treatment, including prosthetic and orthetic appliances, to medical and social rehabilitation, education, vocational training and rehabilitation, aid, counselling, placement services and other services which will enable them to develop their capabilities and skills to the maximum and will hasten the processes of their social integration or reintegration.

7. Disabled persons have the right to economic and social security and to a decent level of living. They have the right, according to their capabilities, to secure and retain employment or to engage in a useful, productive and remunerative occupation and to join trade unions.

8. Disabled persons are entitled to have their special needs taken into consideration at all stages of economic and social planning.

9. Disabled persons have the right to live with their families or with foster parents and to participate in all social, creative or recreational activities. No disabled person shall be subjected, as far as his or her residence is concerned, to differential treatment other than that required by his or her condition or by the improvement which he or she may derive therefrom. If the stay of a disabled person in a specialized establishment is indispensable, the environment and living conditions therein shall be as close as possible to those of the normal life of a person of his or her age.

10. Disabled persons shall be protected against all exploitation, all regulations and all treatment of a discriminatory, abusive or degrading nature.

11. Disabled persons shall be able to avail themselves of qualified legal aid when such aid proves indispensable for the protection of their persons and property. If judicial proceedings are instituted against them, the legal procedure applied shall take their physical and mental condition fully into account.

12. Organizations of disabled persons may be usefully consulted in all matters regarding the rights of disabled persons.

13. Disabled persons, their families and communities shall be fully informed, by all appropriate means, of the rights contained in this Declaration.

Declaration on the Right to Development

G.A. res. 41/128, annex, 41 U.N. GAOR Supp. (No. 53) at 186,
U.N. Doc. A/41/53 (1986).

The General Assembly,

Bearing in mind the purposes and principles of the Charter of the United Nations relating to the achievement of international co-operation in solving international problems of an economic, social, cultural or humanitarian nature, and in promoting and encouraging respect for human rights and fundamental freedoms for all without distinction as to race, sex, language or religion,

Recognizing that development is a comprehensive economic, social, cultural and political process, which aims at the constant improvement of the well-being of the entire population and of all individuals on the basis of their active, free and meaningful participation in development and in the fair distribution of benefits resulting therefrom,

Considering that under the provisions of the Universal Declaration of Human Rights everyone is entitled to a social and international order in which the rights and freedoms set forth in that Declaration can be fully realized,

Recalling the provisions of the International Covenant on Economic, Social and Cultural Rights and of the International Covenant on Civil and Political Rights,

Recalling further the relevant agreements, conventions, resolutions, recommendations and other instruments of the United Nations and its specialized agencies concerning the integral development of the human being, economic and social progress and development of all peoples, including those instruments concerning decolonization, the prevention of discrimination, respect for and observance of, human rights and fundamental freedoms, the maintenance of international peace and security and the further promotion of friendly relations and co-operation among States in accordance with the Charter,

Recalling the right of peoples to self-determination, by virtue of which they have the right freely to determine their political status and to pursue their economic, social and cultural development,

Recalling also the right of peoples to exercise, subject to the relevant provisions of both International Covenants on Human Rights, full and complete sovereignty over all their natural wealth and resources,

Mindful of the obligation of States under the Charter to promote universal respect for and observance of human rights and fundamental freedoms for all without distinction of any kind such as race, colour, sex, language, religion, political or other opinion, national or social origin, property, birth or other status,

Considering that the elimination of the massive and flagrant violations of the human rights of the peoples and individuals affected by situations such as those resulting from colonialism, neo-colonialism, apartheid, all forms of racism and racial discrimination, foreign domination and occupation, aggression and threats against national sovereignty, national unity and territorial integrity and threats of war would contribute to the establishment of circumstances propitious to the development of a great part of mankind,

Concerned at the existence of serious obstacles to development, as well as to the complete fulfilment of human beings and of peoples, constituted, *inter alia,* by the denial of civil, political, economic, social and cultural rights, and considering that all human rights and fundamental freedoms are indivisible and interdependent and that, in order to promote development, equal attention and urgent consideration should be given to the implementation, promotion and protection of civil, political, economic, social and cultural rights and that, accordingly, the promotion of, respect for and enjoyment of certain human rights and fundamental freedoms cannot justify the denial of other human rights and fundamental freedoms,

Considering that international peace and security are essential elements for the realization of the right to development,

Reaffirming that there is a close relationship between disarmament and development and that progress in the field of disarmament would considerably promote progress in the field of development and that resources released through disarmament measures should be devoted to the economic and social development and well-being of all peoples and, in particular, those of the developing countries,

Recognizing that the human person is the central subject of the development process and that development policy should therefore make the human being the main participant and beneficiary of development,

Recognizing that the creation of conditions favourable to the development of peoples and individuals is the primary responsibility of their States,

Aware that efforts at the international level to promote and protect human rights should be accompanied by efforts to establish a new international economic order,

Confirming that the right to development is an inalienable human right and that equality of opportunity for development is a prerogative both of nations and of individuals who make up nations,

Proclaims the following Declaration on the Right to Development:

Article 1

1. The right to development is an inalienable human right by virtue of which every human person and all peoples are entitled to participate in, contribute to, and enjoy economic, social, cultural and political development, in which all human rights and fundamental freedoms can be fully realized.

2. The human right to development also implies the full realization of the right of peoples to self-determination, which includes, subject to the relevant provisions of both International Covenants on Human Rights, the exercise of their inalienable right to full sovereignty over all their natural wealth and resources.

Article 2

1. The human person is the central subject of development and should be the active participant and beneficiary of the right to development.

2. All human beings have a responsibility for development, individually and collectively, taking into account the need for full respect for their human rights and fundamental freedoms as well as their duties to the community, which alone can ensure the free and complete fulfilment of the human being, and they should therefore promote and protect an appropriate political, social and economic order for development.

3. States have the right and the duty to formulate appropriate national development policies that aim at the constant improvement of the well-being of the entire population and of all individuals, on the basis of their active, free and meaningful participation in development and in the fair distribution of the benefits resulting therefrom.

Article 3

1. States have the primary responsibility for the creation of national and international conditions favourable to the realization of the right to development.

2. The realization of the right to development requires full respect for the principles of international law concerning friendly relations and cooperation among States in accordance with the Charter of the United Nations.

3. States have the duty to co-operate with each other in ensuring development and eliminating obstacles to development. States should realize their rights and fulfil their duties in such a manner as to promote a new international economic order based on sovereign equality, interdependence, mutual interest and co-operation among all States, as well as to encourage the observance and realization of human rights.

Article 4

1. States have the duty to take steps, individually and collectively, to formulate international development policies with a view to facilitating the full realization of the right to development.

2. Sustained action is required to promote more rapid development of developing countries. As a complement to the efforts of developing countries, effective international co-operation is essential in providing these countries with appropriate means and facilities to foster their comprehensive development.

Article 5

States shall take resolute steps to eliminate the massive and flagrant violations of the human rights of peoples and human beings affected by situations such as those resulting from apartheid, all forms of racism and racial discrimination, colonialism, foreign domination and occupation, aggression, foreign interference and threats against national sovereignty, national unity and territorial integrity, threats of war and refusal to recognize the fundamental right of peoples to self-determination.

Article 6

1. All States should co-operate with a view to promoting, encouraging and strengthening universal respect for and

observance of all human rights and fundamental freedoms for all without any distinction as to race, sex, language or religion.

2. All human rights and fundamental freedoms are indivisible and interdependent; equal attention and urgent consideration should be given to the implementation, promotion and protection of civil, political, economic, social and cultural rights.

3. States should take steps to eliminate obstacles to development resulting from failure to observe civil and political rights, as well as economic social and cultural rights.

Article 7

All States should promote the establishment, maintenance and strengthening of international peace and security and, to that end, should do their utmost to achieve general and complete disarmament under effective international control, as well as to ensure that the resources released by effective disarmament measures are used for comprehensive development, in particular that of the developing countries.

Article 8

1. States should undertake, at the national level, all necessary measures for the realization of the right to development and shall ensure, *inter alia*, equality of opportunity for all in their access to basic resources, education, health services, food, housing, employment and the fair distribution of income. Effective measures should be undertaken to ensure that women have an active role in the development process. Appropriate economic and social reforms should be carried out with a view to eradicating all social injustices.

2. States should encourage popular participation in all spheres as an important factor in development and in the full realization of all human rights.

Article 9

1. All the aspects of the right to development set forth in the present Declaration are indivisible and interdependent and each of them should be considered in the context of the whole.

2. Nothing in the present Declaration shall be construed as being contrary to the purposes and principles of the United Nations, or as implying that any State, group or person has a

right to engage in any activity or to perform any act aimed at the violation of the rights set forth in the Universal Declaration of Human Rights and in the International Covenants on Human Rights.

Article 10

Steps should be taken to ensure the full exercise and progressive enhancement of the right to development, including the formulation, adoption and implementation of policy, legislative and other measures at the national and international levels.

Directory of Organizations

5

The following is a selected list of national, regional, and international organizations that have as a principal goal the preservation and promotion of human rights. Most are located in North America, and their materials are available in the United States or Canada. It should be noted that most countries and states and even some larger cities have an agency, department, or commission concerned with human rights.

Alberta Human Rights Commission
800 Standard Life Center
10405 Jasper Avenue
Edmonton, Alberta
Canada T5J 4R7
(403) 427-3116
fax: (403) 422-3563
Director: Marie Riddle

The seven members of the Alberta Human Rights Commission are appointed by the Lieutenant-Governor in Council to represent the public at large in this autonomous body established in 1973. The commission is responsible for the administration of the Human Rights, Citizenship, and Multiculturalism Act. In addition to handling complaints of violations of the act, the commission is responsible for educating the public regarding human rights issues. The commission investigates cases of discrimination relating to race, place of origin, color, religious beliefs, physical disability, age, and pregnancy, among others.

Publications: The commission publishes fact sheets on human rights topics.

Website: http://www.gov.ab.ca/~mcd
The website contains the Human Rights, Citizenship, and Multiculturalism Act; the commission by-laws; and a where-to-turn-for-help section, including a description of the complaint process, and fact sheets.

American Civil Liberties Union (ACLU)
132 West 43rd Street
New York NY 10036
(212) 944-9800; (212) 869-9065
Director: Ira Glasser

Although primarily concerned with civil rights, the American Civil Liberties Union works for the protection of basic human freedoms for all individuals, including children, soldiers, welfare recipients, prisoners, and mental patients. It is a network of affiliated and local chapters supported by the national office in New York, which has its own programs on litigation, legislative lobbying, and public education.

Publications: The ACLU has an extensive publications program, including newsletters, handbooks, public policy reports, and books. In 1996 the ACLU started an annual report, *The Year in Civil Liberties,* that highlights the positive and negative events that have occurred during the year. Many of its reports are available online.

Website: http://www.aclu.org
From the home page, there are articles available about current ACLU activities and an index of rights topics. The entire website can be searched by keyword and there are many links to legal resources where decisions can be viewed and downloaded.

American Friends Service Committee (AFSC)
1501 Cherry Street
Philadelphia, PA 19102
(215) 241-7000
fax: (215) 241-7275
Director: Kara Newell

Founded in 1917 by American Quakers to provide conscientious objectors to war with a constructive alternative to military service, the American Friends Service Committee today carries on a program of service, development, justice, and peace under the direction of a Quaker Board and Corporation representing a wide spectrum of Quakers. Through its international headquarters in Philadelphia, its nine regional offices in the United States, and its program operations overseas, the organization works for the abolition of war and the fulfillment of human rights as essential twin goals to creating a nonviolent world in which all may live together. In the United States, the AFSC focuses on questions of exclusion and unequal opportunities in employment, education, administration of justice, land rights, welfare, and food programs. The organization also operates two lending libraries with videos and films (addresses in Chapter 7).

Publications: The AFSC has an extensive publications program, including leaflets, pamphlets, newsletters, and books. Many of the reports are available online. Publications include *Respectful Engagement: Cuban NGO Cooperation in Latin America, Europe, and Canada* ($7) and *Building Movements, Shattering Myths: Arab Women Confront Violence* ($5).

Website: http://www.afsc.org
On the website, in addition to background information about the AFSC, there is information about the archives located in Philadelphia, with some indexing, a book catalog, and links to other sites. Many of the publications are available online. Information is organized around topics and includes fact sheets, prayers, and policy statements from various religious groups.

Americans for Democratic Action
1625 K Street NW, Suite 1150
Washington, DC 20006
(202) 785-5980
fax: (202) 785-5969
Director: Amy Isaacs

Founded in 1947, Americans for Democratic Action monitors the human rights situation in different parts of the world and lobbies the U.S. government and multinational corporations to take action to support human rights. One of the strategies is to attempt to link U.S. foreign aid with human rights records of recipient governments.

Publications: ADA publishes *ADAction News and Notes,* a weekly legislative update; *ADA Today,* a quarterly newsletter; an *Annual Voting Record;* and special reports such as *Simple Human Justice: Increasing the Minimum Wage.*

Website: http://www/adaction.org
Organizational history, information about joining, contacts for regional offices, and information about current projects can be found on the website.

Amnesty International, USA (AIUSA)
322 8th Avenue
New York, NY 10001
(212) 807-8400; (800) AMNESTY
fax: (212) 627-1451
Director: William F. Schulz

Amnesty International is the largest human rights organization in the world. As with Amnesty International worldwide, AIUSA works impartially to (1) free prisoners of conscience (men, women, and children jailed solely for their beliefs, color, sex, ethnic origin, language, or religion, provided they have never used or advocated violence); (2) ensure fair trials for all political prisoners; and (3) abolish torture and executions. Amnesty International, USA, works toward these goals through nationwide "adoption groups" that work for the release of prisoners of conscience, through its Urgent Action Network (letter-writing campaigns on behalf of persons in immediate danger), and through other means designed to raise awareness of human rights violations. AIUSA is supported by research and program staff at the international headquarters in London.

Publications: Extensive publications include full-length books (see the monographs section in Chapter 6), an annual report on human rights in each country, many separate country reports, and special reports on such issues as female genital mutilation. Almost all of this information is available online at the website. Among its most recent reports are *Afghanistan: Reports of Mass Graves of Taleban Militia* ($10) and *Deaths in Custody: How Many More?* ($10).

Website: http://www.amnesty.org
This very extensive website that represents Amnesty International, not just Amnesty International, USA, contains extensive background information about the organization, including many documents outlining Amnesty's mandate. In the library link, there is a vast collection of Amnesty documents, including country reports and special issue reports.

Anti-Defamation League of B'nai B'rith (ADL)
823 United Nations Plaza
New York, NY 10017
(212) 490-2525
fax: (212) 885-5855
Director: Abraham H. Foxman

Dedicated to promoting understanding among peoples of different races, creeds, and ethnic backgrounds in order to further interreligious understanding, the Anti-Defamation League of B'nai B'rith has established relationships with Christian institutions in order to help create programs that reflect sensitivity and concern for the Jewish-Christian encounter. The ADL fights bigotry and discrimination in all its forms and attempts to protect the human rights of Jews throughout the world through its many programs.

Publications: A comprehensive publication program includes reports, books, periodicals, and monographs focusing on topics such as prejudice, discrimination, and intergroup relations, multicultural education, political and social issues, and the Holocaust. Periodicals include *Dimensions: A Journal of Holocaust Studies* ($15 semiannually). Monographs on human rights topics include the following: *High Tech Hate: Extremist's Use of the Internet* ($10) and *Hate Crimes: ADL's Blueprint for Action* ($4).

Website: http://www.adl.org
This site includes breaking news reports on defamation issues, information about publications and programs, and a form for reporting personal knowledge of anti-Semitic harassment or vandalism.

The Carter Center
One Copenhill
453 Freedom Parkway
Atlanta, GA 30307
(404) 420-5117
fax: (404) 420-5145
Director: John Hardman

Founded in 1982 as a nonprofit, nonpartisan, public policy institute by Jimmy and Rosalynn Carter, the Carter Center is dedicated to fighting disease, hunger, poverty, conflict, and oppression, often through partnerships with other organizations. The Carter Center has monitored multiparty elections, established the International Human Rights Council to help prevent human rights violations worldwide, and worked on health issues such as reduction of the Guinea worm, river blindness, and increased child immunizations.

Publications: The center publishes many reports, including *Democratic Challenge in Africa* ($15) and *From Civil War to Civil Society: The Transition to Peace in Guatemala and Liberia.*

Website: http://www.emory.edu/CARTER_CENTER
The website contains extensive program information, reports, publications, and information about the Carter Presidential Library.

Center for International Policy
1755 Massachusetts Avenue NW
Washington, DC 20036
(202) 232-3317
fax: (202) 232-3440
Director: William Goodfellow

Founded in 1975 as a project of the Fund for Peace, the Center for International Policy is a nonprofit education and research group concerned with U.S. policy toward the Third World and its impact on human rights and human needs. In the late 1970s, the center persuaded the executive branch and Congress to extend human rights guidelines to many important but overlooked channels of U.S. aid. The center carries out an extensive research and publication program on the implications of U.S. foreign aid, especially economic and military aid, to countries of Asia, Africa, and Latin America. It has worked for the demilitarization of Latin America and reform of the CIA.

Publications: The center's most important publication is the *International Policy Report* ($1.50 for single issues, $9 for a one-year subscription). These reports are also available online. Recent reports include *Wanted: A Logical Cuba Policy* (February 1998), *Haiti: Democracy Vs. Democracy* (November 1997), and *The Intelligence Community: Time for a Major Overhaul* (July 1997).

Website: http://www.ciponline.org
Many interesting documents are available in the center's current research areas. *International Policy Reports* are also available back to 1990.

Center for the Study of Human Rights
1108 International Affairs Building
Columbia University, Mail Code 3365
New York, NY 10027

(212) 854-2479
fax: (212) 316-4578
Director: J. Paul Martin

The Center for the Study of Human Rights was established at Columbia University in 1977 to promote teaching and research on human rights in national and international contexts. Activities involve all disciplines and address both theoretical and policy questions. An integral part of the university, the center benefits extensively from Columbia University faculty and resources. The center offers a four-month training program for human rights advocates that attracts participants from all over the world to learn advocacy, education, and training skills. Other programs include the religion, human rights, and religious training program; the Africa human rights education project; and internship programs and curriculum development at Columbia. A reading and resource room opened in 1993 that houses a collection of human rights case studies and educational materials.

Publications: The center publishes a series linking specific human rights issues to relevant documents. These titles include *Twenty-Five Human Rights Documents, Women and Human Rights: Basic Documents,* and *Religion and Rights: Basic Documents.* Publications also include *Elements of Constitutionalism* and *The Rights of Man Today.*

Website: http://www.columbia.edu/cu/humanrights
This website offers program and application information for the center's programs, contact information for center staff, information on publications, and a link to a human rights job page.

Center for Victims of Torture
717 East River Road
Minneapolis, MN 55455
(612) 626-1400
fax: (612) 626-2465
Director: Douglas A. Johnson

Founded in 1985, the Center for Victims of Torture provides direct care to torture victims, who come to the center from all over the world. The organization operates an out-patient facility in Minneapolis that offers medical, psychiatric, psychological, physical therapy, legal, and social services to more than 150 clients per year. A lobbying arm in Washington, D.C., works to increase help for victims of torture.

Publications: The Storycloth (quarterly newsletter)

Website: http://www.cvt.org
A valuable site about the problems torture victims face, the website also includes *The Storycloth* online and statistical information.

Center of Concern
3700 13th Street NE
Washington, DC 20017
(202) 635-2757
fax: (202) 832-9494
Director: James Hug

The Center of Concern works with international networks to promote social analysis, theological reflection, policy analysis, political advocacy, research, and public education on issues of global development, peace, and social justice.

Publications: Rethinking Bretton Woods, a five-volume series that includes material on development, the World Bank, the world's monetary system, and world trade, is published by the center ($15.95 per volume or $79.75 for the set). Publications also include *A Guide for Activists: Handbook on African Hunger* ($4.95) and *Center Focus* (bimonthly).

Website: http://www.coc.org/coc
Educational resources, including links to sources appropriate for children, links to lesson plans about human rights, background information, and information about publications, are available on the website.

Colombia Human Rights Information Committee
PO Box 40155
San Francisco, CA 94140
fax: (415) 206-1326

The Colombia Human Rights Information Committee is a volunteer organization composed of Colombians and North Americans concerned with the deterioration of human rights in Colombia that conducts human rights campaigns, development projects, and cultural events to reveal the causes of the human rights crises and to involve other people to work for justice in Colombia.

Publications: Colombia Update(quarterly/ $15 per year)

**Commission for the Defense of
Human Rights in Central America**
Apartado Postal 189-1002

Paseo de las Estudiantes
San José, Costa Rica
213462-33 3326
Contact Person: Mirna Perla de Anaya

The Commission for the Defense of Human Rights in Central America was founded in 1978 to promote and defend human rights in Central America. The commission coordinates and supports national nongovernmental human rights organizations within their respective countries. Activities include human rights education, follow-up on allegations of human rights violations, legal assistance, and coordination of a regional information network.

Publications: The commission's publications include a monthly bulletin on the human rights situation in Central America *(Documentación sobre Derechos Humanos)*, *Brecha* (bimonthly), an annual report, and occasional papers and reports.

Council on International and Public Affairs
777 United Nations Plaza, Suite 3C
New York, NY 10017
(212) 972-9877

The Council on International and Public Affairs conducts research, public education, and advocacy on human rights issues and is especially concerned with violations of economic and social rights in the United States and around the world. The council acts as U.S. secretariat for the Permanent People's Tribunal on Industrial Hazards and Human Rights Violations and focuses on corporate abuse of workers, communities, and the environment in the United States.

Publications: The council publishes books and videos on human rights issues and a quarterly newsletter, *Too Much* ($15), on the topic of income distribution.

Cultural Survival, Inc.
96 Mount Auburn Street
Cambridge, MA 02138
(617) 441-5400
fax: (617) 441-5417
Director: Maria Tocco

Founded in 1972 for the purpose of helping indigenous people survive and adapt to the world around them, Cultural Survival,

Inc., is made up of indigenous people, ethnic minorities, academics interested in the Third World, research institutes and museums, government agencies, and other interested individuals. Cultural Survival sponsors projects designed to promote human rights for indigenous people and to help them become successful ethnic minorities. The organization maintains a library and speakers' bureau and also conducts seminars and research on problems confronting indigenous peoples.

Publications: Publications include *Cultural Survival Quarterly* ($20 year); *World Report on Indigenous Peoples and Ethnic Minorities;* a monograph series that includes *Indigenous Peoples, Ethnic Groups, and the State* ($14); and *Defending the Land: Sovereignty and Forest Life in James Bay Cree Society* ($14); and videotapes.

Website: http://www.cs.org
The website contains *Active Voices: The Online Journal of Cultural Survival,* the table of contents of *Cultural Survival,* and articles, maps, and program information.

Global Exchange
2017 Mission Street, #303
San Francisco, CA 94110
(415) 255-7296
fax: (415) 255-7498
Codirectors: Kirsten Moller and Medea Benjamin

Global Exchange was founded in 1988 to promote people-to-people ties around the world. As part of concern for worker rights around the world, the organization operates a fair trade store where the worker gets a fair percentage of the sales price of merchandise sold. Global Exchange has particular campaigns, including one to further corporate responsibility, country watches, and, uniquely, reality tours—participants tour areas and explore issues related to human rights. A recent tour to Guatemala featured meetings with human rights activists, government officials, citizens, diplomats, and members of political parties from a wide political spectrum. U.S. tours have been conducted at prisons, in bilingual classrooms, at the U.S.-Mexico border, and in agricultural fields.

Publications: Global Exchange publishes a newsletter, *Global Exchanges* (quarterly), and books, including *Corporations Are Gonna Get Your Mama: Globalization and the Downsizing of the American Dream* ($15.95) and *50 Years Is Enough: The Case against the World Bank and the International Monetary Fund.*

Website: http://www.globalexchange.org
At the website are trip itineraries and contact information and information on fair trade merchandise, corporate accountability, and human rights campaigns.

Global Fund for Women
425 Sherman Avenue
Palo Alto, CA 94306
(650) 853-8305
fax: (650) 328-0384
Director: Kavita Ramdas

The Global Fund for Women was established in 1988 as an international grants-making organization that seeks to better conditions for women by making small grants to organizations all over the world. Projects have addressed improving the political situation of women, reducing poverty, increasing women's economic opportunities, enhancing reproductive health, securing lesbian rights, improving women's rights in the context of religious tradition, reducing violence against women, and helping organizations access the media. In the first ten years the fund made grants of over $9,000,000 to over 1,000 organizations in 125 countries. The organization also works to make women's experiences known at conferences and among donors.

Publications: Publications include the semiannual *Newsletter* and the *Annual Report.*

Website: http://www.globalfundforwomen.org
Program information is included at the website.

Guatemala Human Rights Commission/USA
3321 12th Street NE
Washington, DC 20017
(202) 529-6599
fax: (202) 526-4611
Director: Alice Zachmann

A private nonprofit organization that seeks to inform the public about human rights issues in Guatemala and advocate the end of repression and persecution of the Guatemalan people, the Guatemala Human Rights Commission/USA encourages members to become advocates who respond to Urgent Actions that document specific cases of human rights violations and who help to provide assistance to victims of these violations.

Publications: The commission publishes *Updates* ($35 annually), a biweekly news report on human rights and the political and socioeconomic situation in Guatemala; *Urgent Actions* ($5 each), brief reports on individual cases of human rights violations; and *Bulletins* ($10 each), twenty-page reports published twice yearly. All of these publications are available online at their website.

Website: http://www.members.aol.com/PeaceGuate
The website has information about current campaigns, contact information, related links, and publications described above.

Human Rights Center at the University of Minnesota
229 19th Avenue South
Minneapolis, MN 55455
(612) 625-5027
fax: (612) 625-2011
Codirectors: David Weissbrodt and Kristi Rudelius-Palmer

The focus of the Human Rights Center at the University of Minnesota is training effective human rights professionals and volunteers. The center teaches human rights at the university, secondary, and primary level; offers public education in the form of lectures seminars, symposia, and publications on human rights issues; maintains the largest collection in the United States of human rights books, monographs, periodicals, and other materials from around the world; researches topics pertaining to human rights—particularly to improve the effectiveness of human rights activists; runs exchanges with similar centers and human rights activist organizations around the world; provides human rights clinical opportunities to students; provides direct assistance to victims of human rights abuses; and provides internship opportunities.

Website: http://www.umn.edu/humanrts
This is an extremely valuable website with a tremendous number of documents available online and links to other human rights centers. This site has many U.N. documents available online, searchable by keyword. There are also links to other relevant sites, bibliographies, regional materials, and U.S. human rights documents.

Human Rights Internet (HRI)
8 York Street, Suite 302
Ottawa, Ontario
K1N 5S6 Canada
(613) 789-7407

fax: (613) 789-7414
Director: Laurie S. Wiseberg

The Human Rights Internet furthers the defense of human rights through the dissemination of information. It is an international communications network and clearinghouse on human rights with universal coverage. Over 5,000 organizations and individuals contribute to the network. The organization works to support the work of the global nongovernmental organizations community in promoting human rights. It also actively promotes teaching, information sharing, and research on human rights. Its publications and services are among the most useful of any available to those working for the promotion of human rights. It has an extensive publications program and maintains a documentation center rich in publications of other human rights organizations.

Publications: The Human Rights Internet publishes the single most important journal publication in the field—the *Human Rights Internet Reporter* (see the periodicals section in Chapter 6). It has also published *Master List: A Listing of Organizations Concerned with Human Rights and Social Justice Worldwide* (see reference materials section in Chapter 6), *Human Rights Thesaurus*, and *Teaching about Genocide.*

Website: http://www.hri.ca
The website contains information on HRI, fees for using the documentation center, access to *The Tribune,* HRI's quarterly magazine, information about publications, and a section advertising human rights publications by other organizations. A world calendar offers an international snapshot of human rights events occurring each month. The document center offers full text reports on issues such as psychiatric abuses, refugees, the International Criminal Court, housing, and homelessness. Access to HRI databases is available over the internet for a fee.

Human Rights Watch
350 Fifth Avenue, 34th Floor
New York, NY 10118
(212) 290-4700
fax: (212) 736-1300
Director: Kenneth Roth

Human Rights Watch was founded in 1978 as Helsinki Watch (now Human Rights Watch/Helsinki), in response to a call for support from embattled groups in Moscow, Warsaw, and Prague that had been set up to monitor compliance with the human rights provisions of the Helsinki Accords. Today Human Rights Watch monitors the human rights practices of governments all over the world. Through interviews with victims, witnesses, government officials, opposition leaders, local human rights groups, journalists, doctors, and others, Human Rights Watch produces well-documented reports of human rights abuses. The organization lobbies governments and international governmental organizations such as the United Nations and the World Bank to help end human rights abuses.

Publications: In addition to an extensive books publication program (see the monographs section in Chapter 6), Human Rights Watch produces numerous reports of its fact-finding missions, including *Silencing the Net: The Threat to Freedom of Expression On-Line* ($3) and *Building Laser Weapons: The Need to Ban a Cruel and Inhumane Weapon* ($5).

Website: http://www.hrw.org
The website has information about current campaigns, a list of publications and research, and a page of "what you can do" that includes places to write letters about current problems. Publications can be ordered online from the website.

Indian Law Resource Center
601 E Street SE
Washington, DC 20003
(202) 547-2800
fax: (202) 547-2803
Director: Steven Tullberg

The Indian Law Resource Center is a nonprofit law and advocacy organization established and directed by American Indians. The center is devoted to helping Indian nations, tribes, and other indigenous peoples prevent destruction of their cultures and homelands. It works to establish national and international legal standards that uphold the human rights and dignity of indigenous peoples, protect Indian land and resources, and secure their authority for self-government and sustainable futures.

Website: http://www.indianlaw.org
Information about human rights, land rights, law reform, native sovereignty and self-government as well as contact information is contained on the website.

Institute for Policy Studies
733 15th Street NW
Washington, DC 20005
(202) 234-9382
fax: (202) 387-7915
Director: John Cavanaugh

Founded in 1963 as a transnational center for research, education, and social invention, the Institute for Policy Studies critically examines the assumptions and policies that define the American posture on domestic and international issues and offers alternative strategies and visions. One of its areas of concern is human rights. In memory of Orlando Letelier and Ronni Karpen-Moffitt, both strong human rights advocates who were assassinated, the institute established the Letelier-Moffitt Fund for Human Rights, which is designed to explore human rights issues, especially those involving the relationship between economic policy and the denial of human rights.

Publications: The institute's extensive publications program includes monographs and reports. Examples include the following: *Beyond Bretton Woods: Alternatives to the Global Economic Order* ($13) and *Calling the Shots: How Washington Dominates Today's UN* ($18). Reports include *NAFTA's First Two Years: The Myths and the Realities* ($8) and *Consultative Group to Assist the Poorest: Opportunity or Liability for the World's Poorest Women?* ($3).

Institute for the Study of Genocide
John Jay College of Criminal Justice
899 10th Avenue, Room 325T
New York, NY 10019
(212) 582-2537
fax: (212) 491-8076
Director: Helen Fein

The Institute for the Study of Genocide, a nonprofit educational organization, was founded in 1982 to promote teaching and scholarship on the causes, consequences, and prevention of genocide. It supports scholars from various disciplines in the conduct of their research, in the publication of their findings, and in the application of these findings to classroom teaching, using the resources of the John Jay College of Criminal Justice, and also maintains its own library of resources pertaining to genocide.

Publications: The institute publishes the *ISG Newsletter* and occasional pamphlets on current issues relating to genocide.

Inter-American Commission on Human Rights (IACHR). *See* Organization of American States, Inter-American Commission on Human Rights

Intercommunity Center for Justice and Peace
20 Washington Square North
New York, NY 10011
(212) 475-6677
fax: (212) 475-6969
Director: Sister Marie Danaher

The Intercommunity Center for Justice and Peace is a coalition of 38 Catholic religious orders in the tri-state area of New York, New Jersey, and Connecticut that seeks to assist victims of injustice by trying to change the structures that cause violations of human rights. The focus of the center's human rights work is immigration, capital punishment, sweatshops, criminal justice, workfare, and welfare in the United States.

Publications: Universe Update (quarterly)

International Association of Official Human Rights Agencies (IAOHRA)
444 North Capitol Street, Suite 408
Washington, DC 20001
(202) 624-5410
fax: (202) 624-5410
Director: William Hale

Established for governmental human rights agencies in 1949 for the purpose of fostering better human relations and enhancing human rights under the law, the International Association of Official Human Rights Agencies offers extensive services and training for personnel of state and local human rights agencies throughout the United States. It conducts workshops and seminars for human rights administrators and promotes development of state legislation through its technical assistance workshops for state and regional planning agencies.

International Freedom of Expression eXchange
The IFEX Clearing House
489 College Street, Suite 403
Toronto, Ontario
Canada, M6G 1A5
(416) 515-9622

fax: (416) 515-7879
ifex@ifex.org
Director: Wayne Sharpe

The International Freedom of Expression eXchange was founded in 1992 when many of the world's leading freedom of expression organizations met to discuss how best to further their collective goals. The organization is composed of over 25 member organizations from all over the world that support freedom of expression. The main activity is operating an information clearinghouse to coordinate the work of members, thereby reducing overlap among activities to make them more effective in their shared objective. The clearinghouse runs the Action Alert Network where member organizations report free expression abuses in their geographic region or area of expertise to the clearinghouse. The clearinghouse circulates the information to other members and interested organizations all over the world. IFEX also runs an outreach program that provides information, financial and technical assistance, and international support and recognition to fledgling freedom of expression groups.

Publications: In addition to the Action Alert Network, IFEX publishes the *Communique,* a weekly publication about current free expression issues that is available by e-mail or surface mail in English, Spanish, and French. Back issues are available online at the website.

Website: http://www.ifex.org
IFEX uses its website to provide links to all its member organizations and to provide updates on current issues around the world. There is also an archive composed of past action alerts going back to 1995 that is searchable by date and keyword.

International Human Rights Law Group
1200 18th Street NW
Washington, DC 20036
(202) 822-4600
fax: (202) 822-4606
Director: Gay McDougall

The International Human Rights Law Group was established in 1978 as a nonprofit public interest law center concerned with the promotion and protection of international human rights. The organization provides information and legal assistance to organizations and individuals in cases of human rights violations. Funded by foundation grants and individual contributions and assisted in its work by attorneys in Washington, D.C., the Law Group offers its expertise pro bono.

International League for Human Rights
432 Park Avenue South, Room 1103
New York, NY 10016
fax: (212) 684-1696

Tracing its roots to a citizens' league in France in the early 1900s, the International League for Human Rights today provides advice, resources, and publicity to affiliated human rights groups throughout the world. Through its Defenders' Project, the league energetically seeks to protect courageous advocates of human rights in oppressive societies. Among its activities are assisting victims of discrimination, sending special investigative missions to regions where human rights violations occur, negotiating with repressive governments to obtain relief for human rights victims, and sending observers to political trials.

Publications: Human Rights Bulletin ($35 semiannually)

International Rescue Committee, Inc.
122 East 42nd Street
New York, NY 10165
(212) 551-3000
fax: (212) 551-3180
Director: Reynold Levy

Founded in 1933, the International Rescue Committee is a nonprofit, nonsectarian organization that offers relief, protection, and resettlement services for refugees and victims of oppression and violence. Services include resettlement assistance, global emergency relief, rehabilitation, advocacy, and health programs in Africa, Asia, Europe, the former Soviet Union, and the United States.

Publications: Annual Report

Website: http://www.intrescom.org
An abundance of information about refugees is available at this well-organized site.

Lawyers Committee for Human Rights
333 Seventh Avenue, 13th Floor
New York, NY 10165
(212) 551-3000

fax: (212) 551-3180
Director: Michael Posner

The Lawyers Committee for Human Rights was founded in 1978 to protect and promote the most basic and fundamental rights of the individual. In the best tradition of the law profession, the committee gathers facts and demands explanations on behalf of victims of human rights abuses abroad and of refugees seeking political asylum in the United States. Through its International Human Rights Program, the committee has investigated patterns of abuse in Asia, Africa, the Middle East, Eastern Europe, Latin America, and the Caribbean. Its detailed and carefully researched reports, occasionally published with Human Rights Watch, are often used by diplomats, policymakers, the media, and others in the United States and abroad.

Publications: The committee has published many reports of its fact-finding missions in addition to reports on U.S. human rights policy and asylum training materials. Some of its more recent reports are *Islam and Justice: Debating the Future of Human Rights in the Middle East and North Africa* ($15) and *At the Crossroads: Human Rights and the Northern Ireland Peace Process* ($12).

Website: http://www.lchr.org
The website includes information on enforcing the rule of law and protecting the rights of refugees and excellent sections on strengthening nongovernmental organizations through the lawyer-to-lawyer network and on helping nongovernmental organizations to get access to the United Nations and the World Bank.

Madre
121 West 27th Street, #301
New York, NY 10001
(212) 627-0444
fax: (212) 675-3704
Director: Vivian Stromberg

Founded in 1983, Madre supports women's community-based organizations in confronting the devastating effects of war and the harsh economic conditions of women and their families throughout the world. Some projects have included delivery of food and medicines to women in need, a counseling and economic development clinic for women survivors of rape in Rwanda, and Mother Courage Peace Tours, which bring women from affected areas to the United States to speak out for peace.

Publications: Madre Speaks newsletter (quarterly)

Website: http://www.madre.org
Information on programs and issues concerning women all over the world is available on the website.

Meiklejohn Civil Liberties Institute
PO Box 673
Berkeley, CA 94701
(510) 848-0599
fax: (510) 848-6008
Director: Ann Fagan Ginger

Sometimes described as "a grassroots legal think tank for peace and human rights," the Meiklejohn Civil Liberties Institute was founded in 1965 as an archives for attorney papers and court papers filed in civil rights cases, to assist lawyers and others working for civil and human rights causes. The institute is particularly concerned with peace law, including legislation passed by governmental bodies from local to global, believing that it grew out of the universal demand after World War II for the end to war as a method of settling international disputes and for the formulation of procedures to stop the use of force. The Human Rights Project collects data for submission to the U.N. Human Rights Committee to enforce the International Covenant on Civil and Political Rights.

Publications: Publications include *Human Rights and Peace Law Docket,* published occasionally with a digest of 700 cases from around the world; *Peace Law Packets,* an aid for activists and public-interest lawyers; and *Human Rights Organizations and Periodicals Directory* (see the reference materials section in Chapter 6).

Middle East Research and Information Project (MERIP)
1500 Massachusetts Avenue NW, Suite 119
Washington, DC 20005
(202) 223-3677
fax: (202) 223-3604
Director: Judy Barsalou

The Middle East Research and Information Project was established in 1971 to provide independent information and analysis on the Middle East. It has no links to any religious, educational, or political organizations in the United States or elsewhere. Although the main focus is producing the well-respected *Middle East Report,* the organization also has a speakers' bureau; does media work responding to calls for information from journalists; provides research assistance to church leaders, community leaders, and activists; sponsors public events about the Middle East; and does outreach to teachers to help them be better informed about the Middle East.

Publications: Middle East Report (quarterly, $32 individuals, $58 institutions)

Website: http://www.merip.org
In addition to information about the organization, there is a page of links to organizations that specialize in Middle East activism, links to sites about Jerusalem, and information about articles in *Middle East Report.*

National Center for Policy Alternatives
1875 Connecticut Avenue NW, Suite 710
Washington, DC 20009
(202) 387-6030
fax: (202) 986-2539
Director: Linda Tarr-Whelan

Founded in 1975 as a progressive, nonpartisan, nonprofit, public policy center focusing on innovation at the state and local levels, the National Center for Policy Alternatives provides policymakers with field-based services, national resources, and connections to advocates and experts and serves as a catalyst for innovative public policy. Although its focus is on state and local policy, some of its program areas are human rights issues: family and work, women's rights, housing, and environmental security.

Publications: Some examples of publications are *Model Environmental Justice Act* ($12) and *State Progress toward Sustainable Development* ($22).

Website: http://www.cfpa.org
The website includes information on programs and events.

Organization of American States (OAS)
Inter-American Commission on Human Rights (IACHR)
General Secretariat
1889 F Street NW, LL2, 8th Floor
Washington, DC 20006
(202) 458-6002
fax: (202) 458-3992
Director: Edith Marquez-Rodriguez

The Organization of American States is an international organization created by the North and South American states to achieve an order of peace and justice and to promote and defend solidarity, territorial integrity, and independence. The Inter-American Commission on Human Rights was created as part of a resolution adopted in Santiago, Chile, in 1959 and was more clearly defined at an OAS meeting in La Paz, Bolivia, in 1979 as "an organization of the OAS, created to promote the observance and defense of human rights and to serve as a consultative organ of the Organization in this matter." Human rights are understood to be those set forth in the American Convention, "Human Rights and the American Declaration of the Rights and Duties of Man."

Publications: Publications include the bimonthly magazine *Americas* ($18), as well as numerous reports, books, and videos. Most of the videotapes are in Spanish. Reports include *Legal Framework of Education in the Organization of Eastern Caribbean States* ($10) and *Theory, Practice, and the Education of the Person* ($16).

Website: http://www.oas.org
The website includes OAS treaties and conventions as well as contact information and the table of contents of *Americas* magazine.

Peace Brigades International (PBI)/United States
2642 College Avenue
Berkeley, CA 94704
(510) 540-0749
fax: (510) 849-1247
Codirectors: Rebecca Jaffe and Lizzie Brock

Peace Brigades International/United States is a grassroots organization dedicated to exploring and implementing nonviolent approaches to peacekeeping and support for basic human rights. By invitation, PBI sends teams of volunteers into areas of political repression and conflict and provides protective international accompaniment for individuals and organizations who have been threatened by political violence or who are otherwise at risk. In this way, the organization seeks to enlarge the space for local activists to work for social justice and human rights, while at the same time being nonpartisan. PBI has accompanied thousands of human rights workers, *campesinos,* students, union leaders, women's groups, indigenous organizations, and refugees. It trains volunteers from all over the world, operates a speakers' bureau, sends short-term delegations to all sides of conflicts, and has a public education campaign.

Publications: The Project Bulletin (monthly, $25 year) provides analysis of the conflicts in countries where PBI maintains projects.

Website: http://www.igc.apc.org/pbi/
Information about the organization, links to other websites, and country reports are available.

PEN American Center
568 Broadway, Suite 401
New York, NY 10012
(212) 334-1660
fax: (212) 334-2181

The American branch of International PEN (Poets, Playwrights, Editors, Essayists, and Novelists), which also includes historians, critics, journalists, and translators, the PEN American Center was founded in 1921 and has approximately 90 centers throughout the world. Its purpose is to protect the principles of unhampered transmission of free thought and to preserve the concept of a free press, within each nation and among all nations. Members pledge themselves to vigorously oppose any suppression of freedom of expression in the community to which they belong.

Publications: PEN has a substantial publications program, including *PEN Newsletter,* a bimonthly newsletter; *Inked Over, Ripped Out: Burmese Storytellers and the Censors* ($5); and *Liberty Denied: Current Rise of Censorship in America* ($13).

Website: http://www.pen.org
The website contains descriptions of the various PEN programs, including the readers and writers program, writing awards for prisoners, and literature awards. There is an interesting map of the world that is searchable to find out where PEN has campaigns going in its Freedom to Write program.

Physicians for Human Rights (PHR)
100 Boylston Street, Suite 702
Boston, MA 02116
(617) 695-0041
fax: (617) 695-0307
Director: Leonard Rubenstein

Physicians for Human Rights is a national organization of health professionals founded in 1986 to bring the skills and influence of the medical community to the support of international human rights. It works to prevent the participation of doctors in torture, to defend imprisoned health professionals, to stop physical and psychological abuse of citizens by their governments, and to provide medical and humanitarian aid to victims of repression.

Publications: PHR has an extensive publications program. Members receive the *Physicians for Human Rights Record* three times a year and *Medical Action Alerts,* which request that letters be sent on behalf of specific victims of abuse. The organization also publishes very thorough reports of fact-finding missions. These are often cowritten with Human Rights Watch. Three recent publications are *Landmines: A Deadly Legacy* ($25), *Breach of Trust: Physician Participation in Executions in the United States* ($10), and *Dead Silence: The Legacy of Abuses in Punjab* (see Chapter 6).

Website: http://www.phrusa.org
In addition to information about PHR's advocacy and campaigns, many reports are available online, including ones on prisons, torture, forensic science, and refugees. Also included is a complete list and description of publications.

Physicians for Social Responsibility (PSR)
1101 14th Street NW, Suite 700
Washington, DC 20005
(202) 898-0150
fax: (202) 898-0172
Director: Robert K. Musil

Physicians for Social Responsibility was founded in 1963 with the goal of ridding the world of nuclear weapons. The group has since expanded its charter to include ridding the world of global pollution and gun violence. PSR uses its members' expertise, professional leadership, influence within the medical community, and strong links to policymakers to work to find peaceful solutions to interpersonal and local disputes as well as international conflicts. The organization also seeks to promote health on a global level.

Publications: Many reports are available online in three main areas of research: the environment, security and nuclear weapons, and gun violence.

Website: http://www.psr.org
This is a well-researched site, with abundant information on nuclear security, environmental issues, and gun control. A news section provides links to news services with information on these topics.

Science and Human Rights Program
American Association for the Advancement of Science
1200 New York Avenue NW
Washington, DC 20005
(202) 326-6790
fax: (202) 289-4950
Director: Audrey Chapman

The Science and Human Rights Program works to protect the human rights of scientists, to advance scientific methods and skills for documenting and preventing human rights abuses, to develop scientific methodologies for monitoring the implementation of human rights, to foster greater understanding and support of human rights among scientists, and to conduct research on human rights issues. Some examples of current projects include letter-writing campaigns on behalf of scientists who have sustained human rights violations; fact-finding and advocacy missions, including a recent mission to Turkey to help victims of torture there; and the documention of human rights abuses that affect the scientific community. The Science and Human Rights Program is also helping the Truth and Reconciliation Commission of South Africa in the development of an information management system, and its forensic sciences project has worked to investigate suspicious deaths and extrajudicial killings in Guatemala.

Publications: The organization publishes many reports, including many that provide help to human rights organizations in solving technical issues. Some examples are *Preliminary Submission to the Truth and Reconciliation Commission Concerning the Role of Health Professionals in Gross Violations of Human Rights, Who Did What to Whom? Planning and Implementing a Large Scale Human Rights Data Project,* and *Information Technologies for the Human Rights Community: Get On-Line* ($5). The Science and Human Rights Programs also publishes the *Directory of Human Rights Resources on the Internet* (see Chapter 6).

Website: http://www.shr.aaas.org
One of the most useful aspects of this site is a comprehensive directory of human rights internet sites. It can be downloaded or viewed from the site.

Simon Wiesenthal Center
9760 West Pico Boulevard
Los Angeles, CA 90035

(310) 553-9036
fax: (310) 553-8007
Contact person: Rabbi Abraham Cooper

Founded in 1977 to fight anti-Semitism and the rise of neo-Nazi and neofascist groups engaged in racist and religious terrorism, the Simon Wiesenthal Center provides educational materials, including a multimedia program on the Nazi Holocaust, to schools and organizations; conducts public lectures and forums; collects information on the current activities of the Ku Klux Klan and American Nazi party; and participates in international efforts to prevent future occurrences of genocide. The center opened the Beit Hashoah Museum of Tolerance in Los Angeles in 1993. In 1994 Moriah Films was established to make films about Holocaust-related subjects.

Publications: The center produces a quarterly newsletter, *Response,* and has produced *Lexicon of Hate* ($10) and *Racism, Mayhem, and Terrorism: The Emergence of an Online Subculture of Hate* ($10).

Website: http://www.wiesenthal.com
The website includes background information and an online tour of the museum.

Southern Poverty Law Center
400 Washington Avenue
Montgomery, AL 36104
(334) 264-0286
fax: (334) 264-0629
Director: Joe Levin

The Southern Poverty Law Center seeks to protect and advance the legal rights of victims of injustice through civil litigation, educational programs, publications, films, and resource information. One of the major projects of the center is Teaching Tolerance, which is dedicated to helping teachers promote interracial and intercultural understanding in the classroom. Klanwatch works to combat Ku Klux Klan and skinhead activities and hate crimes.

Publications: Publications include *Teaching Tolerance Magazine* (free semiannually), *SPLC Report,* and *Quarterly Intelligence Report.* The center has also produced teaching materials as part of the Teaching Tolerance program.

Website: http://www.splcenter.org
In addition to program information, the center produces an annual list of hate and patriot groups that is accessible online.

20/20 Vision
1828 Jefferson Place NW
Washington, DC 20036
(202) 833-2020
fax: (202) 833-5307
Director: Robin Caiola

20/20 Vision works on peace, environment, and corporate accountability issues. A recent project supported the Campaign to Ban Land Mines. Each month members are sent a postcard asking them to write a public official about a particular issue. These can have a local, regional, or national focus.

Publications: Monthly postcards to members

Website: http://www.2020vision.org
Program information and links to government documents, an internet law library of legal sites, and voting records of U.S. officials are available at the website.

United Nations Centre for Human Rights
8-14 Avenue de la Paix
1211 Geneva 10
Switzerland

Although the U.N. General Assembly and several of its subsidiary bodies deal with human rights, since 1946 the Commission on Human Rights at the United Nations Centre for Human Rights has been the main body charged with the task of preserving and promoting human rights. The organization makes studies, prepares recommendations, and drafts international instruments relating to human rights. It has established a number of subsidiary bodies to assist in this work, for example, the Sub-Committee on the Prevention of Discrimination and Protection of Minorities and the Working Group on Enforced and Involuntary Disappearances. These various groups meet with governments to discuss alleged violations of human rights and, when the offense is sufficiently serious, may launch an investigation by experts in order to initiate a dialogue with the government to bring about change.

Publications: The United Nations has a very extensive publications program in many areas—human rights being one. Most of these are available in the United States from the New York office: Center for Human Rights, S-2914, United Nations, New York, NY 10017.

Website: http://www.un.org/rights/

The site contains updates on current U.N. issues and investigations, information on the High Commissioner of Human Rights, and a treaty database that contains over 1,450 volumes. The database is currently free but will be available by subscription only in the future.

United Nations Public Inquiries Unit
United Nations
Room GA-57
New York, NY 10017
(212) 963-4475

The United Nations Public Inquiries Unit is a resource center primarily serving the North American public that provides answers to questions by mail, telephone, and in person. The resource center also serves as a public relations office, distributing general and detailed information on the work of the United Nations and distributing press releases and all resolutions and documents of the United Nations.

Website: http://www.un.org/pubs/
This site has ordering information and pricing for U.N. publications.

U.S. Department of State, Office of Human Rights
Bureau of Democracy, Human Rights and Labor
201 C Street NW
Washington, DC 20520
(202) 647-2126
fax: (202) 647-5939
Assistant Secretary: John Shattuck

The bureau has the primary responsibility for the development and implementation of U.S. human rights policy. The criteria or broad standards used in assessing any country's human rights performance are integrity of the individual, civil rights, and political rights. The bureau draws upon the reports of the United Nations, human rights groups, information provided by human rights officers in U.S. embassies, and the Universal Declaration of Human Rights for standards, information, and analysis of a country's performance.

Publications: Each year the bureau compiles and presents to Congress *Country Reports on Human Rights Practices.* This report is also available online at the website.

Website: http: //www.state.gov/www/global/human_rights/
index.html
Human rights reports, speeches, and testimony to Congress as
well as statements made to the U.N. Human Rights Commission
are available at this website.

World Policy Institute
New School of Social Research
65 5th Avenue, Room 413
New York, NY 10003
(212) 229-5808
fax: (212) 229-5579
Director: Stephen Schlesinger

Founded in 1948, the World Policy Institute is a not-for-profit research and educational organization that works for the development of U.S. foreign policies that support peace, global security,
human development, and the rights of all peoples to self-determination. Currently the institute supports research fellows; operates the Arms Trade Resource Center, which offers research
and public education on preventative diplomacy and control of
international arms transfers; and is involved in the North American project, which explores democracy, human rights, and environmental quality in the context of North American economic
integration.

Publications: World Policy Journal (quarterly, $17.95) and various
reports

Website: http://www.worldpolicy.org
Table of contents information with some full text articles from
World Policy Journal, program information, and reprints of articles
from a variety of news sources from the North American project
can be found at the website.

World Views
1515 Webster
Oakland, CA 94612
(510) 451-1742
fax: (510) 835-9631
Codirectors: Tom Fenton and Mary Heffron

World Views succeeds Third World Resources, which was
founded in 1984 as a documentation clearinghouse and computer-accessible database on Third World–related organizations
and materials, most of which contain a great deal of human

rights information, with the goal of making these materials accessible through its many publications and with plans to make them available on its website. World Views currently also offers search and document delivery services.

Publications: World Views (quarterly, $25 individuals, $50 institutions) and bibliographical material such as *Africa: Africa World Press Guide to Educational Resources From and About Africa* ($21.95)

Website: http://www.igc.org/worldviews/
As of early 1998, the website had organizational information only; however, there are plans to put the resource database online.

Selected Print Resources

6

The following, except for the indexing and abstracting publications, are reference tools emphasizing human rights. The bibliographies are particularly helpful in locating earlier materials. Many general reference tools can also be helpful in locating useful material on the subject.

Bibliographies and Guides

Bennett, James. *Political Prisoners and Trials: A Worldwide Annotated Bibliography, 1900 through 1993.* Jefferson, NC: McFarland and Company, 1995. 363 pages. $79.50. ISBN 0-7864-0023-4.

Over 3,500 entries, including magazine articles, monographs, and reports arranged by country, and an extensive index.

Center for Human Rights, Geneva. *Human Rights Bibliography: United Nations Documents and Publications, 1980–1990.* New York: United Nations. $95.

This five-volume bibliography lists author, subject, title, and U.N. document numbers by category. It includes over 9,000 entries.

Stanek, Edward. *A Bibliography of Periodicals and Other Serials on Human Rights.* Monticello, IL: Vance Bibliographies, 1991. 9 pages. $3. ISBN 0-7920-0766-2.

A list of periodicals in the human rights fields. Not annotated.

United Nations Reference Guide in the Field of Human Rights. New York: United Nations, 1993. $25. ISBN 92-1-154097-6.

This useful guide provides sales numbers for purchasing materials published on human rights by the United Nations since 1948. Entries are arranged by categories of rights, and an index in the back gives country access.

Walters, Gregory. *Human Rights in Theory and Practice: A Selected and Annotated Bibliography.* Metuchen, NJ: Scarecrow Press, 1995. 459 pages. $55. ISBN 0-8108-3010-8.

Four separate indexes, a broad scope, and long annotations distinguish this work. Works are grouped by subject, including philosophical foundations of human rights, cultural relativism, cross-cultural perspectives, human rights and religious traditions, basic human needs, development and security, human rights and foreign policy, international law, organizations and human rights, group and individual rights, women and human rights, and emerging human rights issues.

Weinberg, Meyer. *World Racism and Related Inhumanities: A Country by Country Bibliography.* Westport, CT: Greenwood Press, 1992. 1048 pages. $125. ISBN 0-313-28109-2.

This bibliography includes racism, slavery, class domination, sexism, national oppression, imperialism, colonialism, and anti-Semitism. The over 12,000 entries span 135 countries and cover ancient history to the present. Bibliographic information only; no annotations are included.

Directories

AAAS Directory of Human Rights Resources on the Internet. New York: American Association for the Advancement of Science, 1998. $8.

Offers descriptions, contact information, and websites for hundreds of human rights organizations worldwide. Entries are organized by site name (other indexes are organized by topic and geographic focus). Also includes articles about using the internet for human rights work. This work is updated regularly.

Ginger, Ann Fagan, et al., eds. *Human Rights Organizations and Periodicals Directory, 1998,* 9th ed. Berkeley: Meiklejohn Civil Liberties Institute, 1998. $60 individuals, $65 institutions. ISSN 0098-0579.

This guide includes over 800 groups, periodicals, and other sources for teachers, students, and researchers seeking information on improving human rights in the United States. This work is updated biennially, making it an excellent referral source for activists and others needing information or assistance on issues and problems affecting public welfare. In addition to the main alphabetic list, there are a federal agencies guide, a list of internships, and periodicals, subject, and geographic indices.

Wiseberg, Laurie, et al., eds. *Master List: A Listing of Organizations Concerned with Human Rights and Social Justice Worldwide.* Ottawa, Ontario: Human Rights Internet, 1994. $35.

This work replaces four regional directories and provides access by country, issue, and region. This work is updated regularly.

World Directory of Human Rights Research and Training Institutions: World Social Science Information Directories. Prepared at UNESCO by the Social and Human Science Documentation Centre and the Division of Human Rights and Peace. Paris: UNESCO, 1992. Distributed by Bernan Associates, Lanham, MD. 306 pages. $30. ISBN 92-3-0027944-4.

Presents basic information on institutions around the world, governmental and nongovernmental, that promote human rights research and training. Programs are identified as to their nature, admission requirements, and scholarships offered. Arranged by geographic region and then by country, subject of research or training, and scholarship aid.

Sources of Human Rights Documents

Brownlie, Ian, ed. *Basic Documents on Human Rights,* 3d ed. New York: Oxford University Press, 1993. $39.95 (pbk.). ISBN 0-19-825712.

This is one of the most useful volumes for basic documents, including those of the United Nations, the European Convention on Human Rights, and other regional documents. Includes introductory notes and biographical references. Index is valuable for tracing specific rights in many documents.

Human Rights in International Law: Basic Texts. Strasbourg, France: Council of Europe, 1995. 464 pages. Distributed by Manhattan Publishing Company, Croton, NY. $18 (pbk.). ISBN 92-871-2039-0.

Contains documents from the United Nations, Council of Europe, Organization of American States, Organization of African Unity, and the Conference on Security and Cooperation in Europe.

United Nations. *Human Rights: A Compilation of International Instruments.* New York: United Nations, Department of Public Information, 1996. $50. ISBN 92-1-154099-2.

This two-volume set is a comprehensive catalog of existing instruments adopted at both universal and regional levels.

United Nations. *The United Nations and Human Rights, 1945–1995.* New York: United Nations, Department of Public Information, 1995. $29.95. ISBN 92-1-100560-4.

The first section of the book is an introduction by Boutros Boutros-Ghali that offers in narrative form a history of human rights with respect to the United Nations. The bulk of the book is U.N. human rights instruments, but the book also contains helpful chronology, indexes, and table showing the ratification status of major human rights declarations.

Indexes and Abstracts

Alternative Press Index. Baltimore, MD: Alternative Press Center, 1969.

Indexes over 200 alternative and radical publications, most not indexed elsewhere. Arranged by subject and then alphabetically by title. Uses the term *human rights,* which makes it easier to search than indexes that use only the term *civil rights.*

Historical Abstracts. Santa Barbara, CA: ABC-CLIO, 1955– .

————. *Part B: Twentieth Century Abstracts 1914 to the Present.* Santa Barbara, CA: ABC-CLIO, 1980– .

Part B is especially useful for human rights issues from a worldwide perspective. Approximately 20,000 articles are indexed in each volume, and beginning in 1980, selected new books and dissertations were added. Arranged by general topic, by more specific topics, and by area or country with a special subject profile indexing system. Also available online.

Index to Legal Periodicals. Bronx, NY: H. W. Wilson, 1908– .

Published for the American Association of Law Librarians, this index covers most English language law publications, many of which have material on human rights. Cumulated volumes contain subject and author indexes. Also available online.

Legal Resource Index (LRI). Foster City, CA: Information Access Company, 1980– .

Sponsored by the American Association of Law Libraries, the LRI provides subject, author, case name, and statute name access to over 875 major law journals in addition to 71 legal newspapers and 1,000 additional business and general interest periodicals. Helpful for many human rights issues. Also available online.

PAIS International in Print. New York: PAIS, 1915– .

One of the best general indexes, the PAIS bulletin is worldwide in scope and surveys approximately 1,400 journals and many other types of publications. It uses the term *human rights*, making searching considerably faster than when the material is grouped with that on civil rights. Also available online.

Religion Index One: Periodicals (RIO). Chicago: ATLA Religion Indexes, 1949– .

Sponsored by the American Theological Library Association (ATLA), this index covers many human rights–related subjects. Over 550 journals are indexed, though a fair percentage are not in English. Its human rights topics are subdivided by country, which is often helpful for gaining a different perspective on human rights abuses in a specific country. Also available on cd-rom.

Social Science Index. Bronx, NY: H. W. Wilson, 1974– .

Similar to the other Wilson indexes, this one covers the more traditional journals in the social sciences. There are author and subject entries and a separate section for book reviews. Also available online.

Dictionaries

Gibson, John. *Dictionary of International Human Rights Law.* Lanham, MD: Scarecrow Press, 1996. 225 pages. $44. ISBN 0-8108-3118-X.

This dictionary covers sixty-four rights in international treaties and four declared rights. Each entry includes the definition of the right, other sources of the right, an expanded definition of the right, landmarks in the evolution of the right, and cross-references to similar rights. This is a great source for getting historical background information on particular rights.

Gorman, Robert, and Edward Mihalkanin. *Historical Dictionary of Human Rights and Humanitarian Organizations.* Lanham, MD: Scarecrow Press, 1997. 296 pages. $44. ISBN 0-8108-3263-1.

This book includes a timeline of human rights events and entries for conventions, concepts, and organizations. Organization entries include contact information. Cross-references, an extensive bibliography, and selected human rights documents make this a valuable work.

Yearbooks and Encyclopedias

Freedom House. *Freedom in the World: The Annual Survey of Political Rights and Civil Liberties.* New Brunswick, NJ: Transaction Publishers, annually. $24.95. ISSN 0732-6610.

At the top of each country entry is a map that shows the location of the country and basic statistics such as income levels, population, polity, and life expectancy. An interesting feature is the ratings that show, on a scale of one to seven, where the country stands with regard to overall political rights and civil liberties. This is followed by a narrative section that gives an overview of the rights situation in the country.

Human Rights in Developing Countries Yearbook. Boston: Kluwer Law International, annually.

Includes thematic studies on human rights and development, country reports on seven countries, and ratification of major human rights documents. Each country report includes a fact sheet, a well-categorized summary of human rights issues, and an extensive bibliography. A table indicates what countries are covered in each yearbook.

Israel Yearbook on Human Rights. Boston: Kluwer Law International, annually. $170. ISSN 0333-5925.

This yearbook is produced under the auspices of the Faculty of Law at Tel Aviv University. It contains articles by different scholars describing aspects of human rights, with particular emphasis on problems relevant to the state of Israel and the Jewish people. It also includes documentary material relating to Israel and the Administered Areas.

Lawson, Edward. *Encyclopedia of Human Rights,* 2d ed. Washington, DC: Taylor and Francis, 1996. 1715 pages. $325. ISBN 1-56032-362-0.

Entries span individuals, organizations, nations, and concepts related to rights and freedoms. This work also includes over 200 international standard-setting instruments dealing with various aspects of human rights.

Osmanczyk, Edmund. *Encyclopedia of the United Nations and International Agreements.* Washington, DC: Taylor and Francis, 1990. 1059 pages. $310. ISBN 0-850666-833-6.

This work brings together in encyclopedic arrangement a compendium of political, economic, and social information related to the United Nations. It contains many references to and some texts of human rights documents and covenants. Useful for identifying various instruments and commissions related to them.

Monographs

The following is a selected list of monographs published since 1990 by governmental and nongovernmental agencies and by research scholars, academicians, and activists.

Amnesty International. *Getting Away with Murder: Political Killings and Disappearances in the 1990s.* New York: Amnesty International, 1993. 126 pages. $8. ISBN 0-939994-82-8.

Documents political killings worldwide with suggested strategies for action. Examines who the victims are and why government forces and armed political groups carry out this terror.

Amnesty International. *India: Torture, Rape, and Deaths in Custody.* New York: Amnesty International, 1992. 195 pages. ISBN 0-939994-73-9.

Documents torture occurring in all 25 states in India. Amnesty International recorded 415 deaths in custody in the period 1985 to 1992. In all 415 cases there is evidence that the victims, who were often innocents or petty offenders and included women and children, were brutally beaten or otherwise tortured to death. This report also examines some of the situations that lead to torture, such as poorly trained police officers with pressure to produce high conviction rates and patterns of abuse in Assam, Jammu, Kashmir, and Punjab, where security forces have immunity from prosecution.

Anaya, S. James. *Indigenous Peoples in International Law.* New York: Oxford University Press, 1996. 267 pages. $49.95. ISBN 0-19-508620-1.

Describes the development of international law and its treatment of indigenous peoples over time. Identifies and evaluates existing mechanisms that could be used to ensure the self-determination of indigenous peoples.

Andreopoulos, George, and Richard Claude. *Human Rights Education for the Twenty-First Century.* Philadelphia: University of Pennsylvania Press, 1997. 636 pages. $26.95 (pbk.). ISBN 0-8122-3388-3.

Addresses training for human rights in many contexts from teacher training, college and adult education to specialized human rights training for professionals, including law enforcement, health professionals, human rights advocates, scientists, and journalists. Also covers fundraising, telecommunications, and the setting up of human rights education resource centers.

An-Na'im, Ahmed, ed. *Human Rights in Cross-Cultural Perspectives: A Quest for Consensus.* Philadelphia: University of Pennsylvania Press, 1992. 479 pages. $17.95. ISBN 0-8122-1568-0.

Reaching consensus about universal standards of human rights is difficult when different cultures value the rights of individuals in different ways. This work explores various approaches to this problem through theoretical consideration and case studies.

Arat, Zehra. *Democracy and Human Rights in Developing Countries.* Boulder, CO: Lynne Rienner Publishers, 1991. 219 pages. ISBN 1-55587-500-9.

Arat argues that the stability of democracy requires a balance between civil-political rights and socioeconomic rights. Uses case studies of Costa Rica, India, and Turkey to examine this interrelationship.

Bailey, Sydney D. *The U.N. Security Council and Human Rights.* New York: St. Martin's Press, 1994. 181 pages. $69.95. ISBN 0-312-12324-8.

Using U.N. documents, the author examines the Security Council's handling of human rights issues. Covers self-determination in Africa, U.N. involvement in elections, international humanitarian law, terrorism, and the connection between human rights and peace.

Battistella, Graziano, ed. *Human Rights of Migrant Workers: Agenda for NGOs.* Quezon City, Philippines: Scalabrini Migration Center, 1993. 282 pages. ISBN 971-8789-03-0.

Nongovernmental organizations have become very active in countries of origin of migration and also receiving countries like the United States and Japan. NGOs combat illegal recruiting, shelter abused women, and offer legal counseling and livelihood programs. This work discusses the role of nongovernmental organizations in general and has case study material about Asia, Australia, the United States, and the new Europe.

Beatty, David, ed. *Human Rights and Judicial Review: A Comparative Perspective.* Boston: Kluwer Academic Publishers, 1994. 361 pages. ISBN 0-7923-2968-6.

This collection features articles written by Supreme Court justices and judges from India, Japan, Canada, the United States, Germany, and Italy that explain the way their courts determine whether a law or activity by an official of the state violates someone's constitutional rights.

Blackburn, Robert, and James Busuttil. *Human Rights for the 21st Century.* London: Pinter, 1997. 168 pages. $79.50. ISBN 1-85567-440-8.

Essays and lectures written for the British Institute of Human Rights. Discusses ways of changing the British system to include a bill of rights, economic aspects of equal opportunity, the European Court of Human Rights, slavery and child labor, naval mines, and international responsibility in the case of human rights abuses worldwide.

Bloom, Irene, J. Paul Martin, and Wayne Proudfoot, eds. *Religious Diversity and Human Rights.* New York: Columbia University Press, 1996. 355 pages. $49.50. ISBN 0-231-10416-2. $18.50 (pbk.). ISBN 0-231-10417-0.

The essays in this work explore a variety of issues, including the applicability and pertinence of the language of human rights in nonwestern contexts; the ways in which relations between individuals and society have been understood over time in the context of several major religions; the relationship among religion, secularism, and religious tolerance; and religion and rights in the contemporary world.

Bobbio, Norberto. *The Age of Rights.* Cambridge, MA: Blackwell Publishers, 1996. 200 pages. $25.95. ISBN 0-7456-15953.

Contains historical and current issue essays discussing the philosophical basis for rights in the works of Kant and Locke. Includes discussion of the death penalty.

Bouvard, Marguerite Guzman. *Revolutionizing Motherhood: The Mothers of the Plaza de Mayo.* Wilmington, DE: Scholarly Resources, 1994. 278 pages. $45. ISBN 0-8420-2486-7. $17.95 (pbk.). ISBN 0-8420-2487-5.

Documents the work and stories of the Argentine Mothers of the Plaza de Mayo who protested the loss of their disappeared children during the military coup from 1976 to 1983. These women have created a model grassroots organization using pacifist means for political change.

———. *Women Reshaping Human Rights: How Extraordinary Activists Are Changing the World.* Wilmington, DE: Scholarly Resources, 1996. 319 pages. $50. ISBN 0-8420-2562-6. $18.95 (pbk.). ISBN 0-8420-2563-4.

Biographical sketches of women human rights activists from all over the world. Sixteen women are featured addressing authoritarian governments, struggling with race and ethnicity, seeking environmental justice, upholding women's rights, and making the world safe for children.

Boyle, Kevin, and Juliet Sheen, eds. *Freedom of Religion and Belief: A World Report.* New York: Routledge, 1997. 475 pages. $74.95. ISBN 0-415-15977-6. $18.95 (pbk.). ISBN 0-415-15978-4.

Arranged in encyclopedic fashion, this volume examines the state of freedom of conscience, religion, and belief in nearly 60 countries. Experts from all over the world contributed the entries, which detail the status of religion and belief, political and legal contexts, relationship between church and state, discrimination against minority groups and women, tolerance of diversity, proselytizing, pressure groups, the media, background statistics, and interreligious relations.

Bronson, Marsha. *Amnesty International.* New York: Silver Burdett, 1993. 64 pages. $13.95. ISBN 0-02-714550-6.

Part of the series Organizations That Help the World, this work chronicles Amnesty International from a one-year project in 1961 to its current status as the largest human rights organization in the world. Plenty of examples and an accessible writing style help high school level readers get a feel for the way the organization works.

Buergenthal, Thomas. *International Human Rights in a Nutshell.* St. Paul, MN: West Publishing, 1995. $17. ISBN 0-314-06532-6.

This is a very readable summary of the legal aspects of international human rights. The work offers historical background, including early human rights treaties and the role of the League of Nations. The United Nations, European System, Inter-American System, African System, and Geneva Convention are discussed.

Bushnell, P. Timothy, et al., eds. *State Organized Terror: The Case of Violent Internal Repression.* Boulder, CO: Westview Press, 1991. 312 pages. $34.95. ISBN 0-8133-8307-2.

This work presents a theoretical template for the phenomenon of state-organized terror. The authors argue that there are four conditions that lead to terror: (1) a distorted concept of the state and society and their interrelationships; (2) disarray of state institutions; (3) presence of deep economic and/or ethnic conflicts in society or between society and state; and (4) state dependence on a foreign power.

Carey-Webb, Allen, and Stephen Benz, eds. *Teaching and Testimony: Rigoberta Menchu and the North American Classroom.* Albany: State University of New York Press, 1996. 391 pages. $71.50. ISBN 0-7914-3013-8.

Various level teachers from high school to graduate school have contributed to this volume about teaching Rigoberta Menchu's autobiography, *I, Rigoberta Menchú.* Articles address teaching about Menchu to white students, middle-class students, and minority students; teaching the Latin American context; and comparative teaching. Includes an extensive resource section.

Cassese, Antonio. *Inhuman States: Imprisonment, Detention, and Torture in Europe Today.* Cambridge, MA: Blackwell Press, 1996. 141 pages. $54.95. ISBN 0-7456-1721-2. $19.95 (pbk.). ISBN 0-74561-722-0.

Well-written account by an inspector for the Council of Europe. Describes visits to police stations, prisons, and psychiatric hospitals, the types of torture used, and inhumane conditions found. A distinguishing feature of this work is the descriptions of the inspection process itself.

Caufield, Catherine. *Masters of Illusion: The World Bank and the Poverty of Nations.* New York: Henry Holt, 1996. 432 pages. $27.50. ISBN 0-8050-2875-7.

Describes how, despite good intentions to improve conditions in the Third World, the World Bank has left a legacy of destruction to indigenous economies, environmental destruction, and resource depletion and has pauperized the Third World while propping up corrupt regimes.

Center for Justice and International Law and Human Rights Watch/Americas. *Honduras—The Facts Speak for Themselves: The Preliminary Report of the National Commissioner for the Protection of Human Rights in Honduras.* New York: Human Rights Watch, 1994. 271 pages. $15. ISBN 1-56432-134-7.

In the early 1980s a Honduran military unit was trained by the CIA. This unit carried out disappearances, interrogations, torture in hidden jails, summary executions, and dumped bodies in unmarked graves. The Honduran government accepted responsibility for the first time in the early 1990s. This is the translated report of findings.

Coliver, Sandra, ed. *The Right to Know: Human Rights and Access to Reproductive Health Information.* Philadelphia: University of Pennsylvania Press, 1995. 391 pages. $26.95 (pbk.). ISBN 0-8122-1588-5.

This work explores governmental interference and failure to provide reproductive health information and the effect of this on the health of women and their families and on the rights of women to liberty, equality, and life itself. International law is presented, along with case studies of several countries from Algeria and Brazil to the United States.

Compa, Lance, and Stephen Diamond, eds. *Human Rights, Labor Rights, and International Trade.* Philadelphia: University of Pennsylvania Press, 1996. 311 pages. $39.95. ISBN 0-8122-3340-9.

Discusses whether worker and trade union rights should be treated as human rights or subordinated to national economics; strategies for improving labor rights; labor rights and trade; worker rights litigation in U.S. courts; and the failure of human rights organizations and trade union groups to forge an effective alliance.

Crelinsten, Ronald, and Alex Schmid, eds. *Politics of Pain: Torturers and Their Masters.* Boulder, CO: Westview Press, 1995. ISBN 0-8133-2527-7.

This book examines the conditions that lead some people to become torturers, the psychological and cultural origins of torture, the use of torture by militaries, new approaches to combating torture, ideas for strengthening human rights to safeguard people from torture, and ways of helping victims of torture. Includes some case study material, including interviews with torturers.

Davidson, Scott. *Human Rights.* Philadelphia: Open University Press, 1993. 212 pages. $99. ISBN 0-335-15769-6. $39 (pbk.). ISBN 0-335-15768-8.

This introductory text on human rights covers historical development, human rights theories, international law and human rights, and the major institutions and systems for the protection of human rights: United Nations, Council of Europe, the Inter-American system, and the African system.

————. *The Inter-American Human Rights System.* Brookfield, VT: Dartmouth Publishing, 1997. 385 pages. ISBN 1-85521-776-7.

Narrative account of the Inter-American Human Rights System, which is part of the Organization of American States. Detailed history and explanation of rights protected by the Inter-American Commission on Human Rights and the Inter-American Court of Human Rights. Includes case citations.

De Brito, Alexandra. *Human Rights and Democratization in Latin America: Uruguay and Chile.* New York: Oxford University Press, 1997. 333 pages. $65. ISBN 0-19-828038-6.

Analysis of how the posttransitional democratic governments of Uruguay and Chile handled the social demands for an official recognition of the truth about human rights violations committed by the outgoing regimes. Authors examine the political conditions that permitted or inhibited the realization of policies of truth telling.

De Varennes, Fernand. *Language, Minorities, and Human Rights.* Boston: Martinus Nijhoff Publishers, 1996. 532 pages. $192.50. ISBN 90-411-0206-X.

Because language is usually difficult for individuals to change and it usually marks the community to which an individual belongs, language becomes a signaling point like race or religion, identifying those who are different and therefore potential targets for discrimination. The author explores language and human rights issues, including language discrimination in international law, ethnicity and race as proxies for language discrimination, the nature of language issues and their importance in human rights, and indigenous peoples and language.

Donnelly, Jack. *International Human Rights.* Boulder, CO: Westview Press, 1998. 216 pages. ISBN 0-8133-99169-6.

This introductory work covers human rights as an issue in world politics, human rights realism versus cultural relativism, multilateral politics of human rights, domestic politics of human rights, human rights and foreign policy, and some case studies of China and the former Yugoslavia.

Ekema, Robbie. *The Right to Development.* Limbe, Cameroon: Presbook Press, 1993. 136 pages.

This interesting work is told from the perspective of someone who has seen development projects up close. In an effort to clarify the right to development, the author outlines key elements of the development process and problems to be avoided. He relates examples from the Yaounde-Nsimalen International Airport and the Mundemba Korup National Park projects.

Feitlowitz, Marguerite. *A Lexicon of Terror: Argentina and the Legacies of Torture.* New York: Oxford University Press, 1998. 302 pages. $30. ISBN 0-19-510635-0.

Author examines the language used during the "Dirty War" of 1976 to 1983 when the Argentinean government embarked on a campaign of kidnapping and torture against citizen "subversives," concluding that the junta's rhetoric deftly reversed all notions of public guilt, making it appear that the victims were the real agents of terror. Interestingly, she compares the rhetoric of that time to the rhetoric of the amnesiac-like response of the succeeding regimes, in which everyone was pardoned or excused for following orders.

Felice, William F. *Taking Suffering Seriously: The Importance of Collective Human Rights.* Albany: State University of New York Press, 1996. 253 pages. $19.95 (pbk.). ISBN 0-7914-3062-6.

Author argues that the most acute and pervasive forms of distress are a consequence of economic, social, and political circumstances that are structural in nature. These structural circumstances impact groups as well as individuals. Therefore a collective ethos is essential for the alleviation of suffering.

Fitzpatrick, Joan. *Human Rights in Crisis: The International System for Protecting Rights during States of Emergency.* Philadelphia: University of Pennsylvania Press, 1994. 352 pages. $42.50. ISBN 0-8122-3238.

Global in scope, this work defines and categorizes various kinds of emergency situations, examining the adverse effects that these situations have on the protection of human rights and the rule of law in a particular society. A standards-setting section compares treaty-based standards with efforts by official and private groups to expand these standards with nontreaty-based guidelines.

Forrest, Duncan, ed. *A Glimpse of Hell: Reports of Torture Worldwide.* New York: New York University Press, 1996. 214 pages. $45. ISBN 0-8174-2665-8. $18.50 (pbk.). ISBN 0-8174-2666-6.

Sponsored by Amnesty International, this volume collects a wide variety of information on torture including the history of torture, methods used, research on what makes individuals become torturers, new trade in technologies of torture and restraint, documentation of torture, and treatment of survivors.

Forsythe, David. *Human Rights and Peace: International and National Dimensions.* Lincoln: University of Nebraska Press, 1993. 206 pages. $40. ISBN 0-8032-1989-X.

Author argues that there are three factors that reduce the probability of international war: (1) attention to civil and political rights; (2) attention to economic and social rights; and (3) modern (post-1945) development. He notes that the U.S. government has generally been opposed to nonwhite and revolutionary regimes and examines Sri Lanka, Liberia, and Romania to determine whether human rights violations contributed to national unrest.

Garfinkle, Adam, et al. *The Devil and Uncle Sam.* New Brunswick, NJ: Transaction Publishers, 1992. 135 pages. $34.95. ISBN 1-56000-012-0.

Authors note that the United States has many dealings with "friendly tyrants." This work offers ideas for balancing U.S. strategic interests with the promotion of human rights. These are presented in the form of 10 maxims for dealing with tyrants: beware dependence, be nimble, promote democracy, chastise with care, define goals, know the country, think it through, coordinate policy, hedge bets, and plan for crisis. Includes examples and a chronology.

Gewith, Alan. *The Community of Rights.* Chicago: University of Chicago Press, 1996. 380 pages. $39.95. ISBN 0-226-28880-3. $19.95 (pbk.). ISBN 0-226-28881-1.

Examines the rights to private property, employment, economic democracy, and political democracy. Author argues that rights and community are mutually supportive and that this relationship can serve to fulfill the economic and other rights of the most deprived members of society and thereby lead to greater economic and political equality.

Gillies, David. *Between Principle and Practice: Human Rights in North-South Relations.* Montreal: McGill-Queen's University Press, 1996. 339 pages. $55. ISBN 0-7735-1413-9. $22.95 (pbk.). ISBN 0-7735-1414-7.

Based on historical case studies of five countries during the late 1980s, Gillies argues that consistent, coordinated, and principled action to defend human rights remains elusive even for nations such as Canada, the Netherlands, and Norway, which have a reputation for humane internationalism. The author finds that states are rarely willing to sacrifice immediate commercial or security interests to protest gross and systematic human rights violations.

Giraldo, Javier. *Colombia: The Genocidal Democracy.* Monroe, ME: Common Courage Press, 1996. 100 pages. $29.95. ISBN 1-56751-087-6. $12.95 (pbk.). ISBN 1-65751-086-8.

Describes the dirty war in Colombia in which the Colombian government perpetuates gross human rights violations under the cover of drug enforcement. Documents how the paramilitary system functions to shield the military from being connected to death squad activity and how the United States is involved.

Goodman, Roger, and Ian Neary, eds. *Case Studies on Human Rights in Japan.* Surrey, UK: Japan Library, 1996. 309 pages. $45. ISBN 1-873410-35-2.

A variety of topics is covered in this volume, including the role of bureaucracy in the enforcement of human rights, Japanese identity and migrant labor, children's rights, the Japanese mental health system, organ transplantation, and exporting of hazardous industries.

Gordon, Neve, and Ruchama Marton, in association with the Association of Israeli-Palestinian Physicians for Human Rights, eds. *Torture: Human Rights, Medical Ethics, and the Case of Israel.* Atlantic Highlands, NJ: Zed Books, 1995. 206 pages. $29.95. ISBN 1-85649-313-X.

This volume is a result of a public conference held in Israel. It addresses the nature of torture, the social response to torture in Israel, participation of health professionals in the practice of torture, the role of codes of medical ethics, and the legal struggle against torture. A large appendix of relevant documents and affidavits by prisoners is included.

Gostin, Lawrence O., and Zita Lazzarini. *Human Rights and Public Health in the AIDS Pandemic.* New York: Oxford University Press, 1997. 212 pages. $29.95. ISBN 0-19-511442-6.

Because human rights policies protect the rights of individuals and public health policies seek to protect the public good, the two are often at odds. Although arguing that honoring human rights will ultimately enhance public health outcomes, the authors examine public health policies and present case studies suggesting ways to improve both human rights and public health.

Griffith, Ivelaw, and Betty Sedoc-Dahlberg, eds. *Democracy and Human Rights in the Caribbean.* Boulder, CO: Westview Press, 1997. 278 pages. $69. ISBN 0-8133-2135-2.

Analyzes the impact of state and nonstate regional and international actors in democracy and human rights. Includes the roles of international law, the Organization of American States, nongovernmental organizations, international government organizations, and illegal drug trafficking.

Haas, Michael. *Improving Human Rights.* Westport, CT: Greenwood Press, 1994. 254 pages. $55. ISBN 0-275-94352-6.

Author studied a comparative body of data on human rights performance from a large group of countries to determine why some countries observe human rights better than others. Using multivariate analysis, the author concludes that poor, undemocratic countries are most likely to violate human rights. Improvements occur when countries achieve solid economic progress, have an informed citizenry, end military rule, and become liberal and later social democracies.

Hey, Hilde. *Gross Human Rights Violations—A Search for Causes: A Study of Guatemala and Costa Rica.* Boston: Martinus Nijhoff Publishers, 1995. 240 pages. $117. ISBN 90-411-0146-2.

Compares the status of human rights in the two countries in an attempt to understand why gross human rights violations occur in some countries and not in others. The author finds that gross human rights violations are rationally planned and occur when state policy requires an enemy-friend dichotomy. She finds further that they are more likely to occur when a regime has declining support, in heterogeneous societies, and in military and military-dominated civilian regimes.

Human Rights Watch. *Human Rights and U.N. Field Operations: The Lost Agenda.* New York: Human Rights Watch, 1993. 173 pages. $15. ISBN 1-56432-1037.

Human Rights Watch argues that human rights abuses have been given low priority by U.N. field operations. Five of the largest field operations are examined: Cambodia, El Salvador, Iraq, Somalia, and the former Yugoslavia.

————. *Human Rights in Iraq.* New Haven, CT: Yale University Press, 1990. 164 pages. $27. ISBN 0-300-04959-5.

Explores the context of repression in Iraq, including the leader, secret police, and constitution. Documents specific human rights abuses such as arbitrary arrest and detention, torture, political killing, disappearances, and deportation.

————. *Human Rights Watch Global Report on Women's Human Rights.* New York: Human Rights Watch, 1995. 458 pages. $15. ISBN 0-300-065469.

Defines and explains different kinds of abuse of women, including rape and sexual assault, as a tool of war and political oppression, abuse against women in prison, trafficking of women and girls into prostitution and coerced marriage, abuses against women workers, domestic violence, and violations relating to reproduction and sexuality. Uses examples from many countries and discusses current status of U.N. attempts to improve conditions for women.

————. *Hungary—The Gypsies of Hungary: Struggling for Ethnic Identity.* New York: Human Rights Watch, 1993. 72 pages. ISBN 1-56432-112-6.

Discusses the status of Gypsies living in Hungary. Although their situation has been much more positive since the fall of the communist regime, this group still faces job discrimination, violence, harassment, and educational discrimination.

————. *Slaughter among Neighbors: Political Origins of Communal Violence.* New Haven, CT: Yale University Press, 1995. 188 pages. $30. ISBN 0-300-06496-9. $15 (pbk.). ISBN 0-300-06544-2.

Studies the causes and strategies to prevent communal violence. Concludes that the origins of many ethnic, religious, or racial disputes stem from political needs of governments that are losing popularity. Covers the role of the military or police; use of state media to foster nationalism, racism, and religious intolerance; government failure to protect victims and prosecute perpetrators; forcible displacement; and the role of other influential governments.

————. *United States—Abuses in the State of Georgia: Modern Capital of Human Rights?* New York: Human Rights Watch, 1996. 214 pages. $15. ISBN 1-56432-169-X.

Although the standards of international law offer better human rights guarantees in some cases than U.S. law, this report shows that many Georgia practices violate both federal and state law. Abuses documented include death penalty discrimination against the poor and against African Americans; drug laws that are enforced disproportionately against African Americans; children confined in overcrowded, squalid, and unsanitary detention and correctional facilities; sexual abuse of female prisoners; inhumane treatment of prisoners; infringement on lesbian and gay rights; and attacks on freedom of expression.

————. Helsinki Watch. *Romania—Ethnic Hungarians in Post-Ceausescu Romania: Struggling for Ethnic Identity.* New York: Human Rights Watch, 1993. 142 pages. $10. ISBN 1-56432-115-0.

Documents treatment of the ethnic Hungarian minority in Romania since the Romanian revolution of 1989. This has included inadequate access to Hungarian language instruction; restriction of minority language broadcasting; less favorable treatment for Hungarian language press; underrepresentation in local government; restrictions on the right to assemble, the right to associate, and freedom of expression; and abusive house searches. Appendix of documents and tables.

————. Middle East Watch. *A License to Kill: Israeli Operations against Wanted and Masked Palestinians.* New York: Human Rights Watch, 1993. 264 pages. $15. ISBN 1-56432-109-6.

Describes pattern of unjustified killings by Israeli undercover security forces in the occupied West Bank and Gaza Strip. Report documents 17 cases in which 20 Palestinians were killed. Although Israel has repeatedly affirmed that the military units are bound by rules of conduct applicable to law enforcement situations, there is little, if any, censure and the principle of using minimum force necessary is not being followed.

———. Middle East Watch and Physicians for Human Rights. *The Anfal Campaign in Iraq-Kurdistan.* New York: Human Rights Watch, 1993. 116 pages. ISBN 0-300-05757-1.

Case study of the Kurdish village of Koremet, one of hundreds of Iraqi-Kurdish villages that were destroyed during the Anfal campaign. Documents the atrocities committed, including large-scale murders, disappearances, forcible relocations, and destruction. Evidence includes interviews, Iraqi government documents, and reports of forensic scientists who undertook studies of mass grave sites.

Human Rights Watch/Africa. *Sudan—Civilian Devastation: Abuses by All Parties in the War in Southern Sudan.* New York: Human Rights Watch, 1994. 279 pages. $15. ISBN 1-56432-129-0.

Documents how all parties to the conflict have preyed on the civilian population. Human Rights Watch argues that the devastation of the Southern Sudan can be halted only if the rules of war are obeyed, or if the war ends. Specific strategies for humanitarian aid are proposed.

Human Rights Watch/Asia. *China: State Control of Religion.* New York: Human Rights Watch, 1997. 144 pages. $10. ISBN 1-56432-224-6.

This report documents the Chinese government's increased efforts to control organized religious activities through registration of religious organizations and regulation of the activities that occur in churches. Christianity and Islam have been especially controlled by the government. Although this constitutes a relatively low level of abuse compared to the selective imprisonment, violence, and physical abuse that occurred in the recent past, this concerted effort at control is frightening.

———. *Indonesia—Human Rights in Indonesia and East Timor: Limits of Openness.* New York: Human Rights Watch, 1994. 145 pages. $10. ISBN 1-56432-140-1.

Describes the evolving human rights situation in Indonesia by documenting six major issues: shutdown of daily newspapers in August 1994; detention and torture in East Timor; lack of labor rights; religion, politics, and torture in North Sumatra; government torture of church ministers; and the work of the Indonesian Human Rights Commission.

Human Rights Watch/Asia and Physicians for Human Rights. *Human Rights Crisis in Kashmir: A Pattern of Impunity.* New York: Human Rights Watch, 1993. 214 pages. $15. ISBN 1-56432-104-5.

Since 1990, there have been clashes between Muslim separatists and the Indian government in the northern states of Jammu and Kashmir. This report documents the extrajudicial executions, rape, torture, and deliberate assaults on health care workers by the Indian government. Appendices document disappearances, code of medical neutrality, and a response to the report from the Indian Embassy to the United States.

————. *Punjab—Dead Silence: The Legacy of Human Rights Abuses in Punjab.* New York: Human Rights Watch, 1994. 103 pages. $10. ISBN 1-56432-130-4.

Documents the extrajudicial killings in the North Indian state of Punjab, where more than 100,000 people have been killed. Includes background information on the conflict and documents violations to humanitarian law by both the government forces and the militants.

Human Rights Watch/Helsinki. *Macedonia—Human Rights Violations in Macedonia: A Threat to "Stability."* New York: Human Rights Watch, 1996. 114 pages. $10. ISBN 1-56432-170-3.

Although human rights principles are encoded in Macedonian law, many national minorities face discrimination in state employment and minority language education. There have also been limitations on the free press, violations of legal rights, and harassment of the political opposition. HRW argues that although Macedonia is politically stable, a lasting peace will be secured only when a democratic system is in place that guarantees full rights for all citizens.

————. *Russia: The Ingush-Ossetian Conflict in the Prigorodnyi Region.* New York: Human Rights Watch. 100 pages. $10. ISBN 1-56432-165-7.

Describes the human rights violations during the November 1995 fighting that erupted between the Ingush militias and North Ossetian security forces. Describes the process of return for the displaced and attempts to bring to justice those who committed criminal acts connected with the conflict. Also examines the Russian government's weak response to events leading to the conflict and its failure to prevent the destruction of thousands of homes and dwellings.

Human Rights Watch/Middle East. *Kuwait—Bedoons of Kuwait: Citizens without Citizenship.* New York: Human Rights Watch, 1995. 105 pages. $10. ISBN 1-56432-156-8.

Bedoons compose one third of Kuwait's native population; yet in 1985 Kuwait declared them illegal citizens and implemented a policy of denationalization. These policies include harassment and intimidation and denial of rights to lawful residence, employment, travel, and movement. This work includes a history of discrimination against Bedoons, the Iraqi occupation, profiles of persecution, and the Kuwaiti government position.

Human Rights Watch and the Natural Resources Defense Council. *Defending the Earth: Abuses of Human Rights and the Environment.* New York: Human Rights Watch, 1992. 106 pages. $10. ISBN 1-56432-073-1.

Authors argue that abuses of human rights often exist in tandem with environmental degradation. Part of the reason for this is that citizens who fear reprisals from the government have no mechanisms for complaining about practices that negatively affect the environment. Case studies are presented from Brazil, Eritrea, Kenya, Malaysia, Mexico, the Philippines, and the United States.

Human Rights Watch Arms Project. *Turkey—Weapons Transfers and Violations of the Laws of War in Turkey.* New York: Human Rights Watch, 1995. 171 pages. $15. ISBN 1-56432-161-4.

Report documents the Turkish Security Forces violations of the laws of war and human rights during its war with the Kurdistan Workers' party (PKK), and its reliance on U.S.- and NATO-supplied weapons to do so. Using investigations of 29 specific incidents from 1992 to 1995, the report links specific weapon systems to individual incidents of Turkish violations. Although the PKK has also engaged in human rights violations during the war, this report focuses on how other countries are perpetuating the Turkish violations through weapons transfer.

Human Rights Watch Arms Project and Human Rights Watch/Africa *Landmines in Mozambique.* New York: Human Rights Watch, 1994. 119 pages. $10. ISBN 1-56432-121-5.

Mozambique was at war almost continuously from the 1960s until 1992 when the government and Renamo, the main rebel movement, signed a cease-fire. Land mines have claimed over 10,000 victims, and by conservative estimate, there are still tens of thousands of unexploded mines. This report documents the origins of this tragedy, its ongoing consequences, and the efforts being made to undo some of the damage.

Human Rights Watch Prison Project. *Human Rights Watch Global Report on Prisons.* New York: Human Rights Watch, 1993. 303 pages. ISBN 1-56432-101-1.

Compilation of six years of investigations of prisons in North America, South America, Europe, Asia, and Africa. The study included prisons in the six largest nations in the world: Brazil, China, India, Indonesia, Russia, and the United States. Human Rights Watch found that human rights problems are endemic in penal systems worldwide. Based on U.N. minimum standards of incarceration, violations were found in standards of medical care, hygiene, activities, treatment of women, contact with outsiders, overcrowding, and food.

Humana, Charles. *World Human Rights Guide,* 3d ed. New York: Oxford University Press, 1992. 393 pages. $ 12.95 (pbk.). ISBN 0-19-507926-4.

This work assesses the human rights performance of 125 countries based on the results of a questionnaire that sought information on 40 items, including such freedoms as peaceful political opposition, political and legal equality for women, travel within and outside one's own country, independent publishing and newspapers, and the practice of one's religion. The report gives each country a percentage rating on its attainment of human rights according to concepts in U.N. covenants.

Hunter, Kenneth, and Timothy Mack, eds. *International Rights and Responsibilities for the Future.* Westport, CT: Greenwood, 1996. 207 pages. $55. ISBN 0-275-95562-1.

These essays center around the connection between rights and responsibilities. Includes justice in the twenty-first century, international cooperation for the environment, population and the environment, knowledge-based development, and the editors' ideas of what actions will improve human rights for the future.

International Committee of the Red Cross. *Landmines: Time for Action.* Geneva, Switzerland: ICRC Publications, 1994. 35 pages.

A thorough discussion of how and why land mines are used, medical consequences of land mines, impact on society, manufacture and trade in land mines, technical control methods, mine clearance, mines and the law, pictures of types of mines, statistics, tables, and photos of victims.

Ishay, Micheline, ed. *The Human Rights Reader: Major Political Writings, Essays, and Speeches from the Bible to the Present.* New York: Routledge, 1997. $74.95. ISBN 0-415-91848-0. $24.95 (pbk.). ISBN 0-415-91849-9.

Book aims to show how conflicting visions of rights have been articulated throughout history and how they have been codified in major legal documents. Author shows that the historical foundation of human rights comes from a "humanist strand" running through the world's great religions.

Jabine, Thomas, and Richard Claude, eds. *Human Rights and Statistics: Getting the Record Straight.* Philadelphia: University of Pennsylvania Press, 1992. 458 pages. $39.95. ISBN 0-8122-3108-2.

Discusses problems quantifying human rights issues, guidelines for reporting violations, role of government organizations, events-based data, standards-based data, and developing and analyzing human rights data. Includes a guide to data sources.

Johnston, Barbara Rose, ed. *Life and Death Matters: Human Rights and the Environment at the End of the Millennium.* Walnut Creek, CA: Alta Mira Press, 1997. 351 pages. $48. ISBN 0-7619-9184-0. $23.95 (pbk.). ISBN 0-7619-9185-9.

Environmental social scientists look critically at how people in communities, organizations, and governmental institutions respond to the human environmental crises that structure their lives. Case studies include biodiversity, global economy, agriculture, development, tourism, and radiation. Also contains a draft of "Principles on Human Rights and the Environment" by the United Nations Human Rights Commission.

Juviler, Peter, et al., eds. *Human Rights for the 21st Century, Foundations for Responsible Hope: A U.S. Post-Soviet Dialogue.* Armonk, NY: M. E. Sharpe, 1993. 288 pages. $72.95. ISBN 1-56324-044-0. $22.95 (pbk.). ISBN 1-56324-110-2.

U.S. and Russian writers share views on the former U.S.S.R. and U.S. progress and regression in the field of human rights, improvements in international law, a stronger United Nations, human rights education, and improving roles for women. Obstacles to human rights are identified as ignorance and indifference; inexperience with democracy; fossilized bureaucracies; economic stagnation; recession and depression; militarism; poverty in rich countries and greater poverty in poor countries; and widespread uncertainty and hopelessness.

Kelsay, John, and Sumner Twiss, eds., for Project on Religion and Human Rights. *Religion and Human Rights: Religion and the Roots of Conflict.* New York: Project on Religion and Human Rights, 1994. 123 pages. $10. ISBN 1-56432-141-X.

Essays cover the role of religion in conflict, the phenomenon of "fundamentalism," tension between universal human rights and cultural relativism, and the potential of religion to advance the causes of human dignity, social justice, and peace.

Lauren, Paul Gordon. *Power and Prejudice: The Politics and Diplomacy of Racial Discrimination,* 2d ed. Boulder, CO: Westview Press, 1996. 433 pages. $25. ISBN 0-8133-2143-3.

Examines the role of race in influencing global politics, diplomacy, and discrimination. Author studies racial issues in the twentieth century and finds that race is at the heart of many human rights issues.

Lavik, Nils Johnson, et al., eds. *Pain and Survival: Human Rights Violations and Human Rights.* Oslo, Norway: Scandinavian University Press, 1994. 244 pages. $39. ISBN 82-00-21907-0.

This collection features essays on the psychosocial aspects of torture, symbolic expression of pain, organized destruction of meaning, individual and familial aspects of human rights violations, religion and oppression, protection of victims, psychological effects of impunity of torturers, justice and revenge, and a case study of the Stasi of the former East Germany.

Levin, Leah. *Human Rights Questions and Answers,* 3d ed. Paris: UNESCO, 1996. ISBN 92-3-103261-5.

Excellent overview of human rights and the United Nations' role in protecting them. Uses a question and answer format and goes through the Universal Declaration of Human Rights article by article to explain what each one means.

Mahmood, Cynthia Keppley. *Fighting for Faith and Nation: Dialogues with Sikh Militants.* Philadelphia: University of Pennsylvania Press, 1996. 314 pages. $18.95 (pbk.). ISBN 0-8122-1592-3.

Ethnographic study of the Sikh culture. Mahmood interviewed many Sikhs, including prisoners in Punjab who had undergone torture in the Indian prisons.

Mahoney, Kathleen, and Paul Mahoney, eds. *Human Rights in the 21st Century: A Global Challenge.* Norwell, MA: Kluwer Academic Publishers, 1993. 1028 pages. $270. ISBN 0-7923-1810-3.

Collection of 75 papers on a range of topics, including discrimination against women, minorities, and the disabled; state violence, nonstate actors and violence, and human rights response to violence; rights to food, health, and sustainable environment; refugees and displaced persons; development and human rights; threats of science and technology to human rights; mass communication and human rights, information technology and confidentiality; medical ethics and human rights; reproduction, technology, and human rights.

Malamud-Goti, Jaime. *Game without End: State Terror and the Politics of Justice.* Norman: University of Oklahoma Press, 1996. 235 pages. $24.95. ISBN 0-8061-2826-7.

Written by one of the architects of the Argentine Human Rights Trials that took place after the "Dirty War" (1976–1983). The author argues that the trials as they were designed reinforced the very authoritarianism they set out to eradicate. Explores the history and background of the trials, the aims and objectives of the trials, and Argentinean society, as well as the actual events.

Millet, Kate. *The Politics of Cruelty: An Essay on the Literature of Political Imprisonment.* New York: W. W. Norton, 1994. 335 pages. $23. ISBN 0-393-03575-1. $13 (pbk.). ISBN 0-393-31312-3.

Author uses writings of torture victims to highlight the nature and politics of torture. Case studies include the Russian gulag, the Nazi camp system, apartheid, the British in Ireland, and Argentina, Brazil, and El Salvador.

Mirante, Edith T. *Burmese Looking Glass: A Human Rights Adventure and a Jungle Revolution.* New York: Grove Press, 1993. ISBN 0-8021-1457-1. Atlantic Monthly Press, 1994. $12 (pbk.). ISBN 0-87113-570-1.

First-person account of Burmese life under dictatorship rule by an American woman who lived among the Burmese people.

Mullerson, Rein. *Human Rights Diplomacy.* New York: Routledge, 1997. 225 pages. $69.95. ISBN 0-415-15390-5. $18.95 (pbk.). ISBN 0-415-15391-3.

Analysis of the reasons for and consequences of the internationalization of human rights. Discusses the use of foreign policy instruments to promote human rights as well as the use of human rights for the sake of other foreign policy aims. Includes discussion of the role of nongovernmental organizations, the media, and the relationship between human rights and international stability.

Nanda, Ved, George Shepherd, and Eileen McCarthy-Arnolds, eds. *World Debt and the Human Condition: Structural Adjustments and the Right to Development.* Westport, CT: Greenwood Press, 1993. 249 pages. $59.95. ISBN 0-313-28531-4.

This work explores the challenge of achieving an international economic order that fosters equitable and sustainable development. Includes discussion of the interrelationship between world development and world debt, social and political consequences of structural adjustments imposed by the World Bank and the International Monetary Fund, and the role of nongovernmental organizations.

Nino, Carlos Santiago. *Ethics of Human Rights.* New York: Oxford University Press, 1991. 323 pages. $29.95. ISBN 0-19-825436-9.

Argues that ethical dogmatism, the belief that self-evident moral truths exist, and ethical skepticism, the belief that reasons cannot exist to support human rights because decisions and emotions are not subject to rationality, are obstacles to improved human rights. What is needed instead is an enlightened moral consciousness that would serve as a bulwark against assaults on human dignity.

———. *Radical Evil on Trial.* New Haven, CT: Yale University Press, 1996. 220 pages. $27.50. ISBN 0-300-06749-6.

Author considers the moral issues as well as the political questions raised by the Argentine trials of human rights violators who committed crimes during the "Dirty War" of 1976 to 1983. Although the author believes that some measure of retroactive justice for massive human rights violations helps protect democratic values, fear of such reprisals can inhibit totalitarian regimes from stepping down. The historical context of the trials is examined and an evaluation of the successes and failures of process is presented.

Oraa, Jaime. *Human Rights in States of Emergency in International Law.* New York: Oxford University Press, 1992. 288 pages. $85. ISBN 0-19-825710-4.

Grave violations of human rights have occurred during states of emergency. The author sets out to examine the extent of the protections of human rights in states of emergency by three main multilateral treaties. He then looks for protections in international law.

Pogany, Istvan, ed. *Human Rights in Eastern Europe.* Brookfield, VT: Edward Elgar, 1995. 255 pages. $80. ISBN 1-85898-333-9.

In every new democracy in Eastern Europe, there are large national minorities. Contributors describe the problems of nationalism, the challenge of recognizing without institutionalizing ethnic differences, refugee law, and the status of Russia, Poland, the Czech Republic, and Hungary.

Ratner, Steven, and Jason Abrams. *Accountability for Human Rights Atrocities in International Law: Beyond the Nuremberg Legacy.* Oxford, England: Clarendon Press, 1997. 368 pages. $95. ISBN 0-19-826550-6.

The authors examine both the international criminal law that can be used to hold individuals accountable for human rights atrocities and also the theoretical and practical challenges to a law's application. A case study of the Khmer Rouge rule over Cambodia from 1975 to 1979 is included to illustrate the practical application of international law.

Reardon, Betty. *Educating for Human Dignity: Learning about Rights and Responsibilities.* Philadelphia: University of Pennsylvania Press, 1995. 238 pages. $24.95. ISBN 0-8122-3306-9.

Geared toward teachers, this work demonstrates how human rights education can be approached throughout elementary and secondary schooling. Curriculum frameworks and rationale, resource listings, and sample lesson plans are provided to support the values of human dignity and integrity, economic equity, equal opportunity, democratic participation, and right to a sustaining and sustainable environment.

Rejali, Darius. *Torture and Modernity: Self, Society, and State in Modern Iran.* Boulder, CO: Westview Press, 1994. 289 pages. ISBN 0-8133-1660-X.

Focuses on political violence and torture in Iran during the period 1950 to 1990. This thoughtful book discusses how torture has changed from being a public to a private act. Author finds the objective has changed from scarring the flesh with marks of infamy to locating, isolating, and crippling the prisoner's soul.

Renteln, Alison Dundes. *International Human Rights: Universalism versus Relativism.* Newbury Park, CA: Sage Publications. 205 pages. $52. ISBN 0-8039-3505-6.

Author attempts to reconcile conflict between cultural/ethical relativism and universal human rights by showing that they are not diametrically opposed. Cross-cultural empirical research to determine which values are shared by all cultures is proposed as the method of reconciliation.

Richburg, Keith. *Out of America: A Black Man Confronts Africa.* New York: Basic Books, 1997. 257 pages. $23. ISBN 0-465-00187-4.

A reporter who spent three years in Africa as the bureau chief for the *Washington Post* discusses his experiences of social conditions and human rights abuses. He witnessed the effects of the genocide in Rwanda and the devastating famine and civil war in Somalia.

Richmond, Anthony. *Global Apartheid: Refugees, Racism, and the New World Order.* New York: Oxford University Press, 1994. 327 pages. $29.95. ISBN 0-19-541013-0.

Describes the increasing mass movements from rural to urban areas as well as the increase in people seeking to move to wealthy countries. Author argues that the restrictive and repressive policies now being implemented in North America, Europe, and Australasia to limit political asylum are a form of global apartheid. Includes tables with statistics.

Robertson, A. H., and Merrills, J. G. *Human Rights in the World: An Introduction to the Study of the International Protection of Human Rights,* 4th ed. Distributed by New York: St. Martin's Press, 1996. 355 pages. $24.95. ISBN 0-7190-4223-2.

Outlines the legal history of treaties and case law with respect to human rights. Notes that we are moving toward a standard where international law applies to individuals and not just states.

Rohde, David. *Endgame: The Betrayal and Fall of Srebrenica, Europe's Worst Massacre Since World War II.* New York: Farrar, Straus, and Giroux, 1997. 440 pages. $24. ISBN 0-3742-542-0.

In 1993 the U.N. Security Council officially named Srebrenica the world's first U.N.-protected civilian safe area. Over 7,000 Muslims were slain when the world did not send sufficient troops to support the safe area. Rohde, a former reporter for the *Christian Science Monitor* who was in Srebrenica covering the Yugoslav war, follows the experience of seven people—three Muslims, two Dutch, one Serb, and one Croat—during the massacre.

Roht-Arriaza, Naomi, ed. *Impunity and Human Rights in International Law and Practice.* New York: Oxford University Press, 1995. 398 pages. $80. ISBN 0-19-508136-6.

Case studies of efforts by people, governments, and international institutions to come to grips with these countries' recent history of repression and of impunity. Considers the difficulties in bringing oppressors to justice, including determination of responsible parties and the risk of backlash or annulment of amnesty law.

Rotberg, Robert, and Thomas Weiss, eds. *From Massacres to Genocide: The Media, Public Policy, and Humanitarian Crises.* Washington, DC: Brookings Institution, 1996. 203 pages. $26.95. ISBN 0-8157-7589-X.

This collection of articles examines the crucial role the media play in preventing ethnic conflicts and massacres. Although the media have no interest in covering anticipated events, media attention is often required in order for a problem to be taken seriously by humanitarians and policymakers. The media also have a brief attention span and have difficulty conveying the history and texture of human rights issues. Authors argue that the relationships among policymakers, humanitarian agencies, and media are complex and chaotic, but they need one another and ought to work together.

Sank, Diane, and David Caplan. *To Be a Victim: Encounters with Crime and Injustice.* New York: Plenum Press, 1991. 481 pages. $28.50. ISBN 0-306-43962-X.

This work examines all types of victims from victims of family violence to victims of government injustice. Authors offer suggestions for eliminating or alleviating their victimization.

Schabas, William. *The Death Penalty as Cruel Treatment and Torture: Capital Punishment Challenged in the World's Courts.* Boston: Northeastern University Press, 1996. 288 pages. $50.00. ISBN 1-5555-3268-3.

Using capital punishment case law from rulings, declarations, and covenants by the world's courts, this work explains the prohibition on cruel treatment. Examines some of the issues surrounding the death penalty, including public opinion, unequal application of the death penalty to the poor and minorities, methods of execution, and prison conditions on death row. Death row prisoners usually experience little outdoor or recreation time, no activities related to work or education, and rare opportunities for visits with families.

Sellers, Mortimer, ed. *The New World Order: Sovereignty, Human Rights, and the Self-Determination of Peoples.* Washington, DC: Berg, 1996. 340 pages. $46. ISBN 1-85973-064-7.

Authors set out to define the proper relationships between national and international institutions after the Cold War, with particular reference to the protection of human rights in different local situations. Also covers human rights and self-determination and U.N. peacekeeping in situations of internal conflict.

Shapiro, Ian, and Will Kymlicka. *Ethnicity and Group Rights.* New York: New York University Press, 1997. 627 pages. $45. ISBN 0-8147-8062-8.

This volume examines whether the familiar system of citizenship rights within a liberal democracy is sufficient to accommodate the legitimate interests that people have as a result of their ethnic identity. Evaluation of strengths and weaknesses of various strategies for resolving ethnic conflict around the world, from secession to nation building to multiculturalism.

Spencer, Michael. *States of Injustice: A Guide to Human Rights and Civil Liberties in the European Union.* London: Pluto Press, 1995. 234 pages. ISBN 0-7453-979-8.

Provides a guide to the decisionmaking structure of the European Union (EU) and relationship between the EU and the Council of Europe. Author warns that there are many unresolved human rights issues, including the treatment of refugees, abolition of internal frontiers and concomitant increase in police surveillance powers, immigration policy, racism and discrimination, police cooperation, and data protection.

Starkey, Hugh, ed. *Challenge of Human Rights Education.* London: Cassell Education Limited, 1991. 264 pages. ISBN 0-304-31943-0.

Recommends age-appropriate curricula and texts for human rights education from nursery school to high school and teacher training. Case studies are presented of Canadian schools; human rights education and women's achievement; children with special needs and human rights education; and nongovernmental organizations.

Thornhill, Teresa. *Making Women Talk: The Interrogation of Palestinian Women Security Detainees by the Israeli General Security Service.* London: Lawyers for Palestinian Human Rights, 1992. 107 pages. ISBN 0-9519610-0-4.

In addition to torture, Palestinians have suffered willful killing, arbitrary arrest, punitive demolition of homes, deportation, and forced separation of their families at the hands of the Israeli security forces. The author conducted interviews with Palestinian and Israeli women who were detained between 1986 and 1990. She documents the torture they withstood, including sleep, food, and basic hygiene deprivation; sexual harassment and threats of rape; and allegations made against the women's children. She further examines the impact of interrogation methods on the defendant's right to a fair trial.

Tibet Information Network and Human Rights Watch/Asia. *Cutting Off the Serpent's Head: Tightening Control in Tibet, 1994–1995.* New York: Human Rights Watch, 1996. 192 pages. $15. ISBN 1-56432-166-5.

Covers the implementation of the Third National Forum on Work in Tibet, which has resulted in dramatic increases in political imprisonment and religious persecution by the Chinese government. An appendix documents many individual cases.

Tolley, Howard. *International Commission of Jurists: Global Advocates for Human Rights.* Philadelphia: University of Pennsylvania Press, 1994. 355 pages. $45. ISBN 0-8122-3254-2.

Describes the history of the International Commission of Jurists based in Geneva, Switzerland, from its founding in 1952 to 1993. This is an interesting look at a well-respected nongovernmental organization that was founded in response to Stalinist totalitarianism.

Tomasevski, Katarina. *Between Sanctions and Elections: Aid Donors and Their Human Rights Performance.* Washington, DC: Pinter, 1997. 251 pages. $85. ISBN 1-85567-470-X.

Reviews human rights policies, use of sanctions, and electoral support and monitoring over the last three decades. Author concludes that there is a lack of correspondence between donor commitment to human rights and aid allocations and that human rights have had a negligible role as an allocative criterion and have been used occasionally as an eliminatory criterion.

————. *Development Aid and Human Rights.* New York: St. Martin's Press, 1989. 208 pages. $45. ISBN 0-312-03139-4.

Author argues that observance of human rights law and related standards is not only required by legal obligations but is a rational basis for working out an overall development assistance policy and implementing individual development projects. She notes that economics and foreign policy interests dominate the design, planning, and evaluation of aid and can be obstacles to including human rights in development aid.

————. *Development Aid and Human Rights Revisited.* New York: Pinter, 1993. 223 pages. $55. ISBN 1-85567-085-2.

Donor nations have adopted strongly worded statements linking development aid to human rights. Author argues that donors are focusing too much on social and economic rights and that the conditionality of human rights has provided an excuse to reduce aid flows. She also examines the United Nations, the International Monetary Fund, the World Bank's role in promoting human rights, donor policies of several nations, the rule of law in development aid, the economics of human rights, and the merging of women and development projects with human rights.

Waltz, Susan Eileen. *Human Rights and Reform.* Berkeley, CA:

University of California Press, 1995. 281 pages. $50. ISBN 0-520-20003-9. $16.95 (pbk.). ISBN 0-520-20154-6.

Describes the role of national human rights groups that started in the 1970s in three North African states: Morocco, Tunisia, and Algeria. Author argues that human rights groups challenge the rules of the political games across North Africa and have changed the political process by their existence.

Weiss, Thomas G. *Humanitarian Challenges and Intervention: World Politics and the Dilemmas of Help.* Boulder, CO: Westview Press, 1996. 239 pages. $69. ISBN 0-8133-2844-6. $19 (pbk.). ISBN 0-8133-2845-4

Addresses the operational, ethical, and legal problems faced by humanitarians working amid active armed conflicts, such as choosing between the provision of humanitarian relief and the protection of human rights. Includes a table of complex humanitarian emergencies that occurred in 1995.

Welch, Claude E. Jr. *Protecting Human Rights in Africa: Strategies and Roles of Non-Governmental Organizations.* Philadelphia: University of Pennsylvania Press, 1995. 356 pages. $39. ISBN 0-8122-3330-1.

Describes specific nongovernmental organizations in Ethiopia, Namibia, Nigeria, and Senegal and shows how they are addressing specific human rights issues. Presents strategies to protect and promote human rights in Africa. Author argues that by documenting the plight of victims and pressing governments for action, nongovernmental organizations both improve the status of individuals but also make significant contributions to the development of new human rights standards.

Winslow, Philip. *Sowing the Dragon's Teeth: Land Mines and the Global Legacy of War.* Boston: Beacon Press, 1997. 167 pages. $21. ISBN 0-8070500-4-0.

A foreign correspondent writes about Angola, one of the world's most heavily mined countries. He chronicles the lives of the victims, discusses the process of mine clearance, the role of international relief organizations, and the campaign to ban land mines.

Wintemute, Robert. *Sexual Orientation and Human Rights: The U.S. Constitution, the European Convention, and the Canadian*

Charter. Oxford, England: Clarendon Press, 1995. 292 pages. $19.95 (pbk.). ISBN 0-19-825972-7.

Describes treatment under the three systems. Argues that the U.S. Constitution, the European Convention, and the Canadian Charter all implicitly contain prohibitions against sexual discrimination.

Wronka, Joseph. *Human Rights and Social Policy in the 21st Century: A History of the Idea of Human Rights and Comparison of the United Nations Declaration of Human Rights with United States Federal and State Constitutions.* Lanham, MD: University Press of America, 1992. 269 pages. $29.95 (pbk.). ISBN 0-8191-8638-4.

Includes a history of the idea of human rights and compares the Universal Declaration item by item against federal and state constitutions. A chart indicates which states offer which guarantees. The author concludes that while the United States conforms to most of the provisions of the declaration, it needs to work on incorporating Article 25, which guarantees the right to a standard of living adequate for the health and well-being of a person, including food, clothing, housing, and medical care.

Periodicals

The following list includes those periodicals that have a strong human rights emphasis. Most are available in academic libraries and some can be found in local public libraries. Many articles can be found in other periodicals, however, and these can be accessed through standard indexes and abstracting journals.

American Journal of International Law
American Society of International Law
2223 Massachusetts Avenue, NW
Washington, DC 20008
Quarterly, $140

Sponsored by a society founded in 1906 to "foster the study of international law and to promote the establishment and maintenance of international relations on the basis of law and justice," this journal is one of the most authoritative and prestigious of the law journals. Published for its members, other lawyers, scholars, and jurists, it includes many articles on human rights issues. It also publishes book reviews and occasionally reprints treaties, conventions, and U.N. publications. It is indexed in law indexes and in general indexes such as *PAIS* and *Social Science Index.*

Columbia Human Rights Law Review
Columbia University School of Law
435 West 116th Street
New York, NY 10027
Semiannual, $26

Formerly the *Columbia Survey of Human Rights Law* (1967–1968), this publication endeavors to illuminate subjects of concern regarding human rights, the law, and people's lives. It focuses on legal issues that are basic to all citizens, such as freedom of religion, freedom of speech, discrimination in employment, and women's rights, but does so more often from the viewpoint of the U.S. legal system than from an international viewpoint. Contains book reviews. Indexed in *PAIS* and *Legal Resource Index.*

CovertAction Information Bulletin (CAIB)
CovertAction Publications, Inc.
1500 Massachusetts Avenue, NW, Suite 732
Washington, DC 20005
Quarterly, $57 (individuals $22)

This quarterly covers the activities of the CIA and other intelligence agencies. Much of the information regarding these activities is difficult to find elsewhere. Many issues concentrate on one topic such as terrorism or misinformation campaigns. Contains occasional book and film reviews. Indexed in the *Alternative Press Index, Human Rights Reporter,* and *PAIS.*

Cultural Survival Quarterly
Cultural Survival Inc.
96 Mount Auburn Street
Cambridge, MA 02138
Quarterly, $60 ($45 individuals)

This journal addresses the immediate and long-term concerns of indigenous peoples throughout the world and attempts to raise public awareness regarding human rights abuses of indigenous peoples. Many of the issues are devoted to a single theme or topic. Also includes information about other groups interested in indigenous peoples and occasional book reviews and news items. Indexed in the *Alternative Press Index.*

Freedom Review
Transaction Periodicals Consortium
Department 3092
Rutgers University
New Brunswick, NJ 08903
Bimonthly, $60 ($30 individuals)

Published by Freedom House, an organization dedicated to strengthening democratic institutions, each issue examines the current status of human rights worldwide, with emphasis on political conditions and economic, social, and cultural factors contributing to freedom and tyranny in all societies. Also included are letters to the editor, news items, and fairly lengthy book reviews. Indexed in *HR Reporter, Historical Abstracts,* and *PAIS.*

Human Rights
American Bar Association
Individual Rights and Responsibilities Section
750 North Lake Shore Drive
Chicago, IL 60611
Three issues per year, $18

This periodical contains features and commentary on human rights issues such as refugees, children's rights, housing, gay and lesbian rights, and women in prison. More popular in style than most of the other human rights law publications, it includes news items and some book reviews. Indexed in several indexes, including *Social Science Index, Index to Legal Periodicals,* and *Legal Resource Index.*

Human Rights
United Nations Division of Human Rights
Palais des Nations, 8-14 Avenue de la Paix
1211 Geneva 10
Switzerland
Quarterly, free

Published in English, French, Russian, and Spanish, this publication carries information on the role of the United Nations in the promotion of human rights. It includes articles, copies of speeches given by U.N. officials, news of human rights events, reports of various commissions and committees relating to human rights, and book reviews.

Human Rights Bulletin
International League for Human Rights
432 Park Avenue South, Suite 1103
New York, NY 10016
Semiannual, $35

The *Bulletin* appears in a newsletter format. It describes violations of human rights all over the world and gives a brief summary of cases that have already been noted by the league. It frequently requests readers to send appeals to authorities in specific cases. News of the league and its activities is also included.

Human Rights Internet (HRI) Reporter
Human Rights Internet
8 York Street
Ottawa, Ontario
Canada K1N 5S6
Quarterly, $80 ($60 individuals)

The *HRI Reporter* is intended to keep the human rights community informed about major international and national developments as they affect human rights worldwide. It seeks to spotlight nongovernmental organizations working for the promotion and protection of human rights; focus attention on human rights defenders under attack; review important decisions and actions of intergovernmental organizations and governmental bodies with a human rights mandate; stimulate discussion, research, and teaching in the field of human rights; and assist human rights advocacy organizations and policymakers. The journal is divided into three main sections: the first includes editorial comments, brief articles by outside contributors, and a calendar; the second includes information on developments of importance to the human rights community, including the work of the United Nations; and the third is the bibliography section, giving lists of fairly lengthy descriptions of human rights literature from all over the world, arranged primarily by geographic region. Material in the bibliography is indexed by geographic region, by subject, and by organization. The *HRI Reporter* is without a doubt the most valuable tool for those interested in human rights; it is probably the most thorough and accurate serial publication in the field of human rights in the world. Indexed in *Alternative Press Index*.

Human Rights Law Journal
N. P. Engel, Publisher
3608 South 12th Street
Arlington, VA 22204
Quarterly, $208

A forum for scholarly debate in the field of human rights law, the *Journal* endeavors to serve as a channel of communication between both sides of the Atlantic. It is published in association with the International Institute of Human Rights in Strasbourg, France, and reports on constitutional and supreme court decisions in the human rights field from all over Europe. Indexed in *Index to Legal Periodicals* and *Legal Resource Index*.

Human Rights Quarterly
Johns Hopkins University Press
Journals Publishing Division
2715 North Charles Street
Baltimore, MD 21218
Quarterly, $85 ($35 individuals)

Tied to no particular ideology, the *Human Rights Quarterly* offers scholars in the fields of philosophy, law, and the social sciences an interdisciplinary forum in which to present comparative and international research on public policy within the scope of the Universal Declaration of Human Rights. Each issue contains scholarly, well-documented articles and book reviews. The journal is sponsored by the Urban Morgan Institute for Human Rights, College of Law, at the University of Cincinnati. Indexed in *PAIS, The Philosopher's Index*, and *Legal Resource Index*.

Index on Censorship
Writers and Scholars International, Ltd.
Lancaster House
33 Islington High Street
London, England N1 9HL
Ten issues per year, $84 ($50 individuals)

A British publication with supporters in many countries, the *Index on Censorship* attempts to raise awareness of such issues as freedom of the press, academic freedom, and freedom of creative expression. The several articles in each issue reflect this purpose. Also included are "News and Notes," book reviews, and a country by country account of censorship and other violations of human rights. Indexed in *PAIS* and the *Alternative Press Index*.

New York Law School Journal of Human Rights
New York Law School
57 Worth Street
New York, NY 10013
Three times per year, $22

This journal is dedicated to the international protection of human rights. Though some of the articles are more properly concerned with civil rights, generally the well-documented, scholarly articles deal with basic human rights. Some of the issues treated are children's rights, the rights of the mentally disabled, and homelessness. Indexed in *HR Reporter, Index to Legal Periodicals,* and *Legal Resources Index.*

Win News
187 Grant Street
Lexington, MA 02173
Quarterly, $40 ($30 individuals)

WIN (Women's International Network) News is a "worldwide open communication system by, for, and about women of all backgrounds, beliefs, nationalities, and age groups." Though not strictly a human rights journal, most of the articles are on the basic rights of women from an international perspective. Indexed in *HR Reporter.*

**World Views: A Quarterly Review
of Resources from and about the Third World**
World Views
1515 Webster
Oakland, CA 94612
Quarterly, $50 ($25 individuals)

Published to alert educators, activists, and others to resources related to Third World regions and problems, each issue has sections on organizations, books, periodicals, pamphlets, articles, and audiovisuals. Almost all are related to human rights issues.

Selected Nonprint Resources 7

Nonprint Media

There are few nonprint materials on human rights as such, but there are many on specific human rights issues such as hunger, imprisonment and torture, disappearances and political killings, refugees, the rights of women, and labor rights. The following are selected films and videotapes that exemplify the types of nonprint materials available. Included at the end is a list of some of the distributors of nonprint materials aimed at raising public awareness of human rights issues. Note that the prices listed are for the item only—there may be shipping and sales tax.

Banking on Life and Debt
Length: 30 minutes
Cost: Purchase: $14.95; rental: AFSC
               Cambridge (see address at
               end of this chapter)
Date: 1996
Distributor: Maryknoll World Productions
               PO Box 308
               Maryknoll, NY 10545
               (800) 227-8523

Narrated by Martin Sheen, this documentary examines the impact of International Monetary Fund (IMF) and World Bank policies on Third World countries. In Ghana, health care services are no longer subsidized; in Brazil, the shift to producing for export has hurt small farmers and led to destruction of the rain forest; and in the Philippines, the people are struggling and it is likely that IMF monies were funneled into Swiss bank accounts by former President Ferdinand Marcos.

Catch 22: The Dilemma of Capturing Bosnia's War Criminals
Length: 21 minutes
Cost: $29.95
Date: 1997
Distributor: ABC News Videos
PO Box 51790
Lavonia, MI 48151
(800) 225-5222

This news segment originally appeared on ABC's "Nightline." It describes the efforts to capture Bosnian war criminals, including Dr. Karadzic, who has been indicted by the War Crimes Tribunal in the Hague. It also touches on the lack of clear procedure once war criminals are captured.

Colombia: Getting Away with Murder
Length: 30 minutes
Cost: Free Loan from Amnesty International
Regional Offices
Date: 1994
Distributor: Amnesty International, 322 8th Avenue,
New York, NY 10001 (212) 807-8400

This Amnesty International production documents the Colombian government's use of the illegal drug problem as a smokescreen for massive human rights violations. Death squads have been following a policy of social cleansing, targeting homosexuals, street children, prostitutes, and the homeless.

Dead Man Walking
Length: 122 minutes
Cost: $19.95
Date: 1996
Distributor: Available at video stores

Susan Sarandon won an Academy Award for her portrayal of

Sister Helen Prejean, a nun who worked with the poor in New Orleans and found herself counseling a death row inmate. This film looks at multiple dimensions of the death penalty, including the feelings of the victim's family, prison officials, the inmate, and his family. Sean Penn plays a remorseless killer.

Deadly Embrace: Nicaragua, the World Bank, and the International Monetary Fund
Length:	30 minutes
Cost:	Purchase: $30, activist guide $6
Date:	1996
Distributor:	Ashley Eames
	Buffalo Road
	Wentworth, NH 03282
	(603) 764-9948

Rental available from the American Friends Service Committee, Cambridge (see information at end of video section). Examines the impact of World Bank and International Monetary Fund policies on Nicaragua. Filmmakers argue that the IMF was founded to rebuild European economics after World War II, not to help poor countries. Heavy debt loads in Nicaragua have caused 60 percent unemployment and 70 percent to live under the poverty level. Three hundred and fifty thousand children cannot attend school because there is no money to pay teachers and cheap imports are destroying small businesses and local identity.

Down Came a Blackbird
Length:	100 minutes
Cost:	$92.99
Date:	1995
Distributor:	Available at video stores

Laura Dern, Raul Julia, and Vanessa Redgrave star in this docudrama about torture. Dern plays an American reporter who is arrested with her husband while covering a political demonstration in Latin America. Her husband is killed and Dern is tortured. She visits a Holocaust survivor's clinic for survivors of torture. This is an interesting look at the lasting psychological effects of torture.

Genocide
Length:	88 minutes
Cost:	$34.95
Date:	1991

Distributor: Simon Wiesenthal Center
9760 West Pico Boulevard
Los Angeles, CA 90035
(310) 553-9036

This Academy Award–winning documentary is narrated by Elizabeth Taylor and Orson Wells. Through narration, interviews, still photographs and footage, the history of the Holocaust in Nazi Germany is portrayed. It includes an introduction by Simon Wiesenthal.

Israel and the Occupied Territories
Length: 20 minutes
Cost: Free loan from Amnesty International
              Regional Offices
Date: 1990
Distributor: Amnesty International
              322 8th Avenue
              New York, NY 10001
              (217) 807-8400

This video shows eyewitness accounts of the human rights abuses that have occurred during the *intifada.* Interviews with a member of Physicians for Human Rights, a *New York Times* correspondent, a Palestinian human rights lawyer, an Israeli human rights lawyer, and the minister of justice in the state of Israel, as well as footage of beatings, describe the problem.

Mama Awethu
Length: 53 minutes
Cost: Purchase: $390; rental price depends on type
              of video screening; film is also available
Date: 1993
Distributor: First Run/Icarus Films
              153 Waverly Place, 6th Floor
              New York, NY 10014
              (212) 727-1711

This beautiful, affecting film shows the lives of five South African women living around Capetown as they go about their daily lives. Although apartheid has officially ended in South Africa, there are still extreme poverty and workplace discrimination. Each of the five women is working to improve her community through activism or community work—one woman serves as a health care worker for her neighbors, for example. This film won the Gold Apple prize and was included in the 1994 Sundance Film Festival.

Mickey Mouse Goes to Haiti: Walt Disney
and the Science of Exploitation
Length:	30 minutes
Cost:	Donation
Date:	1996
Distributor:	National Labor Committee
	275 Seventh Avenue
	New York, NY 10001
	(212) 242-0986

This film examines labor conditions in Haiti at the factories where Walt Disney contracts for workers. Workers receive half of one percent of the sales price of a garment. They make about $2.40 per day, not even enough to cover the cost of food for a family. Workers live in eight by ten foot shacks and there is no money for medicine or milk for children. In the factories the quotas are very difficult to meet, bathroom breaks are discouraged, and workers are fired if they try to organize.

Mostar: Death of a City
Length:	27 minutes
Cost:	$39.95
Date:	1993
Distributor:	ABC News Video
	PO Box 51790
	Lavonia, MI 48151
	(800) 225-5222

This documentary, which aired on ABC's "Nightline," was prepared by BBC reporter Jeremy Bowen. It focuses on the fighting between Muslims and Croats in the city of Mostar, one of the most devastated cities in the former Yugoslavia. Soldiers from both sides are interviewed and footage shows injured and dying civilians, including children, and citizens forced from their homes.

Mustang: The Hidden Kingdom
Length:	90 minutes
Cost:	$29.95
Date:	1994

Distributor: Wellspring Media
65 Bleeker Street, 5th Floor
New York, NY 10012
(212) 674-4912

Narrated by Harrison Ford, this beautiful documentary was originally produced for the Discovery Channel. It shows the visit of
the Dalai Lama to a place nestled high in the Himalayas that is
the only location where pure Tibetan Buddhist culture survives,
because of the persecution by the Chinese. The film discusses the
status of Buddhists in the rest of Tibet.

Nuremberg: Tyranny on Trial
Length: 50 minutes
Cost: $19.95
Date: 1995
Distributor: A&E Home Video
Box HV 1
235 East 45th Street
New York, NY 10017
(800) 625-9000

The film details the Nuremberg trials from accusations to executions. The trials set a precedent for how international tribunals would handle atrocities committed in times of war. This
video examines the evidence, verdicts, and the significance of
the trials. It includes footage of Nazi atrocities and the trials
themselves.

Shadows of Hate, The: A History of Intolerance in America
Length: 40 minutes
Cost: $20.00
Date: 1995
Distributor: Teaching Tolerance
Southern Poverty Law Center
400 Washington Avenue
Montgomery, AL 36104
(334) 264-0286

This historical treatment includes religious intolerance and persecution as well as racial intolerance. This film documents many
cases of persecution, including religious intolerance of Quakers
and Baptists, massacres of Native Americans, Chinese railroad
workers who were massacred and excluded from immigration,
Japanese Americans interned during World War II, an Hispanic

war casualty denied a burial in a white community, lynching of African Americans, and persecution of Jews.

Teaching about Human Rights
Length: 16 minutes
Cost: $14.95
Date: 1991
Distributor: United Nations Publications Sales Section
Room DC-2853, Department I004
New York, NY 10017
(800) 253-9646

The title of this video is somewhat misleading because it is exclusively about the rights of children. The film describes the United Nations Convention on the Rights of the Child and illustrates with footage from all over the world the plight of children who are dying from malnutrition and easily preventable diseases and made to work or serve in the military. The film shows the role of the United Nations and of UNICEF programs.

Valentina's Nightmare
Length: 60 minutes
Cost: $69.95
Date: 1997
Distributor: PBS Video
PO Box 791
Alexandria, VA 22313
(800) 328-7271

This is the story of Valentina Iribagazi, a 13-year-old Tutsi, who survived one of the massacres in the Rwanda genocide by staying hidden for a month among the dead bodies. Over 800,000 people were killed in Rwanda. This video examines the impact on one child and includes interviews with her teachers. Includes a history of the conflict and the position of the United Nations.

War Orphan
Length: 15 minutes
Cost: $29.95
Date: 1996
Distributor: CBS Video
PO Box 2284
South Burlington, VT 05407
(800) 848-3256
Item #SM6110C

Children taken or separated from their rebel parents in El Salvador during the 1980s were put up for adoption. This segment of "60 Minutes" shows the reunification with her parents of a young woman who was adopted in the 1980s and came to the United States.

In addition to the distributors listed for the materials above, the following is a selected list of distributors who also have human rights–related nonprint media.

American Friends Service Committee
1501 Cherry Street
Philadelphia, PA 19102
(215) 241-7000
Video Library

American Friends Service Committee
2161 Massachusetts Avenue
Cambridge, MA 02140
(617) 497-5273

California Newsreel
149 Ninth Street, Suite 420
San Francisco, CA 94103
(415) 621-6196

Cambridge Documentary Films
PO Box 390-395
Cambridge, MA 02139
(617) 484-3993

Carousel Films, Inc.
260 Fifth Avenue, Suite 905
New York, NY 10001
(800) 683-1660

Church World Service
28606 Phillips Street
PO Box 968
Elkhart, IN 46515
(219) 264-3102

Cinema Guild
1697 Broadway
New York, NY 10019
(212) 246-5522

EcuFilm
810 12th Avenue, South
Nashville, TN 37203
(800) 251-4091

Filmmakers Library
124 East 40th Street
New York, NY 10016
(212) 808-4980

Franciscan Communications
1229 Santee Street
Los Angeles, CA 90069
(213) 746-2916

IDERA Films
1037 West Broadway, Suite 400
Vancouver, British Columbia
Canada V6H 1E3
(604) 738-8815

Ladyslipper (Audio resources)
PO Box 3124
Durham, NC 27705
(919) 683-1570

Media Guild
11722 Sorrento Valley Road, Suite E
San Diego, CA 92121
(619) 755-9191

Mennonite Central Committee
PO Box 500
21 South 12th Street
Akron, PA 17501
(717) 859-1151

Social Studies School Service
10200 Jefferson Boulevard, Room 15
PO Box 802
Culver City, CA 90232
(800) 421-4246

World Council of Churches
U.S. Office
475 Riverside Drive, Room 1062
New York, NY 10115
(212) 870-2533

Computer Networks

This section includes general computer information services that link users with indexes and abstracts leading to specific human rights material and two specialized internet networks devoted to peace and human rights issues.

Databases of Indexes and Abstracts

DIALOG Information Services
Knight-Ridder Information
2440 El Camino Real
Mountain View, CA 94040

Dialog includes A-V Online, Historical Abstracts, Legal Resource Index, and PAIS International.

Ovid Technologies Inc.
333 Seventh Avenue
New York, NY 10001
Ovid includes Social Science Index and Legal Resource Index.

PeaceNet
Institute for Global Communications (IGC)
Presidio Building 1012
First Floor, Tourney Avenue
PO Box 29904
San Francisco, CA 94129
(415) 561-6100

PeaceNet is an internet service provider that works with peace organizations. Many peace organizations are located on the IGC server. PeaceNet can be accessed at http://www.igc.org. Once at the IGC homepage, click on PeaceNet for current peace information and links to many human rights organizations.

Wilsonline
H. W. Wilson Company
950 University Avenue
Bronx, NY 10452
(800) 367-6770

The H. W. Wilson Company, a long-time publisher of reference materials, provides Index to Legal Periodicals and Social Science Index online.

The Internet

The Institute for Global Communications provides internet services for many peace organizations, but many organizations are not part of this network. Consult Chapter 5 for websites. Many of the organizations listed have extensive reports available online. These websites were current as of early 1998, but web addresses change frequently. If you are having trouble locating an organization on the internet, try the following strategies:

1. Make a guess at what their address might be. For example, try http://www.organizationname.org. Try this both with www and without. Experiment with using just the initials of the organization.
2. Use a search engine such as Alta Vista or Lycos that has robotic search capabilities. These services cast a much wider net than menu-based search engines like Yahoo because they have robotic search protocols that are continuously updating their databases.
3. Visit a site for a similar subject that perhaps provides a page of links that will give you an address for the organization you are looking for.
4. Consult recent editions of internet organizations guides.
5. Call the organization on the telephone and ask for the address.

Databases

The following organizations have computer databases useful for human rights researchers or activists.

Human Rights Internet (HRI), described in Chapter 5, has established several computerized databases containing all the citations and articles found in the *HRI Reporter.* The databases also contain information on human rights organizations around the world, which is frequently updated in the *Reporter.* Persons wishing to access this information can call or write HRI with their request and the staff will design a search and provide an annotated bibliography of citations. Copies of original documents can usually be provided if they are not readily available elsewhere. Charges are based on the nature of the search, document reproduction, and staff assistance required. HRI has plans to put this database on the internet. Check the website for online searching. The website is http://www.hri.ca.

World Views (see Chapter 5) also has a computer-accessible database on Third World organizations and materials, most of which are human rights related and based on research gathered for the World Views directories and the quarterly publications, *World Views* (see the periodicals section in Chapter 6). World Views plans to have its database searchable over the internet. The website is http://www.igc.org/worldviews/.

Index

ACLU. *See* American Civil
Liberties Union
Activists, women as, 242–243
ADL. *See* Anti-Defamation
League of B'nai B'rith
Africa, 243, 262
and child labor, 20
and nongovernmental agencies,
267
and poverty, 23
and prisons, 256
and self-determination, 241
African Americans,
discrimination against, 252
African Charter on Human and
People's Rights, 41
AFSC. *See* American Friends
Service Committee
Aid, development, 266
AIDS, 20, 250
AIUSA. *See* Amnesty
International, USA
Alberta Human Rights
Commission, 203–204
Algeria, 245, 267
Alien Rights Law Project, 51
American Civil Liberties Union
(ACLU), 204
American Convention on Human
Rights, 37
American Declaration of the
Rights and Duties of Man, 33
American Friends Service
Committee (AFSC), 205–206,
282
Americans for Democratic Action,
205–206

Americas Watch, 50–51. *See also*
Human Rights Watch
Amnesty International, 8, 243,
276, 278
and Mendez, Juan E., 51
and Sagan, Ginetta, 53
and torture, 25
Amnesty International, USA, 54,
206
Angola
and land mines, 267
Anti-Defamation League of B'nai
B'rith (ADL), 207
Antigone (Sophocles), 4
Apartheid, 262
Aquinas, Saint Thomas, 4
Arbitrary arrest, 12, 251
Argentina
and disappearances, 242
and torture, 247, 259
and trials, 259, 260–261
Argentine League for Human
Rights, 57
Aristotle, 3
Arrest, arbitrary, 12
and Iraq, 251
Asia
and child labor, 20
and migrant workers, 241
and poverty, 23
and prisons, 256
*Asociación para la Defensa del
Periodismo Independiente,*
58
Assam, 240
Assaults on health care workers,
254

287

Nina Redman, M.L.S., is a reference librarian at Glendale Community College.

Lucille Whalen, M.L.S., has numerous
publications on human rights issues,
including the first volume of *Human
Rights: A Reference Handbook.* She is also a
reference librarian at Glendale Community
College.